Adolescence:
A Social Psychological Analysis

Custom Edition for
Stony Brook University

FHS71330

Hans Sebald

Taken from:
Adolescence: A Social Psychological Analysis, Fourth Edition
by Hans Sebald

Custom Publishing

New York   Boston   San Francisco
London   Toronto   Sydney   Tokyo   Singapore   Madrid
Mexico City   Munich   Paris   Cape Town   Hong Kong   Montreal

Cover Art: Courtesy of PhotoDisc, EyeWire/Getty Images.

Taken from:

Adolescence: A Social Psychological Analysis, Fourth Edition
by Hans Sebald
Copyright © 1992, 1984, 1977, 1968 by Prentice Hall
A Pearson Education Company
Published by Prentice Hall
Upper Saddle River, New Jersey 07458

This special edition published in cooperation with Pearson Custom
Publishing.

Printed in the United States of America

10 9 8 7 6 5 4 3 2 1

2009500211

MP

**Pearson
Custom Publishing**
is a division of

www.pearsonhighered.com

ISBN 10: 0-558-41838-4
ISBN 13: 978-0-558-41838-0

BRIEF CONTENTS

Preface

This book discusses adolescence as an individual as well as a collective phenomenon. On the individual level, it focuses on the adolescent's reaction to the urban-industrial conditions that have created an environment in which social roots are uncertain and personal identity is vulnerable. This aspect of the discussion is a social-psychological analysis. On the collective level, the book focuses on adolescents' attempts to compensate for uncertainty and vulnerability by engaging in subcultural or even countercultural behavior. This aspect is a sociological analysis. On both levels, adolescent behavior can be understood as a groping struggle—often anguished and drawn out—toward maturity, adulthood, and a stable identity.

In the course of portraying adolescence, I favor an interdisciplinary approach, which includes sociological, psychological, educational, anthropological, and family-life material, plus the occasional use of popular sources.

A full examination of adolescence must be both *analytical* and *comprehensive*—analytical in the sense of showing the causes and consequences of adolescence, and comprehensive in the sense of describing the broader sociocultural context in which adolescence thrives. The text divides this task into five parts:

1. Setting the stage by introducing basic concepts and definitions and providing a historical perspective to the subject.
2. Describing the nature of personality dynamics during the adolescent period.
3. Analyzing the causes of adolescence as they are embedded in the social and cultural matrix of urban-industrial society.
4. Describing the consequences of adolescence as individuals express themselves in compensatory collectivities, ranging from subculture to counterculture.
5. Discussing a range of challenges and social problems strongly associated with adolescents.

The last chapter provides an overview, which highlights the major ingredients of the book, and presents adolescence as an unavoidable crucible of democratic society.

While most readers of this book are probably college students, it is equally well suited for the layperson. This book is not written in academic lingo by professors for professors, but is a straightforward analysis in plain English. Parents who are not in the mainstream of academic life should therefore find it intelligible and helpful.

The book is a guide through the tangle of social and psychological circumstances that have created and now perpetuate adolescence. The route of this journey is reflected in the structure of the book, which provides students with insight into a lifestyle barely outgrown, educators with a systematic introduction to the characteristics and needs of modern youth, and parents with an understanding of the often disconcerting behavior of their offspring.

This is the fourth edition of *Adolescence: A Social Psychological Analysis*. Since the publication of the first edition in 1968, much has changed. Vehement uprisings of restless youth have shaken American society, indeed most of the Western world. Adolescence, as an ingredient of postindustrial society, has become a permanent fixture. The mass media have clamorously claimed more powerful positions in the socialization of the young; new sexual moralities have come and gone; patterns of drug use and abuse have shifted; roles, especially women's, have undergone changes; and colorful New Age movements have soothed many of the weary survivors of the counterculture. This edition reflects these changes.

The material on the counterculture has been reduced, for this upheaval is now part of American history; new attitudes and concerns of young Americans have replaced the once widespread militant resistance against what was then labeled the Establishment. A largely "me"-oriented new generation of adolescents has evolved during the 1980s and early 1990s.

A renewed attempt is made to portray adolescence as the expression of an expected style of behavior that forms a normative stage in the life cycle of modern Americans, indeed of almost all modern urban-industrial people.

Hence there will be less emphasis on the "problem approach" and greater adherence to an objective structural-functional analysis.

This type of analysis of adolescence allows inclusion of positive aspects, as, for example, altruistic volunteerism and creative and artistic achievements by young people who are using their freedom from the restraints of adult roles to explore their personal talents. I am frequently impressed by the quality of musical or dramaturgical performances that can be seen on American high-school campuses, let alone on college campuses. The inner dynamics of adolescence can undoubtedly express superb sublimations.

This volume reflects a continued awareness of the deep-reaching impact of the mass media, especially TV; their effect on personality development can hardly be exaggerated. Renewed emphasis is placed on the dynamics of the modern socialization process, including a reexamination of role expectations, or the lack thereof. Two interesting styles of raising boys and girls are compared: Momism and Dadism.

Further changes from the previous edition include restructuring the material throughout the book. Previously lengthy chapters have been broken up to form new chapters, thereby creating clearer divisions between topics and more manageable limits to discussions. The restructuring resulted in sixteen chapters, which lend themselves as convenient outline for a semester's course.

In addition, the new edition received the usual improvements in style and a thorough updating of figures and statistics.

Finally, a new chapter has been added about some of the challenges that adolescents level at society. Chapter 15 examines the high-school dropout, the inhospitable world of work for the young, sexuality and the teenager, pregnancy and the teenage girl, and teenage drug use.

The preface is also the place to acknowledge contributions. I very much appreciate the help of Karen Y. Murray, who generously provided insight and new ideas. Thanks is due to the reviewers of this and previous editions as well: Marvin R. Koller, Kent State University; John M. Dettoni, Fuller Theological Seminary; Bruce L. Warren, Eastern Michigan University; Alan Krasnoff, University of Missouri—St. Louis; Barbara A. Goodnight, University of North Carolina—Charlotte. Professor Koller's kind and sensitive remarks were particularly appreciated.

Thanks is also due to Nancy Roberts, senior editor at Prentice Hall, and her assistant Pat Naturale: both have smoothed the road to the book's production. Special appreciation is due to Liz Pauw, who with great care guided the book through the various stages of its production; her dedicated midwifery kept birth defects at bay.

Hans Sebald

Adolescence:
A Social Psychological Analysis

Adolescence: Its Time and Place in Social Development

Growing up in a modern urban-industrial society has become a complex venture; traditional ideas social scientists and psychologists have held about the socialization process are largely anachronistic. In a sense, modern *Homo sapiens* no longer is in control of a unitary personality system, but must be understood from the perspective of a number of social-psychological concepts. Some of the major ones are discussed in this chapter.

REFERENCE GROUP

While it is true that the young child depends heavily on an immediate group environment for physical survival, this does not mean that a young person, once he or she has learned how to relate to abstract ideas and images, must remain on the relatively primitive level of relating only to physically present persons. People's effort to understand themselves and their universe is not limited, although highly influenced, by membership groups. *Direct* physical contact with other persons is not necessary to absorb ideas, philosophies, and religions. An actual example is that of a young man with no social connections to Greeks or corresponding ethnic subgroups in the United States, who decided to embrace Greek Orthodox Christianity. His decision was based not on social interaction but entirely on reading and abstract reflecting.

This example illustrates the difference between the reference group and the membership group. Human ability to abstract can free them from face-to-face interaction for information and acquisition of values. The concept of reference group was developed mainly to define the process whereby individuals derive norms and values without necessarily being in physical contact with those persons holding the emulated view. Normally, however, most of a person's membership groups also function as reference groups. In the cases where the two groups do not coincide, serious conflicts may arise for the person involved in both.

The relationship between adolescent behavior and reference groups is complex. Modern urban-industrial environment offers youth a heretofore unknown number of potential reference groups, and value derivation can proceed through ubiquitous images and models presented in the mass media. As a result of the diversity of reference groups, the adolescent's personality development is beset with a number of complications:

Shifting reference groups.   A significant aspect of adolescence is the gradual shift in orientation from teenage standards to adult norms and values. Usually, the adolescent has no choice but to ultimately accept adult behavior patterns.

Multiple reference groups.   Often because of personal preference, but more often because of mandatory conditions, the adolescent is involved in a number of membership groups, which usually constitute reference groups at the same time. Examples of such combinations for the adolescent are family, school, church, and peer group.

Sebald and White's 1980 study found teenagers divided on reference groups and unevenly aligned with peers and parents. Suburban high schoolers clung to their peers' advice on matters of whom to date, which clubs to join, how to dress, choice of hobby, and reading material. Only 10 percent or fewer of the teenagers would turn to parents in these matters. (This was particularly true of boys; significant boy-girl differences are mentioned in Chapter 12.) On the other side, approximately 50 percent sought parental guidance in matters of choosing a career, going to college, and how to spend money. Comparison with 1960 data shows that this juxtaposition has sharpened and nearly polarized, with teenagers of the 1970s and 1980s drawing distinct demarcation lines as to which issue belongs to which reference group.[1]

---

[1]Hans Sebald and Becky White, "Teenagers' Divided Reference Groups: Uneven Alignment with Parents and Peers," *Adolescence*, 15 (Winter 1980): 979–84.

Conflicting reference groups.   Multiplicity of reference groups frequently leads to conflict. Most conflicts stem from the clash between standards of the peer group and those of the parents. Peers represent a powerful reference group, and researchers have found that the clique's expectations often take precedence over norms and values held by family and adults. "The clique, then, acts as a protective structure which may oppose and evade adult authorities and sanctions."[2]

James S. Coleman, studying high school youth, found considerable conflict when a teenager had to choose between standards of peers and demands of parents.[3] The researcher presented the subjects with a hypothetical situation, asking them what they would do if they were asked to join a particular club to which they had always wanted to belong but at the same time were faced with a request by parents not to join. The response pattern of the students depended on the type of community in which they lived. Responses, gathered from ten different schools, had between 45 to 80 percent of the boys and 60 to 85 percent of the girls stating that they would probably or definitely not join the club against their parents' wishes. Greatest regard for the parents' demands was shown in the smallest school, in "Farmdale," a rural community; the least regard was apparent in "Executive Heights," a large suburban school. The four schools in which 70 percent or more of the boys preferred the parents' advice and the three schools in which 80 percent or more of the girls chose the parents as reference persons were located in smaller, nonurban communities. The schools in which girls and boys were least willing to conform to parents' ideas were two suburban schools, "Newlawn," a working-class suburb, and "Executive Heights," an upper middle-class suburb. The findings indicate that in "Farmdale" and "Marketville," the two smallest schools in a predominantly rural area, teenagers enter adult responsibilities earlier and are more familistically oriented, while in "Executive Heights," adolescents assume adult responsibilities later and remain more peer-oriented. These differences between a small farm community and an upper middle-class suburb illustrate the differential influence of the adolescent reference group. "Executive Heights" reflects a style of life that is spreading in the United States. "Farmdale" and "Marketville" reflect a more familistic style that seems to be gradually disappearing.

Conflicting reference groups tend to interfere with the formation of a unified and unambiguous self-conception. A young woman, for example, on being accepted into a sorority, may yield to informal pressure and develop modes of conduct like smoking and social drinking that would cause her family's disapproval. Another example would be the conflict experienced by a teenager simultaneously involved in a delinquent gang and in a family of law-

[2]Ernest A Smith, *American Youth Culture* (New York: Free Press, 1962), p. 9.
[3]James S. Coleman, *The Adolescent Society* (New York: Free Press, 1963), pp. 138–40.

abiding parents and siblings, or the conflict caused by holding membership in a religious congregation and at the same time being a member of a delinquent group.

Unclear reference groups. A majority of modern youths experience difficulty in deciding between different, and often incompatible, reference groups, and are frequently torn between them, unable to clearly identify with any single one. This inability to identify completely with any reference group tends to thwart the formation of a clear and stable identity. In a sense, the social environment functions as a mirror showing the person an image of her- or himself. The powerful influence of social repercussion on the person's identity or "self" has been widely accepted as a basic principle of social psychology.[4] If social images are blurred, distorted, or markedly divergent, personality formation will probably reflect these ambiguities.

SIGNIFICANT OTHERS

One might insist it is not groups and their standards but rather individuals and their attitudes that significantly influence attitudes. Social scientists, in an effort to capture the meaning of this relationship, have suggested the concept of "significant other." H. S. Sullivan[5] first coined this concept and believed that significant persons have decisive influence on the perception (including self-perception) of the socializee. Robert K. Merton also tried to conceptualize this influence and suggested the term "reference person."[6] However, the term can be taken to imply volition, consciousness, and choice of reference on the part of the socializee—an assumption that would limit the application of the concept. The concept of significant other does not convey such limitations and thus allows for a greater variety of types of socializer-socializee relationships.

Those having the greatest impact on personality development are parents. Parental behavior constitutes a potential model for role learning. Since many roles can be learned only by observing others, observability of role enactment is important. In cases of general roles, such as the feminine, masculine, and marital, role taking is largely an informal and unconscious

---

[4]George H. Mead, *Mind, Self, and Society* (Chicago: University of Chicago Press, 1934), p. 164; Charles H. Cooley, *Human Nature and the Social Order* (New York: Scribner's, 1902), p. 184; and Alfred R. Lindesmith, Anselm L. Strauss, and Norman K. Denzin, *Social Psychology* (New York: Holt, 1977), pp. 312–48.

[5]As reported by Dorothy R. Blitsten, *The Social Theories of Harry S. Sullivan* (New York: William-Frederick Press, 1953), pp. 74–75.

[6]Robert K. Merton, *Social Theory and Social Structure* (Glencoe, IL: Free Press, 1957), pp. 302–04.

process. Specific roles, such as professional ones, are learned more formally and consciously.

Generally, the young acquire their role perceptions by unconsciously internalizing norms and values reflected by the behavior of models. The importance of this social psychological process can hardly be exaggerated, since role perceptions form the core of one's identity. It is the internalized roles and their degrees of clarity and meaningfulness that make up one's identity. It follows that individuals who are expected to exemplify certain roles possess an immense influence and, to a large extent, bear responsibility for role behavior of the next generation. Role learning and role transmitting may be influenced or disturbed by acts of commission and/or acts of omission. Acts of commission refer to definite instances exhibiting role behavior, such as exerting parental authority, engaging in adult work, and carrying out adult responsibilities. Acts of omission imply absence of exemplification of role behavior, as, for example, chronic father-absence affecting the child. Failure to provide role models is of concern to many behavioral scientists, since role confusion may arise when important norms are neither formally taught nor informally visible.

Children are highly dependent on their parents' example in acquiring sex role and marital role. These role concepts are part of the cultural heritage; that is, they are *learned* ways of behaving and thinking. In many modern societies, the norms that distinguish between masculinity and femininity are no longer as distinct as they were. Vagueness in sex-role definitions and decreasing visibility of parental models have contributed to problems of identity. Young males in the American middle class seem to be particularly vulnerable to the effects of cultural anomie and father-absence. The traditional family—characterized by patriarchal authority, familistic attitudes, and domicile-work combination—has almost vanished in favor of the modern equalitarian family, which emphasizes individualism over familism. Father-absence from the home has become frequent, and the young male has little or no opportunity to observe his father at work. Home life, *at least from the boy's perspective,* has become matriarchal.[7]

Social scientists have disputed the Freudian distinction between love-object and identification-object, preferring to view the relationship between infant and mother as identification and not as love.[8] Thus, learning cultural norms of masculinity necessitates a shift from the original identification-object—mother—to a culturally more acceptable identification-object—father, or some other adult male image. This is not necessary for the girl. As several social scientists have pointed out, the young female has an initial

[7]Talcott Parsons, "Age and Sex in the Social Structure of the United States," *American Sociological Review,* 7 (October 1942): 604–16.

[8]Orvall H. Mowrer, *Psychotherapy: Theory and Research* (New York: Ronald Press, 1953).

advantage in progressing toward appropriate sex-role identity.[9] The boy faces a more precarious situation for, if he does not make the shift of identification early enough during childhood, it may be difficult for him to achieve a masculine identity. Father-absence complicates the shift in identification, and the boy finds himself learning his role more by trial and error than by consistent imitation. As a result, boys more than girls seek and obtain instruction outside of the family and tend to identify with a general cultural image, or with the male *position* in general, while girls identify with the mother as a *person* and not with an impersonal image or position.

Social scientists seem to agree that physical absence of the father, or presence of a father not providing a clear role model, impedes the development of such traits as independence and achievement orientation.[10] Boys lacking adult role models develop more dependent and submissive personality features. In contrast, father-dominated socialization promotes assertive traits in young males.[11]

A word of caution: these traditional assumptions and findings must be reconsidered in the light of at least two major developments. First, progress made by the women's liberation movement has modified the traditional role definitions and stereotypical behavior. Hence, future social-psychological research may come up with different findings, necessitating modification of theory. Second, increasing power and scope of exposure to mass media, particularly television, constitute a change in socialization patterns that calls for modification of the conventional assumption that physically present role models are irreplaceable. For example, studies have found little evidence that father-absent boys are more feminine, dependent, and less aggressive.[12] It is possible that mass media heroes increasingly function as objects of identification.

[9]Daniel G. Brown, "Inversion and Homosexuality," *American Journal of Orthopsychiatry*, 28 (April 1958): 424–29; David B. Lynn, "Learning Masculine and Feminine Roles," *Marriage and Family Living*, 25 (February 1963): 103–5; and David B. Lynn, "The Process of Learning Parental and Sex-Role Identification," *Journal of Marriage and the Family*, 28 (November 1966): 466–70.

[10]Talcott Parsons and Robert F. Bales, *Family, Socialization and Interaction Process* (Glencoe, IL: The Free Press, 1955); Urie Bronfenbrenner, "Socialization and Social Class Through Time and Space," in *Readings in Social Psychology*, ed. Eleanor E. Maccoby, et al. (New York: Holt, Rinehart & Winston, 1958), pp. 400–25; and Paul S. Ullman, "Parental Participation in Child Rearing as Evaluated by Social Deviates," *Pacific Sociological Review*, 3 (Fall 1960): 89–95.

[11]Lois W. Hoffman, "The Father's Role in the Family and the Children's Peer Group Adjustment," *Merrill-Palmer Quarterly*, 7 (April 1961): 97–105.

[12]Hans Sebald, "Parent-Peer Control and Masculine-Marital Role Perception of Adolescent Boys," *Social Science Quarterly*, 49 (September 1968): 229–36; Alan J. Crain and Caroline S. Stamm, "Intermittent Absence of Father and Children's Perception of Parents," *Journal of Marriage and the Family*, 27 (August 1965): 344–47; and Joan McCord, William McCord, and Emily Thurber, "Some Effects of Paternal Absence on Male Children," *Journal of Abnormal and Social Psychology*, 54 (May 1962): 361–69.

CULTURE AND ROLE LEARNING

Humans are role-learning animals. They lack innate knowledge or feeling as to what their roles are to be and must rely on culture to provide blueprints specifying how to behave in certain places in the social structure. To achieve role skills takes years of effort, persuasion, and even coercion. Much of what is taught meets with initial resistance, for it thwarts the child's natural impulses. Freud expressed a social psychological principle when he said that the id forces must be replaced by the superego, meaning that the unrefined hedonistic approach to gratification must be replaced by culturally acceptable behavior.[13] The time during which this conversion to cultural standards takes place is turbulent and involves emotions of love and hate, conflict and anxiety, rejection and acceptance. Personality emerges not on the basis of the autonomous *action* of the organism, as orthodox instinctivists maintain, nor solely on the basis of the *reaction* to external stimuli, as many behaviorists claim, but on the basis of *interaction* with other individuals.

The human obligation to learn positional blueprints applies even to the most basic roles, such as the sex roles. It would be a misconception to equate biological maleness and femaleness with learned masculinity and femininity. Cross-cultural studies reveal that perception of masculinity and femininity depends on cultural definitions. Each culture postulates values and norms, defining actions and interactions of males and females.

Role definitions are premises from which specific actions and reactions can be deduced, thus allowing prediction of behavior. Role premises and their application in everyday life therefore become integral parts of the social order—in fact, the *foundation* of social order. For the sake of social order, it does not matter greatly *how* the role premise is formulated, just as long as there is consensus. The variety of formulations is exemplified by natives on some Polynesian islands who virtually reverse Western concepts of masculinity and femininity. Men tend the hearth and the children, while females perform the more strenuous outdoor work.

Definitions often change over time, especially in dynamic urban-industrial societies. Many qualities looked on as strictly masculine or feminine fifty years ago are not considered so today. Such changing conceptions invalidate instruments of behavioral scientists that try to measure sex-differentiation criteria. Examination of one of the earliest (1936) sex-differentiating instruments, the M-F (masculinity-femininity) inventory,[14] shows that many items are no longer relevant in determining masculinity or femininity. Cultural conceptions have been modified—generally in the direction of more diffused

[13]See Sigmund Freud's discussion of the repressive and often frustrating aspects of group life in his *Outline of Psychoanalysis* (New York: Norton, 1949), pp. 19, 121.

[14]Lewis M. Terman and Catherine C. Miles, *Sex and Personality* (New York: McGraw-Hill, 1936).

standards. One researcher found that in order to devise a valid and reliable instrument applicable today, more than one-half of the test items of the original M-F inventory would have to be discarded or modified.[15]

Learning to interact in terms of social roles is probably the most important function of socialization. To achieve adequate social participation, the young must internalize role prescriptions as cognitive and affective predispositions; that is, they must look at the world in certain ways and experience certain prescribed emotions. A young boy thus comes to see manliness in terms of courage and physical prowess and experiences profound emotional reactions should he be asked, for example, to wear girls' clothes. However, in order to perform any social role adequately, the boy must also be familiar with the other social roles in his environment. Understanding this network of interacting roles has been conceptualized as the "generalized other."[16] Personality grows concomitantly with role understanding. In fact, internalization of roles is almost synonymous with growth of personality, and internalized roles with which one identifies form the core of one's personality, the "self."

To avoid the mistake of looking for sameness of personality features where two individuals have internalized the same roles, it must be emphasized that a role is characterized by *personal* meaning and by the place it occupies among the other internalized roles and attitudes. The perception of one's role is a *Prägnanz*—and as all Prägnanzes, is highly personalized. The motivation it commands in a particular personality will not be the same as in other personalities. Thus the uniform role requirements are modified by idiosyncracies. For example, the role of girl in a given society is part of the cultural blueprint, but the role internalization of any particular girl is a specific variant and more than just a mirror image of the blueprint.

Another way of looking at the process of role internalization is through a theory describing the relationship between social structure and the personality system as *isomorphic interpenetration*.[17] The theory assumes that cultural norms interpenetrate both the personality system and social structure. In the personality system these norms manifest themselves as motivations, and in the social system they are known as role expectations attached to positions. In an "ideal-type" society, motivations and roles are isomorphic; that is, both exhibit themselves in the same form.

However, "ideal-types" seldom exist in reality. In American society there is considerable confusion concerning the specifics of male and female roles. For example, roles prescribed for college women tend to be contradictory. One study, dealing with college coeds, found that some attitudes necessary

[15]Sebald, "Parent-Peer Control."

[16]Mead, *Mind, Self, and Society*, p. 154.

[17]Talcott Parsons, "Psychology and Sociology," in *For A Science of Social Man*, ed. John Gillin (New York: Macmillan, 1954).

for a woman to successfully play the "feminine" role tended to interfere with her performance in the role of "modern" woman with emphasis on efficiency, independence, and self-assertion.[18] At times it is the independent "modern" female who will chafe under the pressure to conform to the "feminine" pattern, while at other times family and college will thrust the "modern" role on the girl. Generally speaking, American culture confronts the young female with powerful challenges to excel in competitive endeavors and to adopt techniques identical to those of the male. Later in life, however, the very success in meeting these challenges can cause frustration. Psychiatric opinion maintains that the early-learned habit of competing with the opposite sex can cause sexual and marital maladjustments as competitive attitudes are carried into the realm of sexual relations.[19]

The American teenager's task of learning basic roles is complicated not only by absence or rejection of visible models, but also by vagueness of role definition. Vague role concepts seem to be related to at least two conditions: (1) Parents suffer from "cultural lag" and have difficulty in conveying role definitions that fit the technological and social environment of their children. (2) The general culture is nonspecific, emphasizing personal choice.

In sum, the American ethos of individual freedom acts as an agent of uncertainty, leaving the young without clearly differentiated sex-role definitions, requiring them to take extra time to search for clarity. The matter of changing roles applies most acutely to today's young women. Their roles are undergoing more alteration than any other role, and this phenomenon merits additional discussion.

CHANGING SEX ROLES

Traditionally, American society, as most societies, has upheld polarized images of male and female, each with contrasting attitudes and behavior. But postindustrial conditions have challenged these images. Modern science and technology have affected the traditional division of labor between the sexes and brought about a reconsideration of thinking in terms of two essentially different lifestyles. The women's liberation movement feels that there is neither biological nor social justification for dividing humanity into feminine and masculine categories. The movement gained momentum to the point where many young Americans, especially young women, abandoned stereotypical role behavior.

[18]Mirra Komarovsky, "Cultural Contradictions and Sex Roles," *American Journal of Sociology*, 52 (November 1946): 184–89.

[19]Bruno Bettelheim, "Growing Up Female," *Harper's*, October 1962, pp. 120–28.

What is happening in essence is a modification of age-old cultural blueprints, according to which previous generations have patterned their interaction, and inauguration, at least during the transitional stage, of a pronounced degree of interpersonal anomie.

Reference to a "transitional stage" raises the question of what the end (or next) stage will be. In other words, what will be the nature of human interaction after the typical sex-role interaction has been abandoned or radically modified? The answer emphasizes a nonsexist style of *human* interaction expected to replace a sex-stereotyped lifestyle. Some find this starkly individual-centered prospect utopian, while others defend it only as feasible and necessary.

Whatever the future, at this time there is a significant eroding of the traditional stereotypes. Sex-role blueprints have become blurred, and prediction of a person's behavior on the basis of gender is no longer as reliable as it used to be.

This is particularly true for the female role. Role limitations and expectations have been vastly liberated for the girl and the woman, but not for the boy and the man. The male role has remained virtually unchanged and still reflects rigid and stereotypical norms of behavior and appearance.

A striking example has been—and still is—the reaction by the adult society toward "unmasculine" hairstyles of boys. Their ponytails, braids, or simply long hair caused more furor during the counterculture years than any other style or fad that emerged among the teenagers. Antagonism against boys' hirsute deviations has never died down. In 1990, school officials in Bastrop, Texas, daily sequestered an eight-year-old boy into a 10 by 13 foot isolation room, where he was taught by substitute teachers; additionally he was banned from gym classes and from eating in the cafeteria. His offense: refusal to cut his seven-inch ponytail. His parents appealed to the school board to lift the confinement, but it refused to discontinue the disciplinary measure on the basis that it violated the dress code. A state district judge supported the school's decision whereupon the parents threatened to take the case to the U.S. Court of Appeals. Their contention: "If girls are allowed to wear their hair long, boys should be too."[20]

Ludicrous as the case may appear on the surface, it tells us something of sociological significance: (1) Deviation from the traditional masculine role is unacceptable. (2) The vehemence of persecution with which male deviations are met have no parallel in the disapproval, if any, of female deviations from the traditional role.

Boys and men have felt the effects of the changes in the female role. As a result, they have had to reorient themselves, more subconsciously than

---

[20]"Education," *Time*, December 3, 1990, p. 57.

consciously, toward the female role in general, and their girlfriends, lovers, spouses, and other female associates in specific. The reorientation is unfortunately often combined with a good deal of confusion, sometimes resulting in frustration and even hostility.

There are a number of areas in which liberated female behavior has become noticeable. One interesting area deals with competition between men and women. Traditionally, the female tried to understate her intellect and tone down "success" when compared with men. Psychologists termed this attitude "fear of success." Presumably this fear was motivated by fear of deviating from the cultural blueprint, which stressed noncompetition and nonaggression vis-à-vis men. Traditional sex roles had tasks divided in such a fashion that competition was minimal. Postindustrial conditions, however, have brought the sexes closer together in career possibilities and allowed men and women to compete against each other.

Two related studies explored role diffusion and the connected anxieties in a sample of medical students in the 1960s[21] and early 1970s.[22] Whereas the earlier study found that 65 percent of the women had "fear of success" as compared with 10 percent of the men, the more recent study (using the same variables and the same school) found, somewhat puzzlingly, an unchanged percentage of the women but now 77 percent of the men afflicted with achievement anxiety. Details of the study disclosed, however, that the nature of "fear of success" was essentially different between the sexes. While for women the motive to avoid success was in both studies primarily based on the fear of experiencing social rejection or being found unfeminine, for the men the motive was primarily the questioning of the value of the achievement per se, especially in regard to academic and professional success. This type of anxiety had not been found in the 1965 study. Since the follow-up study was conducted in 1971, at the height of countercultural agitation, the heightened sense of questioning the traditional masculine role, the old career definition, and materialism in general may well have been reflected in the phenomenal increase in men's fear of success.

The philosophical base for men's fear of success was apparently still solid after the counterculture years. A late 1970s study supported the earlier findings of women's fear being based on personal-relational considerations, while men's fear was more abstract and philosophical. The latter feared their

---

[21]Matina Horner, "The Motive to Avoid Success and Changing Aspirations of College Women," in *Readings on the Psychology of Women*, ed. J. Bardwick (New York: Harper & Row, 1972), pp. 62–67.

[22]Lois W. Hoffman, "Fear of Success in Males and Females: 1965 and 1971," *Journal of Consulting and Clinical Psychology*, 42 (June 1974): 353–58.

lives might become one-sided and unfulfilled and that they might sacrifice humanitarian concern for self-advancement.[23]

Woman's fear of success was more narrowly based and dealt with fear of affiliative loss, specifically with the fear of being rejected by peers. These peers were mostly female associates (roommates, friends) and so, unlike males, anxiety arose more from same-sex in-group relations than from female–male interaction or competition. This finding introduces a sour note to the hopes of the women's liberation movement since serious obstacles to the free unfolding of talent are apparently generated *within* the female peer group and not necessarily (at least not directly) from the outside by a male group. It seems the Trojan horse of the women's movement is their own in-group.

That women's fear of success is no longer (if it ever was) determined by overwhelming concern as to how they might appear to men is illustrated by Mirra Komarovsky's longitudinal study comparing attitudes of the 1950s with those of the 1970s. In response to the question "When on dates how often have you pretended to be intellectually inferior to the man?" 32 percent reported "very often," "often," or "several times," 26 percent reported "once or twice," and 42 percent said "never" in 1950, as compared with 15 percent, 30 percent, and 55 percent respectively in 1971.[24]

Indeed, a study in the early 1980s discovered a new trend in which men, *not* women, tended to more often play "dumb" and knowingly underplay their intelligence and knowledgeability. The findings showed that more men than women underplayed their intelligence in almost all situations, including interactions with friends, strangers, bosses, coworkers, dates, and children. Understating was most common among persons with more education and high-status careers.[25]

This finding radically deviates from results of previous studies, in which women were consistently found to fake inferior capabilities. Further research is needed to establish whether this indeed is a reversal of a gender-differentiated attitude and whether it is perhaps a sort of male "reaction formation" to changes in women's roles.

[23]Phoebe K. Schnitzer's study reported in *Human Behavior*, August 1977, pp. 51–52. Another study, surveying 20,000 teenagers, corroborates that girls indeed are consistently more interpersonally and affiliatively oriented, have more empathy for their friends, and place greater emphasis on sociability; Daniel Offer, Eric Ostrov, and Kenneth I. Howard, *The Adolescent: A Psychological Self-Portrait* (New York: Basic Books, 1981), pp. 75, 95f.

[24]Mirra Komarovsky, "Cultural Contradictions and Sex Roles: The Masculine Case," *American Journal of Sociology*, 78 (January 1973): 873–84, and *Dilemmas of Masculinity: A Study of College Youth* (New York: Norton, 1976).

[25]Michael Hughes and Walter G. Gove, "Playing Dumb," *Psychology Today*, 15 (October 1981): 74.

Yankelovich's national survey corroborated the trend visible in the above-mentioned studies. For example, the traditional image of what it means to be a man seems to have undergone a change in the eyes of young adults. The old emphases on "good masculine looks," "physical strength," and "being handy around the house," come in last in a list of twelve qualities. The new major preferences heading the list are (1) concern with the sexual satisfaction of the woman, (2) the ability to be a good economic provider, and (3) having strong moral views about what is right and wrong.[26]

Similarly, the view of women's role has undergone change. In a four-year follow-up study of college students, a marked decline in the endorsement of a traditional role definition for women was found. At the time of entry into college in 1967, a national sample of freshmen were asked their opinions concerning the statement "The activities of married women are best confined to the home and family." At that time, 66 percent of the men and 44 percent of the women indicated agreement ("agree strongly" or "agree somewhat"). A resurvey of the same respondents in 1972 showed a sharp decline in endorsement of the traditional position, with only 30 percent of the men and 15 percent of the women agreeing with it.[27]

Statistics indicate that young women are also catching up with men in areas that are eminently destructive—signaling, possibly, that they are now exposed to the same tensions typical of the male role. Such tensions lurk particularly in urban centers. For instance, metropolitan areas across the country have experienced a phenomenal rise in the female suicide rate during the decade of the mid-1960s to the mid-1970s. Los Angeles County, for example, reported that the suicide rate for males under twenty years of age went from 3 to 10 per 100,000 population, a more than threefold increase. However, for females in the same age group the change was from .4 to 8, a twentyfold increase. Similarly, while the suicide rate for males between twenty and thirty years of age slightly more than doubled, the rate for females of the same age increased over fourfold.[28] Girls particularly vulnerable to suicide were "those whose fathers have been either uncaring or long absent from home, and first-born girls, particularly those with younger brothers."[29]

Increase in female suicides appears to be a typical postindustrial phenomenon and can also be illustrated by the German example. In the 1960s and 1970s the proportion of women among the nation's two to three percent

---

[26]Daniel Yankelovich, *The New Morality: A Profile of American Youth in the 1970s* (New York: McGraw-Hill, 1974), p. 39.

[27]Alan E. Bayer et al., "Four Years After College Entry," *ACE Research Report*, 8 (Washington, DC: American Council on Education, 1973).

[28]"Young Suicides," *Society*, 9 (June 1972): 12.

[29]Pamela Cantor's research at Boston University reported in *Time*, January 3, 1972, p. 57.

alcoholics was only 10 percent. Statistics from the early 1990s indicate that the proportion has increased to 30 percent.[30]

An "empathic ecological explanation" of the fluctuations of suicide rates was offered by psychiatrist Daniel Offer and his coworkers, who studied the suicide rate among adolescents over several decades. They hit upon a significant positive correlation between adolescent suicide rates and changes in the proportion of adolescents in the U.S. population. Apparently, density of youth population is significant insofar as "it may be more difficult for an adolescent to gain a sense of self-worth and to find friends in the large impersonal high schools of today than in the smaller schools of the past.[31] The researchers suspect that an isolated and depressed youth may interpret his or her efficiently bubbling environment as a sign that everybody is functioning fine while he or she is not. Observing seemingly well-functioning peers, and assuming they are such without knowing for certain, may further lower already low and vulnerable self-confidence and push him or her into withdrawal. A resulting sense of hopelessness may plunge the youth into attempted or completed suicide.

The ecological explanation may explain why suicides in urban centers are strikingly higher than elsewhere. It may specifically explain the extreme increases in suicides among women in urban settings. Persons with greater affiliative and relational needs—as women are found to have according to pertinent studies—may react more acutely to urban isolation.

In addition, the Offer team found that girls consistently feel worse about themselves on *all* self-image scales, particularly on the self-esteem scale.[32] As if that were not enough, the girls of the 1970s surveys felt worse than those in the 1960s surveys. It is possible that the generally worsening self-image of young women, for whatever reason, contributes to the "catching up" with the male suicide rate.

Another conspicuous symptom of changing life conditions of the American woman is reflected in the number of violent crimes performed by women, which has increased at rates six and seven times greater than that of crimes of violence committed by men. Rutgers University Professor of Criminal Justice Freda Adler did a study of the impact of political and social changes on the criminality of women and found that the "new woman" in crime—from the liberated prostitute to the revolutionary terrorist—is responsible for the striking ascent of the female crime rates especially in homicide, armed robbery, embezzlement, and aggravated assault.[33]

[30]H. W. Goedde and D. P. Agarwal, "Genetic Protection," *German Research*, Fall 1990, p. 10.

[31]Offer, Ostrov and Howard, *The Adolescent*, p. 124,

[32]Ibid., p. 95.

[33]Freda Adler, *Sisters in Crime: The Rise of the New Female Criminal* (New York: McGraw-Hill, 1975).

On the positive side of the women's liberation movement, an influx into formerly male-dominated training and professions, such as medicine, dentistry, law, engineering, and politics has been noted. For example, female enrollment in medical schools increased from 13 percent in 1972 to about 25 percent in the fall of 1974, and more male than female medical students are dropping out during the first crucial year. Similarly, female enrollment in law schools has progressively increased, from 3.6 percent in 1960 to 9.3 percent in 1971 to 20 percent in 1974. The American Bar Association reported that the proportion of practicing female attorneys is sharply increasing, rising from 2.8 percent in 1972 to 7 percent in 1975.[34]

While an upswing in female careerism was sharply noticeable during the 1970s, the 1980s have seen a slowing down of this trend. Taking the decade of the 1970s as a whole, nearly all careers experienced increases in the percentage of female participants. Here are a few examples:

Engineers, .8 to 2.9
Lawyers and judges, 3.6 to 12.4
Physicians, dentists, and related practitioners, 9.3 to 11.9
Social scientists, 21.3 to 34.5
Managers and administrators, 17.6 to 24.6
Construction laborers, .5 to 2.7
Truck drivers, .6 to 2.1[35]

Female influx into professional careers is significantly encouraged by educational achievement—as illustrated by the diminishing differential in male/female completion of higher education. For example, in 1950, 329,000 men and 103,000 women earned bachelor's degrees, the difference being 226,000. The difference has consistently decreased since then, and in 1978 it amounted to only 53,000, with 487,000 men and 434,000 women obtaining college degrees.[36]

The essence of the ongoing changes seems to be that many young women are no longer playing the traditional female role but are working out various types of role combinations and innovations. Teenage girls demand a great deal more than just marriage and motherhood. While they expect to experience some aspects of the old domestic role (spouse, children, home), they also want to complete their education and pursue a meaningful career. Hence the erstwhile dilemma of choosing between one or the other lifestyle is now replaced by the dilemma of trying to combine both. To come to grips

[34]"Women: Still Number Two but Trying Harder," *Time*, May 26, 1975, pp. 40–41.

[35]*Statistical Abstracts of the United States*, 101st ed. (Washington, DC: U.S. Department of the Census, 1980), pp. 418–20.

[36]*Statistical Abstract of the United States* (Washington, DC: Government Printing Office, 1980), p. 165.

with this expanded lifestyle, today's young women must be goal-directed, assertive, and highly adaptable. In order to make the combination of instrumental and expressive roles a creative and happy experience, young women must learn to cope with the tension and confusion that role experimentation usually produces and must be resourceful enough to resolve conflict.[37]

A suggestion was offered by educator Susanne M. Shafer on how to overcome difficulties of role combinations. She suggested a sequential model, whereby girls should plan their lives in phases, for example, school, work experience, career choice, college, marriage, motherhood, reeducation, and reentry into productive work.[38]

The 1980s have seen increasing numbers of women align themselves with this theoretical model. However, some significant deviations are emerging. After college, more and more women prefer to firmly establish themselves in a career, pursue it for an *extended* period, and finally, in their thirties or even forties decide on motherhood—with or without benefit of being married. The proportion of women aged 25 to 29 years who are still childless has jumped sharply. For example, among women born in 1950 (the cohort of 1950), 25 percent had had no children as of 1980 at age thirty, compared with just 14 percent for comparably aged women born ten years earlier. The rate for mothers in their thirties having a first child increased 66 percent, rising from 7.3 first births per 1000 women aged 30 to 34 in 1970 to 12.1 in 1980. The rate for women aged 35 to 39 rose by 33 percent during this period, from 1.8 to 2.4. The steady increase in first-birth rates for women in their thirties has occurred at a time when birth rates for women of other ages have generally fallen, including rates for the traditionally high first-birth categories of women in their teens and early twenties. The desire of many women to complete their education and become established in a career appears to be the important factor in accounting for the high levels of postponed childbearing. In 1979, nearly half of the first-time mothers aged thirty to thirty-four had completed four or more years of college, compared with just 28 percent in 1970.[39]

These postcareer mothers tend to treat motherhood as a sort of second career and attach the dimensions of careerism to the motherhood experience. As a consequence, the child is often metamorphized into a "project" that must prove "successful motherhood" just as the preceding career was meant to yield success and self-realization. It would be worthwhile to specu-

[37]See extensive treatment: David R. Matteson, *Adolescence Today: Sex Roles and the Search for Identity* (Homewood, IL: Dorsey, 1975).

[38]Susanne M. Shafer, "Adolescent Girls and Future Career Mobility," in Robert E. Grinder, ed., *Studies in Adolescence* (New York: Macmillan, 1975), pp. 114–25.

[39]U.S. Department of Health and Human Services, *Monthly Vital Statistics Report*, 31 (May 27, 1982).

late whether or not these postcareer mothers will swell the ranks of those mothers who have come to be defined as "momistic."[40]

While it is true, as we said initially, that the male role has hardly changed, the male nevertheless has had to make adjustments to the more liberated female role. While his options have not changed, those of women have, and the man must adjust to them. Women, on the other side, may evolve their options without needing to consider a changed male role. Their task is to expand their role, and men's task is to adjust. Both tasks require time and patience, and will inevitably produce their share of confusion, frustration, and even animosity.

Mirra Komarovsky introduced the findings of an important study on men's role perceptions by acknowledging that "gender roles today reflect massive institutional and cultural disorganization."[41] She found that although most college men idealistically espouse men's liberation, just as they support women's liberation, they suffer from a dilemma she calls a "double bind." While the young men seem to genuinely favor women's liberation and express a verbal and ideological commitment to it, they experience apparent difficulties in translating this idealism into reality—and, all the while, are unaware of the gap between ideal and real. The double bind arises when they desire a partner who is an equal but who, at the same time, never threatens them or has divergent or contradictory needs—an equal, in short, who is willing to be subordinate. However, by definition, once a woman subordinates herself she is no longer an equal. This contradiction manifests itself in such incongruous expectations as men wanting women to pursue a challenging and creative career, but simultaneously assuming that she will leave her career upon the birth of the first child and, from then on, be a full-time mother and homemaker. Komarovsky concludes that the path of men toward "liberation" is infinitely more complex than that of a mere "escape" from the traditional male role.

In view of the adjustments men have to make, the findings of a study scrutinizing what happens when young men and women meet are pertinent. Overriding the traditional assumption that achieving men and expressive women get along better with each other than men and women whose personalities are less complementary, the study found that it is the androgynous (combining masculine and feminine traits) man and the androgynous woman (measured on the sex-role scale by Stanford University psychologist Sandra Bem) who, when meeting a person for the first time, proved more flexible, communicative, and rewarding. Androgynous people among a sample of college students talked, gestured, smiled, and looked at each other

[40]Hans Sebald, *Momism—The Silent Disease of America* (Chicago: Nelson-Hall, 1976).
[41]Mirra Komarovsky, *Dilemmas of Masculinity: A Study of College Youth* (New York: Norton, 1976), p. 2.

more often than did the traditionally male and female people. The researchers concluded that androgyny makes for more comfortable interaction.[42] However, the study leaves open whether this initially more comfortable interaction will necessarily result in predictable interaction later on.

A skeptic posed the question: Do women really admire the "soft" man? The Alan Alda Syndrome looks splendid on the screen, Sam Allis warned, but women like Alda "not because he epitomizes the sensitive man but because he is a multimillionaire superstar success who also happened to be sensitive." Men are still defined by their performance in the workplace, Allis added. "If women don't like their jobs, they can, at least in theory, maintain legitimacy by going home and raising children. Men have no such alternative ... If women have suffered from being sex objects, men have suffered as success objects."[43]

From the discussion of the various data presented in this section follows a number of implications for the new man–woman interaction: (1) A decrease in predictability of how one or the other party will act, (2) an increase in the necessity to establish a self-definition that is not merely grounded in gender identity, and (3) a demand to base decisions not on rigid role images but on genuine personal feelings and preferences.

In summary, the modern teenage girl will be exposed to a score of changes and will have to orient herself accordingly:

1. She will experience a decrease in the protection traditionally accorded to women and will be more "on her own" than her mother's generation. As a transitional temptation, she may attempt to juggle the old and the new roles to her advantage—often unfairly so.
2. She will be faced with a rapid increase of options and can expand her preferences nearly infinitely. This includes possibilities in professional careers, education, and lifestyles. Within the latter, she is able to choose among the single status, marriage, family, divorce, abortion, birth control, cohabitation, and so forth.
3. She will be faced with a vastly more complex life that is based less on predictable, rigid blueprints and more on uniquely personal encounters and feelings. The skill to make personal decisions will demand independent thinking.
4. She will become involved in an intense search for her true self, since a cultural matrix based on gender will no longer spell out her identity.
5. She will experience a definite increase in demands on her intellect and responsibility. Having to make independent decisions calls for knowledge, insight, and accountability for the consequences.
6. She will have to learn to cope with increasing frustration and anxiety. While frustrations due to inequality will decrease, frustrations due to life's complexity

[42]William Ickes and Richard Barnes, "Boys and Girls Together—and Alienated," *Journal of Personality and Social Psychology*, 36 (July 1978): pp. 669–83.

[43]Sam Allis, "What Do Men Really Want?" *Time*, Special Issue: Women—The Road Ahead, Fall 1990, p. 81.

and the loss of the security of the old role will more than replace the old frustrations.

THE UNPREDICTABILITY OF SOCIAL CHANGES AND REVERSALS

One of the vexing things about sociological observations is that as soon as they are made, published, and deemed trustworthy descriptions of social reality, new changes emerge over the social horizon, making the old observations obsolete. The seemingly firm ground gained by women's liberation is not necessarily an exception. Hence the adoration of androgyny, the acceptance of women as equals in the arena of career competition, and other achievements of emancipation may not be conquered ground that will never be lost again. Historians know that one cannot make such absolute assumptions. Sociologists, more narrowly focusing upon the here and now, sometimes forget this.

The point is that social-psychological dynamics sometimes shift certain processes into reverse gear and, instead of a constant forward motion, regression to earlier stages takes place. Traditional masculinity and femininity may be waiting in the wings of the social stage, ready to reappear and resume the old scripts.

While this is not the place to dwell on the specific ingredients in the social dynamics that may propel the reversal, it suffices to say that they will most likely prominently feature the frustrations young people experience from role uncertainty and role confusion. There is emotional comfort to be found in social certainty, in knowing one's role and place in the social fabric. This emotional need may well play a major role in eroding the emancipation process.

The late 1980s and early 1990s show signs of reassertion of traditional standards of femininity and masculinity, especially as they were and still are cultivated in the mainstream American middle class. A revealing content analysis of *Seventeen*, a slick teen magazine catering to middle- and upper-middle-class girls, shows the fluctuation of and the return to the old traditions. Professor Kate Peirce concluded from her content analysis, spanning nearly 25 years, that the image of the "in" girl presented by the magazine suggests that she concern herself with "appearance, household activities, and romance and dating. 60% of the editorial copy for each issue for the years 1961, 1972, and 1985 dealt with beauty, fashion, cooking, and decorating."[44] In 1972, a year still heavily influenced by the counterculture, the traditional

---

[44]Kate Peirce, "A Feminist Theoretical Perspective on the Socialization of Teenage Girls Through *Seventeen* Magazine," *Sex Roles*, 23 (October 1990): 491.

image was modified and matched by "self-development" concerns of a more feminist nature. However—and this is the important point—in 1985 the proportions of the two types of fare returned to their 1961 lopsidedness, indicating that the feminist influence was not permanent. In essence, the image of the girl was again affined to kids, kitchen, and housework and the man–woman relationship was again cast into the traditional feminine–masculine mold.

Whether the reversal to the traditional feminine role as reflected in *Seventeen* is an anomaly and a nongeneralizable editorial quirk of the magazine or whether it heralds a reversal that will increasingly become applicable to the general female population awaits further observation. In the meantime it might be a good idea to keep in mind that history is replete with examples of the most incredible reversals and regressions.

MOMISM: INFLICTING PERPETUAL ADOLESCENCE[45]

The Nature and Rise of Momism

Momism has arisen as a peculiar perversion of the personality function in the modern family and focuses on the type of mother who uses her child to gratify her neurotic needs. While the mother, to all outward appearance, does a fine job, her child-rearing practice is geared toward retaining the child and converting him or her into a perennial adolescent.

The rationale for treating this clinical issue here is that it deals with an adolescence-producing problem that is increasing in the United States and has assumed regular features in the structure of American society: with amazing frequency, Momism has become a feature of the American middle class. Statistics indicate that increasing numbers of middle-aged women (after having experienced extrafamilial careers), as well as increasing numbers of younger, unmarried women, aspire to enjoy the psychological gratifications expected from motherhood. (Chapter 8 presents related statistics.) In the process they approach motherhood with careerist principles in mind.

Early writers to call attention to Momism included Philip Wylie and Sidney C. Howard.[46] They felt that American motherhood was becoming a public danger, inflicting psychological harm on children. They stimulated investigation by social scientists, and the reference to a "Mom" gradually

[45]The treatment of Momism in this section focuses on a specific application of the concept—its effects on adolescence. A fuller discussion can be found in Hans Sebald, *Momism—The Silent Disease of America* (Chicago: Nelson-Hall, 1976).

[46]Philip Wylie, *Generation of Vipers* (New York: Rinehart and Co., 1942), and Sidney C. Howard, *The Silver Cord: A Satire in Three Acts* (New York: Scribner's, 1928).

became a concept describing the type of mother who retards her child's maturity.[47]

In previous generations, the wife-mother role was more or less the only life task available to women. Although this meant limited freedom, it also meant little anxiety, since women's lifestyle was free from ambiguity. With the advent of women's liberation, the traditional role became only *one* of a spectrum newly available. While this change added freedom to the lives of women, it also added a new worry. It brought restless soul-searching to clarify the question of how the new options could best be used. Liberation from the old-fashioned role introduced the same compulsion toward achievement as has been the psychological torment of the male.

And it is at this juncture that many a half-liberated woman takes an ironic turn: she opts for staying home and becoming an outstanding mother. Motherhood becomes her career, with the output of "perfect" children the tangible evidence of her success. It seems that the visions of liberation did not necessarily match the more slowly changing social structural arrangements that perpetuate the conditions that keep women at home. In other words, psychological emancipation is not fully implemented by structural emancipation. This structural-lag condition inflicts feelings of relative deprivation on the woman who wants but cannot step out into the professional world. Opportunity to compensate for deeply felt deprivation is visualized in a new type of motherhood that establishes evidence of competence. What is overlooked in the haste to preserve self-respect is the fact that the child is not accepted as an end in him- or herself, but only as a means—and a young personality used for the alleviation of a neurosis cannot help but acquire its own.

Focus: The Mother-Son Relationship

Momism usually involves the mother-*son* relationship, since a girl, even if dominated by her mother, can adopt her manners, imitate her, and take on her role. In fact, this is the way many Moms are created: a girl patterning her behavior after mother. She is free to do so since both imitator and imitated are of the same sex. This is reflected in the findings of researchers, who found that girls resemble their mothers in terms of personality much more

---

[47]Edward A. Strecker, *Their Mothers' Sons: The Psychiatrist Examines an American Problem* (New York: Lippincott, 1946); David M. Levy, *Maternal Overprotection* (New York: Columbia University Press, 1943); Erik H. Erikson, *Childhood and Society* (New York: W. W. Norton, Inc., 1963); Martha W. Lear, *The Child-Worshipers* (New York: Crown Publishers, 1963); Margaret Mead, "What Is Happening to the American Family?" *Journal of Social Casework*, 28 (November 1947): 323–30; Arnold W. Green, "The Middle-Class Male Child and Neurosis," *American Sociological Review*, 11 (February 1946): 31–41; and Patricia C. Sexton, *The Feminized Male: Classrooms, White Collars and the Decline of Manliness* (New York: Random House, 1969).

than boys.[48] (The boy's vulnerability to Momism justifies the masculine pronoun when referring to "child" in this discussion.)

Most American fathers are only peripherally involved in socializing their children. This explains why the boy is more vulnerable to Momism than the girl; he lacks a close and daily visible male model. In fact, Momism can occur only if the father fails to enact his part in child-rearing.[49]

The Core Technique

The typical Mom tries to achieve her "success" goal by manipulating the child's behavior by extending or withdrawing love, or by promising to do so. It is powerful "love"-oriented sanction that is responsible for impairing personality growth in the child and establishing a mother-dependency that does not go away when he reaches adolescence; it should be replaced with personal autonomy. Since love is experienced as something *conditional*— contingent on how he behaves and not as something he deserves on the basis of his innate worth—the slightest disapproval of mother (and later of any outside authority) will cause him anxiety. His feeling of acceptability depends on constant approval by others. A mind so conditioned has little reprieve from anxiety.

An important element of this conditioning process is the boy's belief that he *needs* that love. "Not the need for parent love, but the constant threat of its withdrawal *after the child has been conditioned to the need,* lies at the root of the most characteristic modern neurosis."[50] Empirical evidence suggests that maternal achievement pressures are more effective than paternal pressures because of mother's use of the "love"-oriented sanctions.[51]

A tentative profile of the Mom has emerged by now. She (1) is most likely middle class; (2) has a good education, has been steeped in "scientific child-rearing," and has been affected by the promises of the feminist movement; (3) has turned to mothering as a method of producing evidence of competence and "success"; (4) has no husband or one who is merely peripherally involved in the socialization of the child; (5) has a son, usually an only

[48]Ruth E. Hartley, "Children's Concepts of Male and Female Roles," *Merrill-Palmer Quarterly,* 6 (January 1960): 83–91; Lionel M. Lasowick, "On the Nature of Identification," *Journal of Abnormal and Social Psychology,* 51 (September 1955): 175–83; and David B. Lynn, "The Process of Learning Parental and Sex-Role Identification," *Journal of Marriage and the Family,* 28 (November 1966): 466–70; and *The Father: His Role in Child Development* (Belmont, CA: Wadsworth, 1976).

[49]Fitzhugh Dodson, *How to Father* (Bergenfield, NJ: New American Library, 1975); Michael E. Lamb, "Paternal Influences and the Father's Role," in John Keating, ed., *Social Psychology 82/83* (Guilford, CT: Dushkin, 1982): pp. 68–73.

[50]Green, "The Middle-class Male Child and Neurosis," p. 39 (Italics added.)

[51]R. R. Sears, E. E. Maccoby, and H. Levin, *Patterns of Child-Rearing* (Evanston, IL: Row & Peterson, 1957); and Garven Hudgins, "Cheating: Grave Pressures," *AP Education Service,* February 1969.

child, she uses for alleviating feelings of relative deprivation; and (6) uses the "love"-oriented conditioning.

No two Moms are exactly alike, and their styles of manipulation differ widely; they are notably colorful and could fill a museum of psychopathology. While some may meet the above profile only partly, they all seem to have one thing in common: They manipulate the child in such a way that he remains dependent. The "love"-oriented sanction system is patently suited to serve that goal.

Although essentially retaining this core technique, some Moms become specialists in the style in which they apply the leverage. Major types include the overindulgent, overprotective, permissive, domineering, child-worshipping, "star," absolute authority, and "martyr" Moms.[52]

Consequences: From "True Believer" to Suicide

Common elements can be observed among the affected males: (1) the inability to make decisions; (2) feelings of inferiority; (3) a particular brand of anxiety; (4) patterns of irresponsible behavior; and (5) emotional parasitism, that is, insufficiently controlled narcissism and egocentrism.

These consequences do not always become obvious. The Momistically impaired person tends to gravitate toward a "normal" situation, such as a marriage where he locks into complementary interaction. In most instances he marries a Mom type who substitutes for his erstwhile Mom. This constitutes the "silent majority" of which no one takes much notice.

There are also the sensational types: the sexual deviate, drug addict, psychopath, schizophrenic, and suicide. For example, a team of New York City social workers trying to discover why they were unsuccessful in helping young addicts found the latter's mothers employing various stealthy techniques to keep the sons addicted and thereby Mom-dependent. One mother was the "martyr" Mom; another bailed her boy out of jail while he waiting to be admitted to a hospital for addicts.[53] Some mothers encouraged the drug habit by giving their sons ten dollars every day "for a haircut," or fifteen dollars "for a shirt." Similarly, the Family Institute of Chicago, studying heroin and barbiturate addicts, discovered that the stars of the drama were the inefficient father, the domineering-but-protective Mom, and the helplessly dependent son.[54] Additional examples have been described by David

---

[52]These types are discussed in detail in Hans Sebald, *Momism: The Silent Disease of America.*

[53]"Mom Is the Villain," *Time*, May 21, 1965, p. 83.

[54]John Schwartzman, "The Addict, Abstinence, and the Family," *American Journal of Psychiatry*, 132 (February 1975): 154–57.

McCullaugh who sampled the list of famous personages whom he suspects of Momistic affliction.[55]

Other writers focused on extreme cases, such as a thirty-seven-year-old Wisconsin man whose mother took him everywhere in a wheel cart, allegedly because he suffered from polio. Welfare officials finally prevailed and had him examined—he was found capable of walking. It was his mother, not polio, who had disabled him. When the son had been temporarily removed from the mother at age fifteen to attend school, he curled up in a fetal position and remained in this position for twenty-two years, spoon-fed, diapered, and wheeled around by his mother who insisted that "I like him just the way he is."[56]

A common and yet often undetected outcome of Momism is the individual who has always relied on his mother for decision making and who later adheres to a substitute decision making figure. He may become a "true believer," who exhibits a total submission to some supposedly infallible and omnipotent ideology or charismatic leader.[57] It is from people of this temperament that totalitarian movements (be they religious or political) recruit some of their most fanatic followers.

A study in Scandinavian countries discovered correlations between the suicide rate and the style of child rearing.[58] Denmark, with one of the world's highest suicide rates, is characterized by a child-rearing style that creates highly guilt-conscious and dependent personalities. When forced to face an important situation demanding a major decision, a victim of Momism may withdraw from reality to escape pain, guilt, and insecurity—and the ultimate withdrawal can be achieved through self-inflicted death. Norway, with one of the lowest suicide rates, is much like Denmark in most variables, *except* in child-rearing procedures.

The consequences of Momism should be understood with the following points in mind:

1. The effects usually overlap and form combinations.
2. Mother influence can of course be detected in the lives of entirely healthy males, and a pathological connotation should not be attached to all symptoms.
3. Momism should therefore be defined as exceeding normal influence to the point of crippling the personality.
4. Duration of symptoms of Momistic impairment differs from victim to victim, in some cases lasting a lifetime and in other cases disappearing soon after the offspring leaves home.

[55]David McCullaugh, "Mama's Boys," *Psychology Today*, March 1983, pp. 32–38.

[56]"Rehabilitation: Return From the Womb," *Time*, May 17, 1963, p. 93.

[57]This concept was first coined by Eric Hoffer, *The True Believer* (New York: Mentor Books, 1951).

[58]Herbert Hendin, *Suicide and Scandinavia* (New York: Grune and Stratton, 1964).

5. Only a proportion of males suffering from such problems as drug addiction, homosexuality, and suicidal tendencies can be traced to a Momistic experience.
6. Momism can ensue only when the father defaults in helping with child rearing.
7. Diagnosis of a disturbance as an outcome of Momism is often difficult and should be attempted only after careful investigation.

DADISM: WHAT HAPPENS TO PAPA'S LITTLE GIRL

It would be misleading to imply that the stifling influence that a mother can bring to bear on a son is without equivalent in the father-daughter relationship. In that case it is usually the domineering and patronizing father-daughter relationship, a form of Dadism, that can truncate the girl's personality development. But there is a significant cultural difference. As mentioned in an earlier chapter, the boy's masculinity is still upheld, and serious deviation from it is negatively sanctioned in our civilization. Not so with the girl's femininity. The modern female has a vast range from which she can choose her role, ranging from old-fashioned femininity to the modern egalitarian stance. Dadism inculcates the former, that is, he raises, manipulates, and conditions Papa's little girl in the ways of feminine submissiveness. And by cultural dictum, there's not much wrong with that.

> To all appearances it is done in good taste and style: he is merely producing a feminine personality with society's stamp of "good housekeeping." The little girl will receive top grades from her father (later from her teacher, boy friend, and spouse) for growing up to be timid yet "sweet," indecisive yet "compatible," dependent yet "supportive," unsure of herself yet "loving"—in short, "very feminine." This is the way society has camouflaged the stifled personality of females. They cause no problems. They fit a system of male supremacy.[59]

Because these girls are acceptable to our cultural standards—at least to a time-honored set of them—they don't appear to be as pathological as the boys suffering from Momism. The father-dominated girl is cast into the complementary feminine role that does not cause adjustment problems—as long as the traditional role behavior is expected from them. (The traditional acceptability of submissive femininity is also the reason for the sparsity of research done in this interesting area.)

Dadism and its peculiar feminine product may not go unchallenged forever. The attack on the traditional feminine style by the women's liberation movement appears to have made some inroads on raising the subservient girl. With advanced emancipation, this age-old power play may eventually be perceived for what it really is: the interference with the process of a

---

[59]Hans Sebald, *Momism—The Silent Disease of America*, p. 115.

girl's unfolding her true potential and unique personality. It will be branded as hindering a young woman from developing her own personal identity.

SUMMARY

Behavioral orientation is not limited to membership groups, but can be a product of identification with abstract reference groups. Understanding of the behavior of modern adolescents has become difficult because of their exposure to multiple, shifting, conflicting, and sometimes unclear reference groups. This accounts for misunderstood and unexplained behavior patterns, including deviations from adult norms and confused and situationally compartmentalized behavior.

Significant others are models influencing personality development. Traditionally, parents served as such important figures, but modern conditions have diminished the effectiveness of personal models. Among these conditions are the abundance of available reference groups, the relative invisibility or absence of personal models, and exposure to characters portrayed in the mass media.

The traditional sex-specific expectations have become blurred. Nonspecificity has created new freedoms. However, the price for freedom of individuality is uncertainty and anxiety. Erosion of traditional sex-role definitions has come to greatly affect the boy–girl interaction and the personality of the teenage girl. Young women manifest their role change by altered behavior in many areas; for example, in sexual activities, intellectual expression, competition, and such negative phenomena as crime and suicide.

The tendency of many modern mothers to perceive motherhood as a form of career with the corollary of product-centeredness and success orientation has warranted a new concept: Momism. It seems that this new type of careerism affects particularly the mother-son relationship, with great detriment to the boy's personality. Dadism deals with the father-daughter relationship in a different way: the girl's personality is cast into the supplementary feminine role which in our culture is not necessarily perceived as pathological, though close examination may reveal a stifled and limited personality growth.

5

Conditions of Postindustrial Life

The structure of postindustrial society is eminently adolescence-inducing. Super-industrialization has accentuated the discontinuity and the isolation of social positions, converted education into a custodial institution, depersonalized the authority hierarchy, and altered cultural attitudes toward the meaning of work and material achievement. The impact of these conditions on young people is discussed in this chapter.

ISOLATION IN MODERN SOCIAL STRUCTURE

Probably the most striking feature of postindustrial society is its complex network of positions. The division of labor, the way society distributes the functions necessary for its maintenance, includes such fine subdivisions that most people would be unable to identify all of them. An example is the network that regulates automobile use: the operator-licensing office, the auto-licensing office, laws, courts, law-enforcement agencies, the highway department, driver's education classes, insurance companies, and so forth.

Since American working conditions rarely give the individual a chance to do a "whole" job, a sharp discontinuity arises between the life of the child and the life of the adult. The life of the child is more holistic, in that his or her early education and training usually take in the broadest range of different curricula and activities. In late adolescence, when a youth begins a job, this broad range abruptly narrows, and the individual must focus on one particular activity for which he or she probably was not specifically prepared and may require new training and education. The job may be so specialized that, as a child or teenager, he or she may not have had a model or role definition to aid in understanding the new situation. As a result, thousands of teenagers who enter the labor force immediately after, or even before, graduation from high school are unable to decide which vocation will provide personal fulfillment. Their reactions often take the form of discontent and frequent job changes.

To see the multispecific nature of modern social structure in the right perspective, it is necessary to elaborate on two interrelated phenomena. One is the nature of the general culture and the other is the process of achieving personal identity. As already mentioned in Chapter 2, there seems to be a gradual shift of identity-genesis from the culture to one's specific social position. This trend was brought about by diminishing persuasiveness of the culture and, at the same time, by an increasing social-structural specialization. The multispecific social system makes it increasingly difficult to interpret its variegated life experiences into generally understandable terms.

Sociologist Daniel Bell recognized this development and saw the general cultural plateau of postindustrial society undergoing a kind of atrophy because of the outgrowth of technical specialization.[1] He understood culture as a symbolic expression of the common social processes in which people are involved in everyday life. People need such symbolic expression to communicate and share their experiences with one another. But superindustrialization impedes such sharing, and the common ground for symbolic expression is eroding away under the growth of a highly specialized division of labor. Consequences have been felt in all sectors of life and have been symptomized as political alienation, work dissatisfaction, and the general feeling of ignorance and powerlessness vis-à-vis an unfathomable and amorphous industrial-scientific complex. In short, culture is failing in its function to serve as a forum through which people can find common expression. Our advanced technology, with its finely divided and isolated work patterns, inhibits the formulation of common symbolic expression and fosters isolation and alienation.

What modern society fails to provide in terms of ideational guidance it tries to make up in bureaucratic guidance. But this effort is of little help. Indeed, it worsens the situation because it adds to *anomie* an element of unfreedom that blocks the search for new principles and prohibits experi-

---

[1]Daniel Bell, "The Post-Industrial Society," in *Technology and Social Change*, ed. Eli Ginzberg (New York: Columbia University Press, 1964), and *The Cultural Contradictions of Capitalism* (New York: Basic Books, 1976).

mentation with new behavior patterns. Thus, as Peter Berger, Brigitte Berger, and Hansfried Kellner pointed out, alienation through bureaucratization turns modern humans into "homeless minds" in search of a meaningful culture.[2]

As a consequence, people depend on discrete social positions for personal identity and partially ignore a culture that is too general to represent the wide spectrum of life experiences. In fact, in this type of society, culture *cannot afford* to be specific, since it would contradict or discriminate against the life experiences of many members.

It is true, however, that the superficial and sensate ingredients of postindustrial culture are widely shared, creating the impression of a culture of substance and viability. But a close look reveals that most messages and images are geared toward sensate appeals or common anxieties and not toward an ideational union or commitment. The common cultural denominator intelligible to the masses of the postindustrial society is the sensate. (Echoes of Sorokin's philosophy of history!) Postindustrial people compensate for *anomie* and superficiality by clinging to social positions for directions and goals.

This situation creates identity problems for youth. While still generalists, dependent on vague and nonspecific cultural "blueprints," young people suffer from *anomic* conditions that create difficulty in answering "Who am I?" unless parental guidance and value indoctrination compensate for cultural nonspecificity. It is not until the young person enters and feels at home in a specific position that a sense of trustworthy identity develops. This, then, is the dilemma of modern adolescents.

The above generalizations, applicable as they may be to the majority of American youth, require several modifications. The first deals with the institution of apprenticeship, a process whereby the young are systematically introduced into the adult division of labor. An apprentice had a defined status, with rights and obligations specified in a contract, and spent from three to six years under the supervision of a master. After successful completion, he or she was initiated (by rite of passage) into the rank of journeyman and henceforth regarded as an adult.

The United States tried to encourage the tradition of apprenticeship through the National Apprenticeship Act of 1937, wherein the Secretary of Labor was "authorized to formulate and promote the labor standards necessary to safeguard the welfare of apprentices, to encourage the inclusion of such standards in contracts, to bring together employers and labor for the formulation of programs of apprenticeships."[3] About 420,000 Americans

---

[2]Peter Berger, Brigitte Berger, and Hansfried Kellner, *The Homeless Mind* (New York: Random House, 1973).

[3]*United States Congressional Record*, Chapter 663, Washington, DC, August 1937, p. 664.

benefited from this legislation in 1980 and were trained as carpenters, electricians, iron workers, barbers, butchers, painters, printers, roofers, and in many other skills. The number of such registered apprentices had substantially increased over the preceding ten years which was only 155,000 in 1962.[4] The Bureau of Apprenticeship and Training of the United States Department of Labor suggested a composite portrait of the "typical apprentice": he is a "married 25 year old male high school graduate with no physical handicap, presently in his third year of apprenticeship, and whose father does not work in the same trade. Prior to his apprenticeship he did have a full-time job, and his chances of being a veteran are about even."[5] While apprentices are still predominantly male, the 1981 Report shows that the proportion of women is steadily increasing; it was 4.3 percent in 1978 and 6.4 percent by 1980.

The second qualification deals with the widespread custom of teenagers working part-time during their school years. This practice sometimes prepares them for positions and hence reduces the "culture shock" when entering the adult position. The important functions of part-time work experience for a teenager include: (1) a feeling of economic independence; (2) a feeling of self-reliance; (3) a strengthening of self-respect; (4) acceptance of proper sex-role behavior; (5) rehearsing and practicing socially responsible behavior; and (6) facilitating the process of selecting and preparing for a final occupation.

Another modification must take into consideration the direction young people often obtain through their families. This is particularly true for youngsters growing up in families strongly bonded to religious belief and/or subcultural tradition. For example, a youngster growing up and taking active part in a Mormon community, or one following the Amish way of life, or one integrated in a fundamentalist Christian tradition may not have the problems of forming a personal identity as those growing up in a more liberal and secular family. (Though it must be added that such identity transmission may mean foreclosure of a more individualistic identity formation.)

PURSUIT OF INSTANTNESS

One of the most cherished goals of supertechnology is *instantness* of result and gratification. One may view the achievement of instantness as the acid test of a postindustrial society's capability of providing goods and services. The rationalization of processes of manufacture and service creates a soaring productivity, and postindustrial economy holds out at least two promises: the

---

[4]U.S. Department of Labor, *Employment and Training Report*, Government Printing Office, Washington, DC, 1981, pp. 45, 46.

[5]U.S. Department of Labor, Apprentice Survey, Code 321, Government Printing Office, Washington, DC, March 1975, p. 8.

promise of instantness of gratification and the promise of elimination of scarcity.

Given the American obsession with time and efficiency, it comes as no surprise that this society has become the prototype of *technological instant-ness* and has assumed virtual world leadership in this capacity. Promises of instant results abound and have become an ever present feature of consumerism. Numerous products and services are promoted with the adjective *instant*. Examples include drugs ("instant relief" through Dristan/Aspirin/Excedrin/Rolaids/and so on, "instant sleep" through Sominex), food ("instant" coffee/rice/breakfast/pudding/potatoes/and so on), transportation ("instant transportation" through Boeing 747), communication ("instant communication" through satellite relay), finance ("instant credit" by supermarkets), religion ("instant prayer" by dialing a number), cosmetics ("instant hairsetting" by Clairol), recreation ("instant dancing through dance studios), and so forth.[6] The range of modern instancies has created the impression that instancy is unlimited. This is an illusion. While in many sectors of modern life the expectation for immediacy is realistic, in some sectors it is unrealistic. Hence the vision of and the insistence on instantness in *all* aspects of life are delusory.

Modern adolescents are particularly receptive to this delusion. The inventions and miracles of modern science are no longer awesome to adolescents; they are taken for granted and expected to be available whenever desired. In short, youthful attitudes include the naive belief in and the unabashed demand for instantness in *all* areas of life. This includes the extrapolation of the principle of *instant results* from the feasible to the nonfeasible.

One area where instancy is not feasible is mental achievement and psychological maturity. There are no instant "knowledge pills."

Adolescents are involved in an intense process of mental development and must learn a culture, memorize a vast body of technical knowledge, and, at the core of all these mental tasks, form a personal identity. Our technocracy's ethos of instantness seduces them into believing that shortcuts and instant achievements can be had in these intricate processes. In the process, the American ethos of the right to the pursuit of happiness becomes corrupted into the assumption of the right to *instant happiness*, and deferment of gratification becomes unintelligible and repugnant to American youth.

The postindustrial promise of instantness and youth's natural hedonism coalesce into the tenacious inclination to eschew delay and tedious effort. Postindustrial adolescents grow up with a vastly diminished concept of the scarcity of goods and services. The pioneer era and the hardships of the Great

---

[6]See details in Hans Sebald, "The Pursuit of Instantness in Technocratic Society and Youth's Psychedelic Drug Use," *Adolescence*, 7 (Fall 1972): 343-50.

Depression are to them mere historical anecdotes, encountered only when an instructor insists that they read assignments or when a grandfather relates "stories." Emphasis in American life is no longer on producing, but on consuming—and on being able to do so instantaneously. These changes have had impact on the American mentality for already two to three decades, and the symptoms have become noticeable in many sectors of public life.

The educational institution is an example. College education has increasingly come to be viewed as just another "right," the ingredients of which a student should be able to enjoy instantly. Students intuitively try to make it palatable and add it to the list of American "fun and instantness." Americans, accustomed to instantness in life, experience difficulty in coping with exceptions. As Bruno Bettelheim observed: "The expectation is that education can hand over knowledge and skill, and this nearly instantly."[7]

DIVORCING THE HOME FROM THE WORKPLACE

In industrialized societies, the setting for raising children and the setting for employment have become separate realms. The practice of commuting from the home to the place of employment seems to be directly correlated with the degree of a country's industrial development. For example, in the 1950s West Germany had roughly 3 million people commuting to jobs in communities outside their own. In 1965, with progressing technology, industrialization, and affluence (but the same national population figure), the number of commuters was 6.3 million.[8]

Most urban families no longer practice the tradition whereby the son takes on the occupation of his father and the daughter that of her mother. (However, most girls still learn the wife-mother role through the mother.) James S. Coleman found that in the city and the suburbs less than one out of ten boys intended to pursue the occupation of his father.[9] In most cases, the children are not familiar with the specific type of work their fathers do, and when they assume their own vocational activities they are received into a completely new surrounding. The abrupt change from primary socialization in the nuclear family to secondary socialization in the job can create considerable confusion.

Conditions of modern society have gradually changed the family from a production unit to a consumption unit. Each member is *individually* engaged in the production process. This is strikingly different from the tribal or folk

---

[7]Bruno Bettelheim, "Student Revolt, The Hard Core," *Vital Speeches of the Day,* 35 (1968–69): 406.

[8]*The Bulletin,* Press and Information Office of the Federal Republic of Germany, Bonn, November 9, 1965, p. 6.

[9]James S. Coleman, *The Adolescent Society* (New York: Free Press, 1963), p. 7.

societies where the consanguine family is a production unit as well as a consumption unit and where only the most elementary division of labor exists. The network of positions may comprise merely a few simple status definitions, such as hunters, warriors, chiefs, housekeepers, and so on. This type of social structure prevents discontinuity between the position of the child and of the adult, since children experience early involvement in visible and imitable work. Primary and secondary socialization are merged into one process.

In contrast, in a rapidly changing and highly rationalized society education within the family has been replaced by formal institutions covering an ever longer span of time. Nonfamilial education and training has resulted in a by-product: the evolution of *social systems* that resemble subcultures with norms and values of their own. As a result, not only have education and job training been removed from parental supervision, but so has youth. They now belong to a society of peers, a society whose natural habitat is the campus of the high school or college.

The population of this youth habitat has risen sharply over the last decades. In 1900, only 11 percent of America's high school-aged youth were *in* high school; in 1930, the proportion was 51 percent;[10] today it is estimated at well over 90 percent. The emphasis on formal education is directly correlated with industrial development—a correlation observable the world over.

When it is the mother who works away from home, especially in a one-parent situation, a by-product sometimes is the so-called latchkey child who returns from school in the afternoon and spends unsupervised hours until mother comes home. (An alternative is the day-care center child, discussed below in the section on Home away from Home.) The number of latchkey children in the U.S. has been estimated to be roughly 10 million,[11] and for many years researchers have talked about the psychological pros and cons for this type of child. They have arrived at divergent conclusions. The negative view held that the child is prone to experience feelings of neglect, even rejection, and thus develops behavior problems. More recent findings seem to suggest that such concern is usually overdrawn. One study compared children who spent after-school hours unsupervised with a matched group of children who were cared for by adults. The researchers found no significant differences. Latchkey children were as high in self-esteem as were those under adult supervision.[12] Cornell University psychologist Urie Bronfenbrenner, a researcher of the latchkey situation for many years, basically agreed with this finding and concluded that what really matters is whether there are expectations about how children occupy themselves during unsupervised

---

[10]James S. Coleman, *Adolescents and the Schools* (New York: Basic Books, 1965), p. 7.
[11]Amitai Etzioni, "US Needs," *U.S. News and World Report*, January 9, 1984, p. 59.
[12]Jeff Meer, "Children—Alone but not Neglected," *Psychology Today*, August 1985, p. 11.

time. Moreover, each child is different, and structured self-care arrangements need to be individually adjusted.[13]

Nonetheless, the opportunities to get involved with peer groups and possibly with subcultural activities of course increase with the amount of time children are on their own.

EDUCATION IN POSTINDUSTRIAL PERSPECTIVE

The modern educational institution plays a salient role in the lives of the young and calls for a separate examination. Hence the major discussion is deferred to Chapter 9. A brief summary preview is offered at this time for the purpose of indicating that the topic has an important place in the array of postindustrial conditions.

Nonfamilial Education

Modern education has assumed a ghetto existence away from most adult institutions. This is particularly true of high school campuses, the Teenland America, where students pursue their own values, styles, and lingo. Never before have the institutions of the family and of education been such separate experiences. Many families do not see the values they cherish reflected in the schools. Such nonfamilial education has aroused opposition in ethnic groups, who fear their children might be unduly exposed to worldly and decadent influences. One example is the Amish, who have opposed "worldly" education persistently enough to persuade the authorities to grant them their own Amish-run schools. Obviously, the vast majority of American school-aged children do not have such a unitary experience. They continue to experience a parallel socialization process with family and school remaining separate, if not opposing, institutions.

Longer Education

There has been a steady increase in years added to the formal education of Americans. Roughly half of the American population now has finished high school *and* spent some time in college. Prolonging the sojourn in academia means prolonging adolescence by offering a moratorium on social responsibilities, allowing time for psychological growth, and delaying career decisions.

The extended segregation of the young from adult life unintentionally created a setting conducive to: (1) peer influence and subculture formation;

---

[13]Ibid.

(2) freedom of sexual experimentation; and (3) mate selection beyond the constraints of parental control.

Custodial Education

While longer education is in part a function of the necessary preparation for sophisticated careers, it is in part also a holding pen to keep the young from invading the labor market too soon and adding to unemployment pressure. The increasing concern voiced over the educational dropout is motivated less out of awe for the presumed knowledge disseminated through the educational process than out of worry of not knowing what else to do with the masses of America's young.

HIGH MOBILITY

Urban-industrial Americans are among the world's most mobile people. Precisely how this trait affects American youth and their adolescent experience is not yet fully understood. Probably the best that can be done is to suggest plausible hypotheses.

First, what is meant by mobility? The term has several meanings. One refers to movement within the social structure, either vertically or horizontally. Changing from the occupation of waiter to that of doctor would be an example of vertical mobility, while changing from factory worker to construction worker would be an example of horizontal mobility. Mobility can also refer to geographic movement—a kind of mobility that is remarkable among Americans.

Vertical Social Mobility

This type of mobility compares members of one generation with those of the next (generational mobility) or compares different stages in the life of one individual (career mobility). The focus here is on generational mobility and the resulting discontinuities. Part of the American heritage is the Protestant ethic, which includes a mobility ethic that encourages Americans to achieve "success" in life. Hence, the young are not necessarily encouraged to follow in parental footsteps, but to improve on the latter's lives.

In most industrial societies, the placement function of the family has declined. While it is true that children identify and are identified by status and prestige of their families, as teenagers and young adults they become detached from familial influence, and social standing depends increasingly on personal achievements. The status eventually achieved may be on a different level from that of the parents. In postindustrial society, family origin affects the status of the individual only indirectly, by influencing opportunities for educational and occupational achievements.

Research in American generational mobility has shown widespread discontinuity between the careers of the parents and the offspring. Sociologists Cecil C. North and Paul K. Hatt surveyed sons' deviations from fathers' occupations and revealed that, with the sole exception of farming, no occupational category achieved more than one-third generational continuity.[14] It should be noted that those who classified their occupation in the same general class as their fathers' did not necessarily occupy the *same specific* occupation, implying that a great deal of horizontal mobility existed *within* the broad occupational classes. Coleman found that few boys planned to follow in the occupational footsteps of their fathers. His survey showed 23 percent of boys in small towns and only 9.8 percent of boys in city and suburban schools planning to enter their fathers' occupation.[15]

The mobility ethic can have a devastating impact on those adolescents who fail, as some must, in the process of status striving. In a society that encourages all to strive and that promises success to those who are capable, failure is considered evidence of personal inadequacy. For those who achieve upward mobility, difficult adjustments are required. This problem is frequently evident in both the research literature and the popular "success" story, describing the situation of the rich and successful but unhappy and maladjusted man or woman.

Lack of family continuity and tradition may present teenagers with an obscure future for which they have no visible models. They are called upon to make one of the most vital decisions in life—choosing a career. The mobility ethic, expecting the teenager to go beyond the family's level of achievement and improve his or her level of social prestige, contributes additional pressures. By ruling out parents as occupational models, a familiar sociocultural orientation is rendered irrelevant. Most teenagers who choose an occupation or vocational training that differs significantly from their parents' undergo a shift in life orientation often comparable to "culture shock."

Horizontal Social Mobility

The 1980s reflected a typical postindustrial phenomenon: high mobility of American workers within the general confines of their vocational categories. Rapid economic and technological changes prompted over 11 million workers, roughly 10.5 percent of the work force, to change jobs during a

[14]Cecil C. North and Paul K. Hatt, "Jobs and Occupations: A Popular Evaluation," *Opinion News*, 9 (September 1947): 3–13.
[15]Coleman, *The Adolescent Society*.

year's time. This has been computed to mean that, on the average, the American worker changes jobs 11 times during his or her life.[16]

Geographic Mobility

Approximately 17 percent of the American population changes address each year,[17] compared with about 12 percent in Europe and 8 percent in Japan.[18] If we accept the theory that development of a stable personality depends on a consistent environment, disruption of life patterns through frequent moving should negatively influence the adolescent experience, prolong it, and aggravate confusion. Research has revealed that children and adolescents whose families move are dismayed about losing friends, worried about making new ones, and show a decline in scholastic achievement. Highly mobile youths (who have moved twice or more) exhibited notable maladjustments to peers and were less frequently chosen as playmates than youths with local roots.[19]

Military families are prototypes of this mobility, and their children have been found to be characterized by social and psychiatric troubles. Psychiatrist Don M. LaGrone found 12 percent of all children and adolescents on a base in need of psychiatric help and diagnosed 4 percent of them as psychotic. Causal to these conditions, he felt, were extensive father-absence, the families seeing themselves as transients with no roots, and children moving from school to school so frequently that they had to break into peer groups repeatedly as the "new kid" and were often the school's scapegoats.[20]

Other studies of youngsters of military families have found that lengthy separation from one parent, usually the father, caused interesting psychological upheavals. For example, navy personnel may ship out for six to ten months at a time. How children react to these separations, virtually creating temporary one-parent families, depends largely upon their age. Tom, a high-school junior, reports that his father was on the ship twice, each time for eight months. The first time, Tom was a toddler and can't remember when his father returned. The second time, Tom was a teenager and cast into the role of being "the man of the house" during father's absence. Upon father's return, father and son experienced a power battle, for now father resumed

[16]"Tomorrow," *U.S. News and World Report,* August 15, 1983, p. 12.

[17]"US Census," *U.S. News and World Report,* May 14, 1984, p. 24.

[18]U.S. Department of Labor, *Economic Forces in the United States* (Washington, DC: Government Printing Office, 1973); and AP report (Washington, October 20, 1975).

[19]Joseph Schaller, "The Relation Between Geographic Mobility and School Behavior," *Man–Environment Systems,* 5 (May 1975): 185–87.

[20]Don M. LaGrone, "The Military Family Syndrome," *American Journal of Psychiatry,* 135 (September 1978): 1040–43.

being "the man of the house." Certain privileges, such as staying up late with mom to watch television or escorting her to certain functions, were rescinded and Tom reacted with confusion and resentment. A daughter may similarly react upon the return of a uniformed parent.[21]

It seems that the worst stress resulting from moving or from the temporary one-parent situation occurs during the junior or senior year in high school, for this is the time of strongest involvement and identification with peers. It is feared that after having to leave close friends repeatedly, these teenagers learn to establish superficial friendships.[22] Studies have found that military adolescents spend more time with their parent or parents—whether completing homework, playing games, or doing chores—than with other adolescents. "Both groups showed the normal adolescent break from parents, but it came somewhat later for the military youth."[23]

Vance Packard takes this contention a step further and, in A *Nation of Strangers*, expresses concern that too many Americans move too often, become rootless, and contribute to the decline of a sense of community.[24]

While the effects of frequent moving can be interpreted as disruptions of identification processes, they can also be interpreted as providing the young with extra opportunities for learning and greater variety of reference persons. One could argue that adolescents subject to mobility acquire more information and better insight. This may make the process of identity growth more complex (compared with the process of the nonmobile youths who stay in one community), but not less valid or stable in its final outcome. In fact, one might argue that for the nonmobile, roots become ruts. At this time, the statistical question waiting to be researched is: How many people adapt easily to and grow emotionally and intellectually by moving, and how many suffer and how seriously?

HOME AWAY FROM HOME

Many American children are raised, partially or wholly, away from the parental home. Some children are entrusted to the care of a partial home while their mothers are employed full-time. Others are victims of disabled or delinquent parents and grow up in welfare institutions. Still others are delinquent youths who serve time in juvenile or rehabilitative institutions. This discussion deals with those children in day-care centers part-time and those in welfare institutions full-time.

21Patricia Long, "Growing Up Military," *Psychology Today*, December 1986, p. 34.
22Ibid., p. 35.
23Ibid., p. 36.
24Vance Packard, A *Nation of Strangers* (New York: David McKay, 1972).

The Day-Care Center

Day-care centers enable mothers to simultaneously pursue motherhood and an occupation outside of the home. Day care was available in 1987 for nearly 25 percent of the almost 10 million preschool children whose mothers worked. In 1970 only 13 percent of the 5 million preschool children of working mothers were in day-care centers. This means that within one decade the proportion of the children in day care nearly doubled.[25]

Effects of maternal employment on children's personalities have been studied by many investigators. Examination of the research literature by Edith H. Grotberg revealed a diversity of findings regarding the correlation between mother's employment and children's delinquency, school and personal adjustment, and academic achievement.[26] While some studies demonstrated the positive functions of day care, such as increased language skill and a sense of security within a group setting, others concluded negatively, pointing up reduced capacity for emotional attachment, diminished sense of autonomy, and stifled creativity.[27]

The findings fail to add up to a consistent picture, and suspicion is warranted that research has ignored important variables. There are many relatively unexamined conditions that play an intermediary role between a mother's work away from home and the personality formation of the child. For example, one study discovered that a mother's liking or disliking of her job is significantly associated with how she interacts with her children. Mothers liking their work had more positive relationships with their children, though their children exhibited nonassertive and dependent attitudes. Mothers who disliked their work had more negative relationships with their children, and their children exhibited assertive and hostile attitudes.[28]

Correlations of this nature remind us of the complexity of the matter and of the many variables that enter into the picture. Such variables must be explored before we can obtain a clearer view of maternal employment and its impact on children.

The Full-Time Institution

Full-time institutions are for youths who have no, or no adequately functioning, parents. Information derived from studying youths in such

[25]U.S. Bureau of the Census, *Current Population Reports*, "Child Care Arrangements," Series p-70, No. 20, U.S. Government Printing Office, Washington, DC, 1990, p. 5.

[26]Edith H. Grotberg, *Review of Research, 1965–69, of Project Head Start*, U.S. Department of Health, Education and Welfare, Office of Child Development, 1969.

[27]Bruno Bettelheim, *The Children of the Dream* (New York: Macmillan, 1969).

[28]Lois W. Hoffman, "Effects of Maternal Employment on the Child," *Child Development*, 32 (March 1961): 187–97.

settings is more conclusive than that concerning day-care-center children. Clinicians have long agreed that substituting the parental home with the anonymous crowd in an institution has detrimental effects on children.

The case has been stated by Dr. Lauretta Bender, who observed approximately 6,000 children in New York's Bellevue Hospital for more than a decade and noted that children parentally deprived for one or more years were rarely able to adjust in foster homes: they all appear retarded, untrained, and impulsive in their behavior. As they grow older and the demands of society increase, their behavior becomes progressively more asocial.[29]

Another study reported the transfer of thirteen orphaned children, less than three years old, from the state institution where they had been living to a home for retarded women.[30] Two years later, the children showed a surprising increase in intellectual proficiency, while children who had remained at the state orphanage retained marked impairment of mental abilities. A follow-up study showed that the transferred children grew up to be normal members of the community, while most of the children in the orphanage were retarded and spent the major part of their lives in institutions. The explanation for the different outcomes was ascribed to the love and attention that the thirteen children received from the retarded inmates. The two reports are typical of numerous observations of what can happen to children reared in institutions.

A crucial shortcoming of institutional homes is the number of youths per adult supervisor or nurse. The Child Welfare League of America recommended no more than approximately six children per adult. In most institutional settings, this suggestion remains utopian. Consequences of serious understaffing and parental deprivation include the following:

1. With understaffing, anonymity is unavoidable. The child with its needs, opinions, and dreams does not receive sufficient attention *to feel known*. In fact, it is usually necessary for the nurse or supervisor to avoid emotional involvement with individual children. To carry the emotional burden of each child would be beyond the staff member's endurance.

2. The child may be disturbed by the perfunctory atmosphere of the institution and wonder whether he or she is really wanted. The feeling of *full acceptance* is immensely significant to a child, and its absence can result in feelings of personal worthlessness.

3. The experience of *physical affection* is of utmost significance in the development of a healthy personality. The effect of the caressing touch has been demonstrated in laboratory animals. In experiments with two sets of

[29]Lauretta Bender, *Aggression, Hostility and Anxiety in Children* (Springfield, IL: Thomas, 1953), p. 153.

[30]Stephen A. Richardson, "Retarded Children," *Trans-Action*, 6 (September 1969): 6.

rats, all variables were kept constant, except that the experimental group received physical caresses daily. The fondled rats gained weight faster, matured earlier, appeared healthier, and generally expressed greater vitality than the rats in the control group.[31] The basic condition underlying this finding can be extrapolated to humans. Its significance applies to the institutional setting insofar as it rarely affords conditions where the child finds sufficient physical intimacy.

4. Children have an interminable need for *question-answer* interaction. Their constant "why," "how," and "what-is-this" can hardly draw adequate responses in an institutional environment and their curiosity must go unsatisfied. This may generate indifference, dullness, and, in extreme cases, even retardation.

5. Human qualities appear to be the product of the primary family group—a sense of loyalty, cooperation, affection, and consideration. As Charles H. Cooley pointed out, these qualities are universal because of the universal primary-group experience and they constitute essential elements of what is loosely called "human nature."[32] The question arising in conjunction with the substitution of institutional homes for the primary familial home is: what modifications, if any, does the institutional substitute have on the *human nature* of the child? Will the child's sense of kindness, sympathy, and affection be reduced? Will the child develop characteristics of the sociopathic personality, showing little regard and sympathy for the suffering of others? A vast amount of research findings, a few of them already mentioned above, point to example after example of sociopathic products of institutional child rearing.

6. Institutional upbringing may add complications to the process of transition from child to adult status. A common criticism of subjecting the child to constant adult supervision is that it *prolongs dependency*. The child is deprived of the opportunity to make independent decisions, lacks opportunity to roam about, cannot escape from constant adult supervision— conditions that are inimical to developing an independent personality. Under constant supervision, the child becomes passive and prefers to let others take the initiative. Such attitude patterns cause serious problems when the individual tries to assume adult responsibilities.

7. Institutional upbringing may fix the child's loyalty and value-orientation on the institutional *peer group*. They learn early to adhere to norms and values different from those of the home and the adult world.

---

[31]Victor H. Denenberg, "Animal Studies on Developmental Determinants of Behavioral Adaptability," in *Experience, Structure and Adaptability*, ed. O. J. Harvey (New York: Springer Publishing Co., 1966), pp. 123–47.

[32]Charles H. Cooley, *Social Organization* (New York: Scribner's, 1915), pp. 23–24.

ADOLESCENT AFFLUENCE

The boost that teenager affluence has on the youth subculture was recognized years ago. Sociologist Jessie Bernard went as far as seeing the relationship in terms of strict causation: "Our teenage culture is a product of affluence. It is possible because our society can afford a large leisure class of youngsters not in the labor force but yet consumers on a vast scale, or, if in the labor force, free to spend their earnings on themselves."[33]

The causative implication of this statement is overdrawn. Affluence does not cause the teenage subculture; it has its origin in adolescence. While the affluence of late twentieth-century America causes neither adolescence nor the subculture, it effectively promotes the spread and survival of the collective expression of adolescence—the teenage subculture. This is achieved through teenagers' buying patterns, the interests of the business world, and reinforcement of stereotypical teenage behavior.

Reinforcement of teenage behavior is primarily the result of rewards obtained through conforming to peer norms. These rewards are popularity and prestige in the peer group. Adherence to peer patterns often necessitates material implementation and may involve a car, "in" clothes, electronic gadgets, cosmetics, recreational paraphernalia, and other goods and services. In order to buy the latest fads and fashions of the subculture, a teenager must have financial means. Statistics indicate that such means are available and modern teenagers control a large share of society's affluence.

Estimates from national surveys show that spending by teenagers (thirteen to nineteen years old) grew from $29 billion in 1977 to about $39 billion in 1980.[34] "From cosmetics to pizzas and from electronic games to records, teenagers and young adults make up a huge market . . . that seems resistant to recession and inflation."[35] The majority of youngsters enjoy parental safeguarding of their basic needs (housing, food, insurances, clothing) and hence are free to spend their money on leisure and luxury. The University of Michigan's Institute for Social Research found that about 40 percent of college-bound high school graduates already owned cars and that 50 percent of those not going to college owned theirs. The presumedly financially struggling American college student has, on the average, $173 per month to spend on pleasure, after room and board are paid.

High school youngsters also have an impressive consumption record. While it is impossible to cover all the market habits of American teenagers,

[33]Jessie Bernard, "Teenage Culture: An Overview," *Annals of the American Academy of Political and Social Science*, 338 (November 1961): 3.

[34]"Youth on the Move," *U.S. News and World Report*, January 5, 1981, pp. 72–76.

[35]Ibid., p. 77.

studies have provided enough data to form a general picture. Some of these data are mentioned below. The *Media Book* '79 lists the following items:

> About half of the teenagers own cameras (40 percent of the boys, 55 percent of the girls)
>
> 80 percent go to movies on a more or less regular basis (Gallup Report 1981 indicates that only 2 percent of American teenagers "never attend")
>
> 15 percent have traveled abroad within three years prior to the survey
>
> over 40 percent play tennis
>
> about 20 percent ski
>
> 86 percent of the boys and 77 percent of the girls have driver's licenses
>
> 39 percent of the boys and 53 percent of the girls buy records
>
> in comparison, a relatively low 29 percent of the boys and 43 percent of the girls buy books
>
> 52 percent of the boys and 62 percent of the girls have bicycles
>
> 42 percent eat at fast food restaurants once or more a week, with eight out of ten of them buying hamburgers[36]

Do teenagers spend their own money on such consumption? Not necessarily. The Sacramento Metropolitan Teenage Market Study disclosed that teenagers usually pay out of their own pockets for records, radios, and entertainment. This tendency increased during the 1970s, with 19 percent of the teenagers spending "parents' or others' money" in 1970, but only 10 percent did so by the mid-1970s. On the other hand, the proportion of parents or others buying jewelry, shoes and clothes for teenagers sharply increased during that period, going, for example, from 33 to 43 percent for jewelry, 37 to 52 percent for shoes, and 54 to 70 percent for clothes.[37]

To what extent do teenagers make their own buying decisions? Over 90 percent of the teenagers themselves—and not their parents—make buying decisions for almost all items.[38]

How do teenagers acquire their financial resources? One of the most common sources is the weekly allowance. The Sacramento surveys indicate that allowances have kept pace with inflation. During the 1960s, 95 percent of high school students received up to $15 a week; in 1970 and 1974, 92 and 80 percent, respectively, fell into this category. Conversely, the proportions receiving $15 or more increased from 5 percent in the 1960s to 8 percent in 1970 to 20 percent in 1974. There were no significant allowance differences between boys and girls.[39] Many students hold part-time jobs to boost their finances. Surveys in 1964, 1970, and 1974 found weekly earnings up to $15,

---

[36]*The Media Book* '79 (New York: Barlow & Papazian, 1979), pp. 469, 471.

[37]H. Nicholas Windeshausen and Paul A. Williams, *Sacramento Metropolitan Teenage Market Study* (Sacramento: California State University Center for Research, 1974), p. 26.

[38]Ibid., p. 22.

[39]Ibid., p. 8.

respectively, for 67, 45, and 42 percent of those responding. Conversely, again reflecting inflation, the over-$15 group increased from 33 to 55 to 58 percent. There were significant gender differences in income: 77 percent of the boys earned above $15, but only 28 percent of the girls fell into this category.[40] Another estimate of teenagers' (fifteen to nineteen years old) income put it at $2,370 per year during the early 1980s—all of it discretionary income that could be spent on leisure and luxury.[41]

It is interesting that despite differential income girls outspend boys early in life, a lead they apparently never relinquish. In a Rand Youth Poll's charting of twenty years of fiscal habits of America's youth, girls have consistently held a spending lead over their male counterparts. In the late teens, the gap is widened further. This raises intriguing questions. Since they earn *less* but spend *more* than boys, where and how do they get their finances? A plausible answer may be that parents buy more of the necessities for girls than boys. In addition, their boyfriends pay certain luxury and social expenses for them. Thus they can more freely spend the money they have.

Traditional male chivalry in paying for date expenses is now frequently modified by a more egalitarian philosophy. But this cannot be generalized. As in so many other realms of male-female interaction, also the expectations concerning financial responsibilities have increasingly assumed a more individualistic character. Nonetheless, it is usually reserved for the female to indicate—subtly or bluntly as it may be—what the expectations are to be. The male usually has little choice but to adjust to them.

Aware of the teen buying potential, the American business world is trying to cater to youth's tastes. It would be misleading, however, to understand the teenage influence as a one-way causality. Merchants, ad writers, and market researchers grasp the enormous potential available for exploitation and are manipulating, if not actually creating, the tastes and styles of the young. Therefore the marketing system consists of a complex interrelationship between preferences of teenagers and manipulations of the marketeers. In exactly which proportions the etiology of styles evolves is not known at this time. In any case, the teen market is a volatile one. Sometimes, a few youngsters will suddenly wear something to school, and then everybody has to have it. Sometimes the fad is grubby work pants ("gas station" pants), and a year later it is printed turtlenecks.

Predictably, the American business establishment tries to profit from teenagers' buying power and their apparent need for their own styles and fads. What are the industry's means of exploring and exploiting? A premium is on sheer inventiveness. For example, in the 1980s a San Francisco firm

---

[40]Ibid., p. 7.
[41]"Youth on the Move," p. 78.

came out with rock concert souvenirs such as T-shirts selling for $8.00 a piece to the crowds worshiping their idols. Signifying that their necessities are somehow taken care of, teenagers provide an immensely profitable market for sports equipment. Some of the best-selling items during the early 1980s were skis and equipment for racquetball, jogging, and exercising. Of perennial profitability are soft drinks, and manufacturers—while addressing all ages—direct their appeal particularly at the young. The Coca-Cola Company developed Mello Yello, a low-carbonated drink, to sell to teenagers who are into sports. Marketing experts seem to agree on the principle that if you want to capture youth, you must lure them with a gimmick. Hence theaters and pizza parlors have pinball machines and arcade and video games; department stores use disco music, blinking lights, and space-age displays; fast food restaurants almost exclusively use children and teenagers in their advertisements; sports stores use champion skaters, skiers, and swimmers in their commercials; beer brewers display hardy, youthful outdoor people "slamming down" a Lite; ads in college papers read, "You didn't get the courses you wanted. But you got Friday off . . . Now comes Miller time."

This brings into play the power of the mass media. Many advertisement specialists believe the best way to reach teenagers is via the radio. Rock stations still draw the biggest audiences and hence are favorites for advertisers. Of course, there is also the advertising power of TV. In any case, an enticing mass-medium depiction of consumption patterns can establish and sustain the marketing plans of the industry.

The economic power of teenagers is not limited to their actual financial means; it includes their psychological power, manifesting itself through the peculiarly youth-oriented market in the United States. Teenagers stimulate most mass buying trends by functioning as persuasive agents in their families. Surveys have indicated that teenagers have weighty influence on their parents' purchases of automobiles in 69 percent of the cases, on 68 percent of vacation plans, 66 percent of the food buying, and 54 percent of television purchases.[42] A 1989 Roper Report found that children decide 74 percent of the time what leisure activities their families will pursue, and approximately $50 billion a year in household spending is influenced by children.[43]

In summary, adolescents' expenditures are not made randomly but are selectively invested in goods and services that enhance popularity among peers. The selections are usually in accord with short-lived fashions of the subculture and they create a feeling of belonging. Material implementation furthers identification with subcultural standards and in this way promotes the survival of the subculture. Also, material implementation facilitates com-

[42]"Millions of Young Adults, A New Wave of Buyers," *U.S. News & World Report,* 72 (January 17, 1972), 16.

[43]Richard Corliss, "Kid Power," *Time,* January 6, 1991, pp. 81–82.

munication within the subculture—communication that does not have to be verbal, but can speak through the visible common style and fashion. Faded jeans, therefore, are not just clothes but a symbol.

It is through this reinforcement that adolescence has obtained structure and internal statuses and become a way of life. This way of life is not wholly acceptable to the adult world and is viewed with ambivalence. In the final analysis, adolescent "status" is paradoxical in that it is relatively structured from the *inside* of the subculture, but is uncertain *within* the adult world.

SOCIOSOMATICS: SOCIETAL INFLUENCES ON BIOLOGICAL DEVELOPMENT

The sociological view of human beings is regrettably limited. It tends to regard them as interactional units or status entities but rarely as biological creatures. And, yet, we are both. Because of this neglect, the relationship between societal (social, cultural, and technological) factors and the human body is insufficiently studied. While psychologists and clinicians study the relationship between mental states and physiological responses (classified as *psychosomatic*), few social scientists have explored the impact of social and cultural conditions on the human body. One might call this influence *sociosomatic*, referring to sociocultural variables on one side and the human body on the other. Sociosomatic processes accelerate and become noticeable under conditions of rapid social change or cultural innovation.

Since young people are always in the chronological front line, they are the first to experience the impact of innovation—not only as social units but also as biological organisms. The following discussion attempts to recognize some of the important influences on the biological development of adolescents.

The most significant biological process during the period of adolescence is pubescence. (*Pubescence* is derived from Latin *pubertas*, "age of manhood," and *pubescere*, "to grow hairy.") While adolescence refers to the period of social maturation, pubescence refers to the physiological development during which the reproductive system matures. Pubescence normally corresponds with early adolescence and ends with the appearances of secondary sex characteristics and the achievement of reproductive ability. These changes usually take place over approximately two years. The exact age at which reproductive maturity is achieved varies widely and is influenced by many factors.[44]

Of these factors, gender difference plays a major role. Girls mature

---

[44]Phyllis B. Eveleth, "Timing of Menarche," in Jane B. Lancaster and Beatrix A. Hamburg, eds., *School-Age Pregnancy and Parenthood* (New York: Aldine, 1986).

about two years earlier than boys. Climate, however, seems to make little difference. It was once thought that girls who grew up in a hot climate developed earlier than those who grew up in a cold one. Actually, researchers found a tendency toward earlier maturation in the temperate zone rather than in either tropical or arctic regions.[45] In general, however, scientists reject assumptions of climatic determination. Race seems to have even less effect than climate. In two studies, age at menarche (first menstruation) for black girls did not vary significantly from that of white girls who lived in the same places and had similar socioeconomic backgrounds.[46]

The most influential factors seem to be nutritional and medical ones.[47] This is where sociosomatic processes enter the picture, where social and cultural conditions have marked influence on biological development and age of maturity. A social environment that uses recent scientific insights in these areas—as is typical of postindustrial society—usually lowers the age of pubescence. Among the various aspects of scientific progress, better nutrition is the most significant factor. Scientific standards of nutrition, hygiene, and medication are more common in urban-industrial societies than in tribal or agricultural societies and more common in the middle and upper socioeconomic classes than in lower classes. This is why a consistent difference of menarcheal age exists between higher and lower socioeconomic classes, a difference verified by international studies. Menarcheal difference between higher and lower classes was found to be two months in Copenhagen, Denmark; three months in Bristol, England; eight months among blacks in New York; six months among Hindus; ten months in Durham, South Africa; and five months among South African Bantu.[48]

A related study found Japanese girls born in Japan but reared in California to be one-and-a-half years ahead of Japanese girls born in California but reared in Japan. The racial factor was constant between the groups, and the groups were large enough to include comparable cross-sections of social

[45]David P. Ausubel, *The Theory and Problem of Adolescent Development* (New York: Grune and Stratton, 1954).

[46]Comradge L. Henton, "A Comparative Study of the Onset of Menarche among Negro and White Children," *Journal of Psychology*, 46 (July 1958): 65–73; and N. Michelson, "Studies in Physical Development of Negroes, Onset of Puberty," *American Journal of Physical Anthropology*, 2 (June 1944): 151–66.

[47]Ann C. Petersen, "Can Puberty Come any Earlier?" *Psychology Today*, February 1979, p. 45.

[48]K. W. Boylen, G. Rasch, and M. Weis-Bentzon, "The Age Incidence of Menarche in Copenhagen," *Acta Obstetrica et Gynecologia Scandinavica*, 33 (1954): 405–33; R. C. Wofenden and A. L. Smallwood, *Annual Report of the Principal Medical Officer* (Bristol, England: City and County of Bristol Education Committee, 1958); E. Kark, "Puberty of South African Girls, III, Social Class in Relation to the Menarche," *South African Journal of Laboratory and Clinical Medicine*, 2 (1956): 84–88; and A. G. Oettlé and J. Higginson, "Age at Menarche in South African Bantu Girls," *Human Biology*, 33 (May 1961): 181–90.

stratification. The researcher concluded that the difference was due to the better diet of the girls who grew up in California.[49]

Heredity contributes to the determination of the time a girl experiences menarche. Daughters of early-pubescent mothers tend to reach menarche earlier than those of late-pubescent mothers.[50]

Effects of various factors reinforce each other and at other times neutralize each other. For example, if a German girl whose mother matured at eleven was brought up during the war and experienced nutritional deficiencies, she may have started menstruation at a later age. But the daughter of a late-maturing mother of a poor family may reach menarche earlier if the family moves up the socioeconomic ladder and provides a better diet. A double effect is experienced by the daughter of a late-maturing mother deserted by the husband and living under depressed economic standards. The girl is prone to reach menarche at an even later age than her mother.

Intergenerational comparisons of menarche have revealed an ever-decreasing menarcheal age in most societies. This especially is true of societies with improved standards of nutrition and sanitation. Complete records are available in Norway, covering the period from 1840 to 1950. Average menarcheal age in 1840 was seventeen years, one month. This age decreased consistently, until in 1950 it arrived at thirteen years, three months—a decrease of almost four years.[51] Similar changes have been found in Sweden, Germany, Denmark, England, Finland, Japan, and the United States.

In the United States, a study comparing mothers and daughters found the average menarcheal age for the mothers to be 13.99 years and for the daughters 13.61 years.[52] Another study found that American college women born around 1920 reached menarche six months earlier than those born around 1900.[53]

The reason reference is made almost exclusively to the pubescent process of girls is that there is no clearly defined method for determining the onset of pubescence among boys. There is no equivalent sign as unmistakable as menstruation. Indications of male pubescence are appearance of pubic hair, voice change, and nocturnal emission. However, not all of these male pubescent characteristics appear at the same time; several may go unnoticed for some time.

[49]Paul D. Ito, "Comparative Biometrical Study of Physiques of Japanese Women Born and Reared under Different Environments," *Human Biology*, 14 (September 1942): 279–351.

[50]Harley N. Gould and Mary R. Gould, "Age of First Menstruation in Mothers and Daughters," *Journal of the American Medical Association*, 98 (April 1932): 1349–52.

[51]V. Kiil, "Menarche-alderen hos skolepeker i Oslo og sammenhengen mellom menarche-older og fysiskutwicklung statistiche," *Kvartalashelft*, 43 (1954): 84–88.

[52]Gould and Gould, "Age of First Menstruation."

[53]Clarence A. Mills, "Further Evidence on the Reversal Human-Growth Tide," *Human Biology*, 13 (September 1941), 365.

Conditions of urban-industrial society have influenced not only timing of maturation but also quality. In 1961, researchers compared measurements of thirteen-year-old white Iowa schoolgirls with those of girls of the same age taken in 1880, 1899, 1916 to 1919, and 1937 to 1939.[54] Comparison showed progressive increase in all physical aspects except head width. Comparison of measurements taken in 1880 and in 1960 showed that girls of 1960 were taller by four inches in mean stature, heavier by twenty-two pounds in mean weight, and not different in head width.

The average boy of mid-twentieth century is five inches taller and twenty-four pounds heavier than his counterpart of 1880.[55] The average soldier in the United States army during World War II was three-fifths of an inch taller, almost ten pounds heavier, and better nourished than the average World War I soldier.[56] College students today are taller and heavier than their counterparts of twenty-five years ago. Today's athletes outstrip yesterday's stars in nearly every discipline. In the eighteenth century, the king of Prussia, Frederick the Great, had to search all over Europe to find enough men six feet tall to serve as his special guards. Today, he could find that many in almost every large high school. Visitors to museums are frequently astounded by the size of armor and other garments worn by medieval knights; they give the impression that twelve-to-fourteen-year-old children went on the Crusades. Actually, armor was worn by adults who on the average were several inches shorter than today's adults. The measurements of recruits in countries that have had universal military draft show consistent increases in both height and weight over the past generations.[57]

The examples given show that these increases are due to greater availability of food, a more balanced diet even among the poor, more equitable distribution of the countries' wealth, improved medical care, the resulting decrease in illness and epidemics, and virtual elimination of child labor.

"Natural experiments" tested the role of nutrition in the maturation process and revealed a direct correlation between quality of nutrition and physical development. Adverse effects of inadequate nutrition were observed during three socio-economic upheavals: World War I, the Great Depression, and World War II. All three catastrophes had a direct impact on the growth of children and teenagers. During World War I, there was a slowing of growth among the children of nations that were intensely involved in the war.

Reliably documented correlations between nutrition and physical measurements come from Stuttgart, Germany, where children were measured

[54]Howard V. Meredith and Virginia B. Knott, "Descriptive and Comparative Study of Body Size on United States School Girls," *Growth*, 26 (December 1962): 283–95.

[55]Luella Cole and Irma N. Hall, *Psychology of Adolescence* (New York: Holt, Rinehart & Winston, 1965), p. 23.

[56]Ibid.

[57]Ibid.

every year since 1910, with records available for both the *Volksschule* (elementary school) and the *Oberschule* (secondary school).[58] The records show marked reductions in weight and height during times of national crisis. For example, around 1925, the average weight for all age levels declined sharply. These were years of severe inflation. Concomitantly with recovery from the national economic disaster, there was an upswing in physical measurements. During the first years of World War II there was an increase in weight, probably because Germany acquired food supplies through conquest. Over the subsequent four years, however, the average weight declined rapidly and remained low for two or three years after the end of the war.

An additional insight grew out of this study. There was a consistent difference between pupils in the two types of schools. Since the German system allows youths of the same age to attend either the *Volksschule* or the *Oberschule*, comparison between pupils of the same age was possible. The *Oberschule* draws enrollment primarily from upper socioeconomic classes. Regardless of national crises, the average measurements of the *Oberschule* pupils *always* remained above those of the *Volksschule* pupils.

The direct correlation between socioeconomic background and physical growth has been verified in Germany as recently as the 1980s. A survey showed that students from unskilled working-class families had the smallest measurements, while those from professional and business families had the largest. Students from the middle of the socioeconomic range—from skilled working-class and farm families—had in-between measurements.[59]

The influence of a national crisis on the growth pattern of children was observed in America during the Great Depression. The greatest impact was among the children of middle-class parents, who met the crisis by reducing the quality of food rather than relying on public relief. Interestingly, the children of the lowest income groups actually gained weight during those years, probably because the food given to them in public kitchens or through charities was better than the diet their parents had been able to provide.[60]

Rate and quality of growth correlate positively with socioeconomic status. The differences are small but consistent from one study to another. Children of professionals or business executives are on the average taller and heavier than those from middle-class homes, who, in turn, exceed in all aspects of growth the children from the lowest socioeconomic class.

American society is characterized by factors favoring earlier maturation and superior physiological development, with a concomitant intensifying

[58]Paul E. Howe and Maria Schiller, "Growth Responses of the School Child to Change in the Diet and Environmental Factors," *Journal of Applied Physiology*, 5 (August 1952): 51–61.

[59]"Karlsruhe: Studenten immer länger," *Mitteilungen*, Deutsche Akademischer Austauschdienst (DAAD), Bonn, November 1982, p. 17.

[60]C. E. Palmer, "Height and Weight of the Depression Poor," *United States Public Health Reports*, 50 (1935): 1106–13.

effect on adolescence. While earlier maturation creates a longer period of adolescence, and while superior maturation produces a youth with the capabilities and physical appearance of an adult, he or she is not allowed to act as an adult.

Although the age of pubescence has begun to level off in the United States, we can assume that the teenage subculture will soon include ten-to-nineteen-year-old youths rather than thirteen-to-nineteen-year-old youths.

Postindustrial society is delaying adulthood for educational, economic, and other reasons, and improved biological care shortens the period of childhood. In-between lies an expanding period in which a person's physical and sexual maturity is out of phase with his or her social position.

SUMMARY

Postindustrial life accentuates the adolescent experience. Most influential in this aggravation is the complex network of positions making continuity from child to adult status difficult. The division of labor in postindustrial society requires specialists to occupy a vast range of highly specific positions. Children are "generalists." When they enter adolescence, the generalist standing becomes dysfunctional and they must choose a specific but relatively unknown position. Most teenagers know little about their parents' occupational responsibilities, and only a small proportion follow the occupation of their parents. This situation calls for nonfamilial preparation for the adult position. High schools and other institutions have replaced traditional preparation within the family setting and assumed *in loco parentis* authority. Since technological progress is continuously eliminating the need for unskilled manual labor and creating new technical and managerial positions, training and education of adolescents have become more complex and time consuming. This adds more years of poorly defined status to the adolescent experience.

American schools have become holding pens trying to prevent the onrush of millions of sixteen-year-olds into the labor market. The holding-pen nature of modern education has been sensed by the students and has created among them a sense of meaninglessness. Students' resentful attitudes are compounded by many young Americans' expectation that postindustrial society's promise of "instantness" can be applied to mental tasks.

In addition to geographic mobility, extensive social mobility increases uncertainty by inducing the teenager to improve, strive, and enter a career with prestige.

Frequently, socialization of the young takes place in nonfamilial institutions. Clinicians have found that parental deprivation disables the young, inducing defects in achievement, identity, assumption of adult responsibilities, and acquisition of normal emotions.

Adolescents' affluence allows them to materially implement peer standards. They signify membership in the subculture by material implementation and thereby reinforce a collective identity.

Modern medicine, technology, and especially nutrition have lowered the age of puberty. Since the upper limit of adolescence is not lowered, increasing proportions of America's youth experience adolescence.

6

American Culture and Its Imprints

CULTURE: A SOCIOLOGICAL EMPHASIS

While the preceding chapter discussed the impact of major structural, tech nological, and biological conditions on the adolescent experience, this chapter explores the influence of a more abstract phenomenon: culture.

The concept of culture varies with the frame of reference. For example, the colloquial connotation usually deals with the "finer things" in life, such as art, music, theater, dance, literature, etc. Anthropologists refer to either physical or nonphysical culture or to both, including all human creations. Physical aspects of culture refer to the products of technology; nonphysical aspects to ideas, knowledge, and common symbolic expressions.

The latter dimensions of culture are important to the sociological discussion, since they emphasize *rules, expectations, and values of society,* making up the "blueprint" for behavior that society imposes on its members. This blueprint consists of cultural dicta and is enforced by social sanctions (by punishment for deviation, reward for conformity). It is a powerful force, capable of evoking compelling reactions, such as guilt and shame in cases of violation, and pride and self-esteem in cases of adherence. The following discussion uses the term culture primarily in the sense of a blueprint for behavior maintained by formal as well as informal sanction systems.

THE NATURE-NURTURE CONTROVERSY

Although social scientists agree that modern teenagers are characterized by restless and confused behavior, they differ in explaining this behavior. While most sociologists and psychologists argue for an environmental, primarily cultural, explanation, a few opt for a biogenetic hypothesis. The question of whether *nature* (biological conditions) or *nurture* (social environment) is responsible for a given behavior pattern is an old one and has been asked in relation to various stages of life. The assumption that a causal relationship exists between the physiological, especially endocrinological, changes during pubescence and the adolescent's behavior has been largely discarded in favor of the cultural explanation.

It is for historical interest that we refer to G. Stanley Hall, frequently called the father of the psychology of adolescence. He promoted a biogenetic theory that became well known in the 1910s and 1920s and became the credo of many educators and psychologists.[1] In fact, the concept of adolescence was brought to the attention of the public through Hall's writing, starting during the last two decades of the nineteenth century.

Hall's psychology of adolescence assumed a causal relationship between pubertal changes and social-psychological adjustment problems. It translated Darwin's concept of evolution into a psychological theory of individual recapitulation, asserting that the experiential history of the human species had become part of the genetic structure of each individual. The law of recapitulation maintained that the individual organism, during its development, passes through phases that simulate the developmental stages of the human race from early animal-like primitivism through an era of savagery to the more recent, allegedly more civilized, ways of life that characterize maturity. "Ontogeny recapitulates phylogeny" is the famous adage derived from this theory.

Hall's first major developmental phase includes the first four years of life, when the child is still crawling. Presumably this corresponds to the animal stage of the human race, when the species was using four legs. The period of childhood, ranging from about four to eight, corresponds to the epoch when hunting and fishing were humans' main activities. This primitive way of living is reflected in children's play preferences, such as playing cowboys and Indians, using toy weapons, and building caves, camps, and other hiding places. The latter activities putatively parallel the cave-dwelling culture of early history. Youth, from eight to twelve, recapitulates the life of savagery of several thousand years ago. Hall considered children in this stage to be receptive to learning skills and discipline. Adolescence ranges from puberty to the attainment of full adult status, which occurs between twenty-

[1]G. Stanley Hall, *Adolescence*, 2 vols. (New York: Appleton-Century-Crofts, 1916).

two and twenty-five years of age. Hall ascribed the idiom *Sturm und Drang*[2] (storm and stress) to this stage and likened it to the time when the human race was in a turbulent, transitional stage. In late adolescence, the individual recapitulates the initial phase of modern civilization and enters the end phase of the process: maturity.

These developmental stages are presumably brought about by biologically innate forces that control growth and behavior. Human behavior was thought to manifest itself therefore in unchangeable patterns regardless of differences in the cultural environment.

Cultural anthropologists challenged this assertion in the light of cross-cultural observations.[3] They pointed to societies where adolescence did not exist, thereby invalidating Hall's claim that the adolescent's dispositions are universal expressions of innate drives.

However, Hall and his followers continued to insist that socially unacceptable behavior, the type held analogous to earlier historical phases, must be tolerated by parents and educators, since it is part of unavoidable stages in the social development of the individual. These psychologists reassured parents and teachers that objectionable behavior would vanish of its own accord in subsequent stages of development and that corrective measures were neither necessary nor advisable. Remnants of this theory still occupy a place in American educational philosophy embedded in such ideas as Gesell's concept of maturation.[4] In fact, Hall's theory played a role in the formation of the educational philosophy of permissiveness—a child-rearing style that has become widespread in America. Like Rousseau, whose educational philosophy is illustrated in *Émile,* Hall believed that the adult should not interfere with the natural course of development, which is determined by directional forces innate to humans.

Although G. Stanley Hall has almost been forgotten, if not rejected, he has left his mark on the theories of adolescence. His critics denied the validity of conceptualizing personal growth in terms of "stages," yet this is still done.

---

[2]Hall was strongly influenced by a movement in German literature that was led by Schiller and Goethe. The literary trend extolled idealism, search for goals, revolution against the old, expression of personal feelings, passion, and suffering. Hall drew an analogy between the objectives of this group of youthful writers at the beginning of the eighteenth century and the psychological characteristics of adolescence.

[3]One of the first and most incisive challengers was Margaret Mead, *Coming of Age in Samoa* (New York: William Morrow, 1983). However, recent reexamination of Mead's data revealed her "nurture" bias and her consequent misrepresentation—albeit unintentional—of growing up in Samoa. See Derek Freeman, *Margaret Mead and Samoa: The Making and Unmaking of an Anthropological Myth* (Cambridge, MA: Harvard University Press, 1983).

[4]Arnold Gesell maintained that maturation and growth is a process that should not be interfered with. He assumed that time alone will solve most of the normal problems of the child and that difficulties and deviations will be outgrown. Arnold Gesell and Frances L. Ilg, *Infant and Child in the Culture of Today* (New York: Harper & Row, 1943).

His critics charged him with exaggerating the "storm and stress" symptoms, yet this is the preoccupation of many psychologists of adolescence today.

A realistic assessment of the nature-nurture question will probably result in neither an extreme environmental nor an extreme biogenetic statement, but rather in a balanced view. Without doubt, the physiological upheavals during early adolescence are capable of profoundly influencing the psychological processes and the social behavior of the young individual. However, the vast majority of modern behavioral scientists ascribe greater influence to the cultural environment's interpretation of this physiological turbulence than to the physiological processes per se.

Cultural interpretations establish the meaning of an event, thing, or physiological process. Humans, as creatures who interpret symbols, do not react to things and happenings as such, but mainly to the meanings attached to them. From a cross-cultural point of view, it is possible to observe a nearly endless *differential interpretation of neural impulses*; that is, one and the same physiological process can be perceived in totally different ways.

PUBESCENCE AND CULTURAL VALUES

As mentioned in the preceding chapter, urban-industrial society tends to cause earlier onset of pubescence and extends the adolescent period into younger age groups. This implies that concomitant sexual needs occur at a progressively younger age.

The young adolescent's awareness of physiological changes—even if they were not accompanied by any particular cultural interpretation—would be enough to cause him or her alarm. Bodily changes take place too rapidly to give the child enough time to adjust. When a negative cultural interpretation of the sexual maturation process is added, it leaves a powerful and often lasting impression.

American culture turns pubescence into an adolescence-reinforcing event by making the young feel that they go through a stage that should not be mentioned. Both girl and boy develop ambiguous perceptions of their bodily changes that often result in nonacceptance of themselves.

In contrast, in many so-called primitive tribal societies, pubescence is celebrated. For example, the Apache Indian girl's menarche is celebrated by a priest who kneels before her to obtain her blessing.[5] Four ceremonial days honor the Navajo girl's puberty. She is bathed and decorated; relatives bake corn cake; songs and chants are offered; and young men run the dawn races.[6]

---

[5]Ruth Benedict, *Patterns of Culture* (New York: New American Library, 1950), p. 26.
[6]Charlotte J. Frisbie, *Kinaaldà: A Study of the Navajo Girl's Puberty Ceremony* (Middletown, CT: Wesleyan University Press, 1967).

DISPARITY BETWEEN BIOLOGICAL ADULTHOOD AND SOCIAL ADULTHOOD

American culture prescribes sexual neuterness at a time the young have just achieved sexual potency and are characterized by intense sexuality. Biologically, the vast majority of adolescents are as capable of the reproductive act and as much in need of erotic release as the adult. But, while teenagers are sexually adult, they are not yet socially adult; they are called "minors," and this cultural norm is legally edged: not one state in the union permits marriage under the age of eighteen without the consent of the parents.

The social immaturity ascribed to teenagers has serious implications for their sex lives. American mores discourage young adolescents from expressing their sexual interests; sexual expression, be it heterosexual, homosexual, or autoerotic, is disapproved. Yet the majority of adolescents have been both sufficiently informed and encouraged by mass media fare to choose actual sexual experimentation over passively limiting themselves—as utopian cultural standards would seek—to fantasies or nocturnal emission. Without exception, survey data have shown high rates of masturbation, petting, sex play, and intercourse.

Representative survey findings of 1979, collected by UCLA sex researcher Aaron Hass and based on samples across the nation, show that among fifteen-to-sixteen-year-olds 43 percent of the boys and 31 percent of the girls have had intercourse. Approximately 28 percent of the boys and 7 percent of the girls report ten or more sexual partners. In the same age group, 80 percent of the males and nearly 50 percent of the females report they masturbate at least once a week. Nearly 70 percent of the girls and 90 percent of the boys approve of oral sex, and, among seventeen-to-eighteen-year-olds, over half of each group has performed it.[7]

The Kantner-Zelnik surveys, corroborating many others, show that teenage sexual activities have increased over the past decades. National samples indicate that the proportion of fifteen-to-nineteen-year-old girls having premarital intercourse has grown from 30 to about 50 percent in 1979.[8] These figures confirm the findings of various surveys showing increases in premarital intercourse rates for all groups of young Americans, but particularly for women, who now roughly match the men's rate.

Since premarital sexual behavior deviates from cultural norms, most sexually active teenagers experience feelings of guilt and shame. Recognizing that they have violated standards imposed by adults, they develop a sense of alienation. Feelings of shame and guilt are easily converted into feelings of rejection and hatred against those causing the self-punishing emotions. Ulti-

---

[7]Aaron Hass, *Teenage Sexuality* (New York: Macmillan, 1979), pp. 53, 54, 67, 68, 86.
[8]"Contraception," *Psychology Today*, November 1980, p. 100.

mately, a reinforcing vicious cycle forms between the rejector and the re-jectee. This holds especially true when the parties involved are collectivities, since feelings of rejection toward outsiders thrive most vigorously if an in-group supports and rewards hostile attitudes. The rejection that teenagers perceive because of their sexual attitudes and activities is in this way trans-formed into feelings of belonging to the peer group, which accepts them as they are.

THE LACK OF RITE OF PASSAGE INTO ADULTHOOD

Life in society consists of a series of passages from one age group to another, from one occupation to another, from one institutional membership to the next—in other words, from one status to another. In parts of the world, the progression from one status to the next is accompanied by ceremonies publicly proclaiming entry into the new status. Sometimes the ceremonies are of a sacred nature, suggesting divine sanction of the new role and entrusting the individual with rights and obligations. In all cases, these rites are public rituals, manifesting the consensual quality of the transition.

Certain transitions are universal. Birth, puberty, assumption of adult responsibility, marriage, parenthood, and death are examples of universal experiences. These and other crises are usually accompanied by *rites of passage*, designed to carry the individual from one phase of human experi-ence to another. Although the celebrations may differ in detail and manner from one culture to another, wherever they are present they essentially serve the same three functions:

Informing. The initiate is informed of his or her new rights and obliga-tions. Sometimes this may involve a special period of training and indoctrina-tion supervised by qualified elders of the community.

Announcing. The community is alerted to the fact that a given person assumes a new status and that the actions and reactions of its members must now fall in line with new role interaction.

Emotionally anchoring. Humans respond to rituals profoundly. More persistent loyalty and commitment can be elicited through them than through almost any other means. Taking on a new role in the eyes of the public and witnessing its decisive approval presents the young with a vali-dated reinforcement that gives him or her a feeling of belonging to the new status. The initiate does not *play* the new role; he or she *becomes* the role. (Points 1 and 3 are obviously not implemented in birth and death, where the rite is solely for the benefit of the community.)

The rite of passage in the context of adolescence concerns the transition from the status of child to the status of adult. It is popularly held that the transition is indicated, if at all, by puberty rite. However, it is necessary to distinguish between the rite of passage concerning physiological puberty and "social puberty"; they are different and only occasionally converging phenomena.

Many privileges, such as sexual expression, marriageability, and adult responsibilities do not depend on puberty but may be experienced earlier or later, depending on the individual and the social environment. Nonsynchronization of physiological puberty and social puberty can be illustrated by many examples, such as the fact that in Italy girls are legally marriageable at age twelve, when barely 10 percent of Italian girls have started menstruating. In France it is legal to marry at sixteen and one-half years of age, but the average age of puberty is around fourteen.[9] Thus, in Italy social puberty precedes physiological puberty, while in France it follows.

Among the Salish Indians of British Columbia, membership in an endogamous adult class begins with a name-giving ceremony, which always comes later than the ceremony of puberty. The father prepares an elaborate feast and invites the relatives. When all have gathered, the father leads his son, together with sponsors, onto the roof of the house and begins a prescribed dance and song. This is followed by distribution of gifts in the name of ancestors. Then the father asks forty nobles to act as witnesses, while two elder chiefs step forward with the young man between them and announce the name and the titles of that ancestor after whom the father wishes the son to be named. In most cases it is the grandfather. The crowd expresses consent through hand clapping. Once more, gifts are distributed, and a meal follows; afterward the young man is known by the name and title received at the ceremony.[10]

This custom is not as unique as it may appear. For example, in Japan and Europe during the Middle Ages, the coat of arms corresponded to the totem and sacred symbols and tatoos for age groups or secret societies. Bestowing of the coat of arms, like that of the totemic emblem, is a rite of passage into an adult group.[11] Among the Masai of Kenya, circumcision as a ritual of social puberty occurs as soon as boys are considered strong enough to undergo the elaborate rite, usually between twelve and sixteen. The date sometimes depends on the affluence of the boy's family. Circumcision may be performed earlier if the parents are rich; if the parents are poor, the ceremony is delayed until they can pay the cost. The ritual of circumcision

[9]Arnold van Gennep, *The Rites of Passage* (Chicago: University of Chicago Press, 1960), p. 66.

[10]Ibid., p. 101.

[11]Ibid., pp. 101–02.

takes place every four to six years; all boys who are circumcised at one time belong to an age group bearing a special name chosen by the chief. Simultaneously with or prior to the rite of passage for the boy, the father must undergo the rite of "passing the fence," signifying acceptance of the status of "old man," after which he is called "father of (name of his offspring)."[12]

Another example of the independence of initiation rite from puberty is the bar mitzvah. It takes place when the Jewish boy is thirteen and presumably enters the age of responsibility and religious duty, thereby acquiring adult status. The bar mitzvah has been reduced to mere religious ceremony with little or no bearing on the public and secular life of the boy. Obviously, a thirteen-year-old boy is not eligible for marriage and may not assume adult status in the larger American community.

Because of discrepancy between physiological maturation and ascription of adult status, it is incorrect to refer to *initiation rites* (entry into adult status) as puberty rites. In virtually all societies the age at which young men and women are allowed to marry does not coincide with physiological puberty, and if one day the two moments, one social and the other physiological, come to coincide, they will do so only as a result of deliberate planning.

American culture lacks *both* puberty and initiation rites. Puberty is a taboo issue and is not accompanied by a public ritual with status-clarifying effect. Likewise, there is no definitive rite of initiation into the adult world, although a legal age is set for marriageability and franchise. However, prior to these particular privileges, there is partial assumption of adult responsibilities and privileges through military service, employment, driving an automobile, and so on. One cannot speak, therefore, of a *certain age* at which the young of our society move from one status to the other.

Clarity of one's social position and integration into the system is a recognizable human need. To meet this need, a number of prerequisites must be completed, one being a clear introduction into one's status. Absence of a transition rite reduces awareness and clarity of one's status and can create maladjustment.

If society is to prevent this type of maladjustment, it must (1) clearly define roles, (2) cultivate consistent responses toward role incumbents, (3) respect the importance of each role, and (4) observe a transition procedure that clearly signals the change of role.

These principles are not available for the majority of American teenagers. There is role confusion, condescension toward their age group, inconsistent response patterns on the part of the larger society toward the young, and lack of transition procedure.

---

[12]M. Merker, *Die Massai, Ethnographische Monographie Eines Ostafrikanischen Semiten-Volkes* (Berlin: Reimer, 1904), p. 55.

VALUE CONFLICT: THE ALL-AMERICAN DICHOTOMIES

Although dualism in value patterns can be observed in most modern societies, American society appears to subject its members to extreme contrasts. Some deserve special mention because they cause confusion and uncertainty for all Americans, whether young or old:

Competition versus cooperation.   American society maintains the value of fierce competition and glorifies a "winner"—whether it is a beauty queen or a farmer raising the finest cattle. The goal of economic success has been heavily stressed and has strained institutional regulations and the permissible means for its attainment. In extreme instances, only questions of technical effectiveness have entered into the choice of means for the goal, and "business is business" has been the apology of robber barons, organized crime, and racketeering.

However, the generosity of the American people is proverbial. There exists an enormous range of voluntary humanitarian activities in America such as the Community Chest, service clubs, public welfare agencies, religious charities, private philanthropies, and the Peace Corps.

The polarity of competition and cooperation is part of many situations involving young people. In school, boys and girls become aware very early that they are competing with one another. The typical American grading system, the "curve" method, automatically converts students into competitors. Yet students are expected to cooperate when it comes to other aspects of interaction, such as dating, courting, and marriage. Necessity of frequent, abrupt switches from one attitude to the other and unclearness of when and how to do so introduce confusion into the boy–girl, and later man–woman, relationship.

Work versus leisure.   Puritan tradition viewed successful work as a sign of divine grace. The metaphysical directive to work was the norm in the older rural culture of America and is still extant in rural areas and subcultures that have not yet assimilated postindustrial attitudes toward leisure and consumption.

Modern American youth's attitude toward work mirrors the economic conditions of the nation. During the early 1970s, propelled by idealistic counterculture philosophy, youth took material security for granted and looked for psychological rewards ("self-realization") when choosing a career. The attitude was reflected in Yankelovich's survey findings: 57 percent of college and 52 percent of noncollege youth felt confident that they would "make as much money as they want." Yet their confidence apparently was not based on the Protestant ethic, since their belief in "hard work always pays off" declined from 79 percent in the 1960s to 56 percent in the 1970s.[13]

With worsening economic conditions, the 1980s and early 1990s saw a return to basic material concerns by American youth. College students realized that they were facing hard times in which the work ethic again played a role. But a modification had also developed: Young people expected the work ethic to be supplemented, if not replaced, by social welfare programs.

At the same time, we have observed continuing conspicuous consumption. For example, despite gas prices, hotel fees, and import duties, America's lakes still teem with speed boats, hotels still show "no vacancy" signs, and young people are saturated with foreign-made goods. The last decade of the twentieth century still reveals the contrasting values of hard work and of consumption patterns anchored in post-industrial affluence.

Piety versus freethinking. Public opinion polls have shown that freedom is repeatedly mentioned as one of the most cherished advantages of American life. Most Americans are proud to remember such freethinkers as Walt Whitman, Ralph Waldo Emerson, and Henry Thoreau. When it comes to concrete instances, however, "free thought" rapidly loses its appeal. It is often said that America is a land of freedom of religion, but hardly *from* religion. For example, one who publicly admits being an atheist often meets with suspicion and rejection. This conflict between "free thought" and Christian piety has been visible in long, drawn-out battles and polemics concerning prayer in public schools.

Individualism versus conformity. The "individual" in American life is conceptualized as an independent and inventive agent, morally responsible only to him- or herself. While theoretically this idea is still maintained, considerable dependency and conformity has developed in American life. Regulations have been introduced, presumably guaranteeing economic well-being for all, including social security, Medicare, and obligatory retirement funds. Critics call these measures "welfare state practices" and claim that freedom is no longer tied to a system of private property and passive government.

American youth are introduced to many glorified, historical exposés of "rugged individualism" and encouraged to emulate this "truly American" trait. On the other hand, they are constantly challenged to conform to national and patriotic standards. Although conflicting values have been part

[13]Daniel Yankelovich, *The New Morality: A Profile of American Youth in the 70s* (New York: McGraw-Hill, 1974), pp. 84, 87, 103.

of any era, they were particularly visible during the 1960s and early 1970s when dissent against the Vietnam War ran high. A powerful faction of public opinion, the "silent majority," recognized dissent not as an expression of individualistic thinking but as subversive and un-American. It is interesting to note that factionalism also split the youth population, dividing them into "hawks" and "doves."[14]

New national and international issues will continue to challenge youth. They will have to decide whether to adhere to or dissent from governmental policies. Each generation of young Americans will have to learn anew that the cultural blueprint for individualism is ambiguous and situational—imposing on them the nongeneralizability that prevents simplicity and predictability in social life.

Sex versus chastity.   One of the most vexing clashes of values in American life deals with sexuality, and its corollary of sex appeal and youthful prowess, on one side, and the virtue of chastity, with its corollary of Christian asceticism generally, on the other side. Shifting emphasis on the continuum between these poles makes generalization difficult. The past several decades have seen interesting oscillations.

From the 1960s to the late 1980s young Americans have expressed what might have been the freest sexual standards in American history, possibly warranting the label of Sexual Revolution for a part of that period. But even during those years the battle between American values never abated, the virtue of chastity was propounded by concerned parents, educators, and, above all, clergymen. Strangely enough even voices from the New Left chimed in, joining conservative views by pointing out that American culture promotes commercialized "sex and love" and made it part of the all-American fun syndrome. In the process—says Herbert Marcuse, a leader of the socialist fraction of the counterculture—the liberalization of sexualization has been taken advantage of by the capitalist system and used as a repressive means, dulling the political sensitivities of the masses. In a sense, commercial sexuality has taken over the role of religion as the opium of the masses.[15]

At the same time, however, puritanical values refused to surrender and were still able to oppose sexual liberation and inflict those well-known control emotions of guilt and shame on young Americans.

Then an unexpected element entered the scene: the sexually transmittable condition of AIDS. This lethal condition suddenly rejuvenated Puritan attitudes. AIDS accomplished virtually overnight what years of preaching

[14]Hans Sebald, "Voices of War and Peace—What Do They Know? Attitudes and Knowledge about the War in Southeast Asia," *Pacific Sociological Review*, 14 (October 1971): 487–510.
[15]Herbert Marcuse, *An Essay on Liberation* (Boston: Beacon Press, 1969).

from the pulpit had failed to achieve: reconsideration of standards of chastity. One could, however, argue that embracing chastity during the last years of the twentieth century was less an endorsement of a value and more the heeding of medical warning. The official tolerance, even promotion, of the sale of condoms on campuses seems to indicate that reining in liberal sexual behavior is more an issue of health than of virtue.

Implications. In summing up the meaning of such polarities in American culture, one could say that the American mentality is beset with contradictory values. These inconsistencies add vexation to the lives of adolescents, whose learning must proceed situationally instead of holistically. This means they must assess each situation as to which side of the polarity is to be implemented. Erving Goffman used the term "frame analysis" to describe the nature of charting one's journey through American life: each situation, like one picture in a film strip, must be analyzed individually and independently from the previous or following frame.[16] If the theory is accepted that a healthy personality at peace with itself requires an integrated *Gestalt* of views and attitudes, then contradictory cultural values will have confusing and possibly even pathological effects.

VALUE CONFLICT: THE CHILD-ADULT DICHOTOMIES

No culture ascribes the same blueprint to all participants. Humans at different chronological stages have different needs and capabilities; nowhere is a child required to act like an adult, and neither is a mature and healthy adult allowed to act like a child for any length of time. The differences that various cultures have with respect to time of role transition and to degree of role distinction vary greatly. In some societies, mostly the small and so-called primitive societies, children assume adult roles at an early age, while in the large and modern societies children grow into adulthood via a nondescript phase that separates adulthood from childhood by as much as ten years. With respect to degree of role differentiation, American culture goes to great lengths to emphasize contrasts between the roles of child and adult, prescribing for each distinct sets of expectations. This principle can be exemplified by a number of specific opposing role expectations.

Responsibility versus nonresponsibility. In many tribal societies, child-rearing techniques achieve a continuity of activities that is not limited to daily nurturing patterns but is extended to include responsibilities that, in

---

[16]Erving Goffman, *Frame Analysis: An Essay on the Organization of Experience* (Cambridge: Harvard University Press, 1974).

our society, are reserved for adults. For example, in the United States a child is declared nonresponsible with respect to serious adult work. Americans consider it a rule that the child wants to play and that the adult has to work, forgetting that in many societies the mothers take their babies along to their daily work, carrying them in shawls or baskets close to the body. The child thus has an opportunity to observe adult work and, as soon as the child is old enough, he or she takes on tasks that are important and yet suited to his or her strength—thereby precluding formation of a dichotomy between work and play.

In American society, the law enforces the child/adult dichotomy. For example, a child cannot be accused of a crime but only of "delinquency." The legal and moral burden is the parents' because the child presumably has not yet reached the "age of legal responsibility." The question of *when* the social and legal reaction to a child's "delinquency," either in terms of penalty or correction, is commensurate with the child's understanding raises a difficult issue. There has been suspicion that permissive and "understanding" attitudes and counseling will only reinforce the delinquent pattern. What is needed, according to some psychiatric experts, is "reality therapy" that makes social reactions commensurate with the juvenile's understanding of his or her acts.[17] Readjustment of the legal machinery in this direction would assure that the juvenile would be held more responsible for his or her behavior.

The brutal killing of an infant by three boys, the oldest a ten-year-old, illustrates the nonresponsible status of a minor's action in American society. The boys were held in 1987 in the Milwaukee Child and Adolescent Treatment Center after they were found to have beaten to death a two-year old girl whom the oldest had been baby-sitting. When she dirtied her diapers, they were so irritated that they beat her with wooden slats pulled from a bunk bed, and also kicked her and jumped on her, causing fatal injuries. Legal consequences were limited to removing the boys for up to one year from their homes, but because of their ages they could not be sentenced to any form of detention. On the other hand, the girl's mother, a 26-year-old woman, was charged with child abuse for leaving the child in the care of a ten-year-old.[18]

Another example deals with Atlanta city officials' effort to stem the tide of juvenile gang activities, which had claimed the lives of scores of young people, including a four-year-old girl who was fatally hit while asleep in her bed when teenagers invaded a housing project in the middle of the night and sprayed it with bullets. Outraged by the killings, the authorities passed a new citywide curfew law, taking effect in November of 1990 and requiring teenagers under 17 to be off the streets by 11 p.m. weekdays and by midnight on Fridays and Saturdays. But it is not the perpetrator of the new law that is

---

[17]William Glasser, *Reality Therapy* (New York: Harper & Row, 1965).
[18]UPI Report, *The Arizona Republic*, March 15, 1987, p. A8.

being punished, rather it is the parents of the offenders who face up to sixty days in jail or a fine as high as $1000.[19]

Jerome S. Bruner, head of the center for cognitive studies at Harvard, thinks we grossly underestimate the perceptual and comprehensive capability of children. Bruner holds that children can learn any subject at any stage of their development and advocates that they be required to perform far more complicated tasks than they do. By not expecting much from children, we in fact condition them not to give much, thereby perpetuating the American myth that nonresponsibility for children is necessary.[20]

Sex versus sexless. Sexual attitudes and activities are the most complicated discontinuities in cultural learning. In virtually all societies the child must seriously modify his or her behavior at puberty or at marriage—these two occasions representing universal discontinuities in both sexual capability and sexual standards. At such times, the cultural prescriptions for sex may, for example, change preadolescent sexual license to marital fidelity or, as in a few societies, premarital virginity in either male or female to marital status with considerable sexual license.

Although some degree of discontinuity in sexual behavior is a universal condition, there can be continuity in one aspect: *continuity in sexual expression means that the child is taught nothing he or she must unlearn later.* Therefore, in spite of the universal conditions of puberty and marriage, one can classify some societies as facilitating continuity and others as imposing discontinuity.

For example, adults among the Dakota Indians observe great privacy in sex acts and in no way encourage children's sexual activities.[21] Yet one cannot speak of discontinuity, since the child is not indoctrinated in ways he or she must unlearn later. In a culture with this type of sex pattern, adults view children's sexual experimentation as in no way wicked but rather as innocuous play.

But the same *laissez-faire* attitude may be taken by adults in societies where such play is encouraged among young children. This is true of Melanesian cultures where adults exhibit sexual permissiveness and children feel free to indulge in sex play that is autoerotic, homosexual, or heterosexual. Although modified by marital regulation, the same open and hedonistic style is carried over into adult status, and no discontinuity is experienced.[22]

If society's emphasis is on reproduction, as for instance it is among Zuñi

[19]Chicago Tribune report, "Atlanta Hopes," *Arizona Republic,* November 25, 1990, p. B7.

[20]Jerome S. Bruner, *The Process of Education* (Cambridge, MA: Harvard University Press, 1963), pp. 33ff.

[21]Ruth Benedict, "Continuities and Discontinuities in Cultural Conditioning," *Psychiatry,* 1 (May 1938): 164–65.

[22]Ibid.

Indians, sexual expression among children is not encouraged. Although the Zuñi child is impressed with the prohibition of premature sex, the prohibition is not associated with sex itself but only with sex at a young age.[23] In Anglo-American culture the association is with sex as such and the adult often fails to unlearn the evil connotation of sex.

Dominance versus submission.   Americans tend to accept as universal the custom of viewing the adult–child relationship as dominant-submissive. This ethnocentric assumption has been exposed by anthropologists who studied cultures with different modes of intergenerational relations. In some cultures the terminology of address between father and son reflects a reciprocal relationship; the two are equal and the terms of their relationship will never change. When the son becomes a parent, he will establish the same relationship with his child. In societies with this type of equalitarian father–son relationship, the figure with a disciplining function usually is a close male relative, such as the mother's brother.[24] Such kinship conventions provide the individual with a behavior code he or she can follow from childhood through adulthood with minimal discontinuities.

In American society the child lives under parental authority by informal custom and formal law, reinforced by religious dictates of the Judeo-Christian heritage that threaten with damnation everyone who disobeys parents. This generational polarity raises questions for young people about when and how to shift from one mode of the relationship to the other.

Unrealism versus realism.   The culture of the American child, as well as probably of the entire Western Civilization, includes a fantasy world populated by fairies, ghosts, aliens, and other entities of doubtful empirical existence. While these figures are more or less straightforward figments of imagination and children have relatively little difficulty in recognizing them as such during their transition into the more empirically grounded older age, additional figures have been imposed on them through the mass media, especially television, that are far harder to identify as purely imaginary entities. There are two types of figures that are not so readily demystified. One deals with roles pretending superhuman abilities, stamina, and good luck. Our detective, adventure, and Wild West movies show an abundant load of these pretensions. The other deals with occult entities, the main fare of increasing numbers of thrillers and pseudoscience programs. Here is an exploitation of deep-seated human desires for external powers of whose good services we could possibly avail ourselves in times of need. They range from serious or semiserious claims of the existence of ghosts, apparitions, extrater-

---

[23]Ibid.

[24]Reference is to the Trobriand Islanders. Bronislaw Malinowski, *Magic, Science, and Religion, and Other Essays* (New York: Doubleday, 1954).

restrials, and the more abstract forces contactable through meditation or esoteric ritual.

The Youth Survey carried out by Gallup Organization, Inc. has provided data about young Americans' belief in supernatural phenomena, especially about the kind generally defined as occult. Questions were asked concerning belief in angels, astrology, ESP, witchcraft, Bigfoot, ghosts, clairvoyance, and the Loch Ness Monster. The samples represented two teenage categories, girls and boys separately, and the years of 1978, 1984, and 1988. When examining the latest available data of 1988 and comparing the proportions of believers between the age brackets, we notice that occult beliefs tend to increase with age; out of the eight categories, five showed increases, one stayed the same, and only two showed (relatively minor) decreases. When comparing the responses between the boys and the girls, we find that the boys reflect significantly higher proportions in six categories. Only when it comes to believing in astrology do the girls show a significantly higher proportion. (See Table 6-1.)

Teenagers' beliefs in the occult areas show mixed changes over the ten-years' span of the surveys. It appears that angels, ghosts, witches, and astrology gained, whereas ESP, clairvoyance, Bigfoot, and the Loch Ness Monster lost in credibility. (See Table 6-2.) Topping the list is the belief in angels, which interestingly enough should be classified more properly as a religious belief, showing a 74 percent belief record of the teenage population. Second on the list is now astrology with 58 percent, having moved up from third in the 1984 distribution. ESP comes in third; and witchcraft fourth.[25]

It is this kind of occult genre that stubbornly sticks in the minds of the young and is often difficult to dislodge when adult status begins to demand reorientation to more empirical and substantial approaches to life and life's

TABLE 6-1 Teens' Supernatural Beliefs—1988

	National %	Male %	Female %	Ages 13-15 %	Ages 16-17 %
Angels	74	73	74	74	73
Astrology	58	53	64	60	56
ESP	50	54	46	47	54
Witchcraft	29	30	28	26	34
Bigfoot	22	33	11	22	24
Ghosts	22	28	16	19	25
Clairvoyance	21	24	19	15	30
Loch Ness Monster	16	22	10	16	16

Source: The Gallup Youth Survey, Princeton, NJ. Reprinted by permission.

[25]Based on a report by Kendrick Frazier, "Gallup Poll of Beliefs: Astrology Up, ESP Down," *Skeptical Inquirer*, Vol. 13, Spring 1989, pp. 244–45.

TABLE 6-2   Trends in Beliefs

	1988 %	1984 %	1978 %
Angels	74	69	64
Astrology	58	55	40
ESP	50	59	67
Witchcraft	29	22	25
Bigfoot	22	24	40
Ghosts	22	20	20
Clairvoyance	21	28	25
Loch Ness Monster	16	18	31

Source: The Gallup Youth Survey, Princeton, NJ.
Reprinted by permission.

tasks. Exposure to and indoctrination with occult and supernatural phenomena at a tender age may hinder their unlearning at a later age and may partially explain why adults adhere to occult imaginations with perennial persistence. In other words, some persons never accomplish the transition from the child's unrealism to the adult's realism.

Hollywood has been playing a powerful role in cultivating the unreal in American life. The Hollywood connection is influential not only because this center of phantasmagoria produces unrealism, but also because many of its famous actors and actresses have made no secret of their occult convictions. Ghosts and poltergeists enliven not only the screen, but seem to populate many a celebrity's brain. These famous persons—bright, attractive, and lively as they are—present persuasive models to Americans, especially young Americans.

Implications.   The above list of child–adult value dichotomies could probably be extended to include play vs. work, dependence vs. independence, and irrationality vs. rationality, but the additions would largely overlap with the ones already discussed. In conclusion, American culture contains striking discontinuities between age groups to confuse the individual and strain interpersonal processes. The brunt of the impact of this situation is felt by adolescents who find themselves *between* two relatively well-defined roles. During their transitional existence they have to struggle with ambiguity, constantly trying to decide which set of values and which set of corresponding behavior they should endorse.

ANOMIE IN AMERICAN LIFE

Effects graver than those caused by conflicting values can result from a culture's failure to spell out *any* values or norms. Deviation from known norms or compromise between conflicting norms seems to be less destructive to personality and the social system than vagueness or lack of norms, since deviation or compromise at least starts with a stable point that potentially provides direction.

Humans need structure, a *Gestalt* that conveys a sense of direction, orientation, and stability. Such guides are intimately dependent on clear norms and expectations. A person not realizing any norms would be shiftless and unstable. Emile Durkheim recognized this principle in his classic study on suicide, and conceptualized one type of suicide as *anomic,* the result of a person feeling meaningless in a normless environment.[26] Anomie, derived from the Greek *anomia,* originally meant "lack of order" and was used by Durkheim to describe a social milieu in which control over the members has broken down. This breakdown liberates the individual from moral authority of the community, but at the same time results in personal disequilibrium manifested by a variety of antisocial behavior patterns that may include suicide, delinquency, and formation of subcultures.

Values, usually tied up with basic cultural goals suggesting *what* is to be valued, and norms, the rules of conduct spelling out *how* to go about achieving the values, can be considered two different phenomena. The relationship between them varies and can be classified in a number of ways. Robert Merton developed a typology and showed anomie to be a result of preoccupation with cultural goals in the absence of clear norms and means. In terms of American culture, values are suggested, but feasible ways of achieving them are not indicated. As a general example, American culture stresses monetary success, but fails to extend "a corresponding emphasis upon the legitimate avenues on which to march toward this goal."[27] This type of anomie can cause apathy, manifested by the rejection of goals and norms altogether. A prominent type of apathy results after a cultural goal is not attained in spite of intense striving. Reaction to failure may be anxiety expressed in moral fatigue and indifference. The individual may be left in a social vacuum, without direction or meaning.

The significance of anomie for adolescence is that it strikes hardest when social-structural security is not yet obtained, when the young individual is still a "generalist" trying to find orientation in the *general* culture. "General" is emphasized because youth lacks *specific* norms and directives, which come with adult positions. It is in the general culture that anomie operates, and the teenager is bound to suffer anxiety when attempting to derive direction from it.

Adults are faced with the same anomic condition when trying to orient

---

[26]Emile Durkheim, *Suicide: A Study in Sociology,* trans. J. A. Spaulding and G. Simpson (Paris: F. Alcan, 1897; reprint ed., Glencoe, IL: The Free Press, 1951).

[27]Robert K. Merton, "Social Structure and Anomie: Revisions and Extensions," in *Social Theory and Social Structure* (Glencoe, IL: The Free Press, 1949), p. 133.

themselves by abstract cultural features. However, adults have established clarity by means of concrete living patterns—patterns that are guided by positions in the social structure. Since the young are largely excluded from the division of labor of the adult world, they tend to group together and compensate for cultural vacuum by forming a culture of their own.

In conclusion, the psychological reaction to anomie is *anxiety*, the feeling of being lost in an amorphous surrounding. The reaction to conflict, on the other hand, is *frustration*, the feeling of anger against opposing points. American teenagers suffer from both. The attempt to escape from them leads to subculture formation, where teenagers find norms and values that fit together, thereby eliminating, at least temporarily, anomie and anxiety.

POINT OF ORDER: THE PROBLEM OF SELECTIVITY

This chapter attempted to identify causes of adolescence as they exist in American culture. To accomplish this, I focused on negative aspects of our culture to extract examples necessary to accomplish the analysis. The task can be compared to the job a medical doctor has to do when tracing the causes of a certain condition. The report may point to several physiological problems to explain the illness. For example, he or she may diagnose a malfunction of a certain organ, a deficiency in nutrition, and low resistance. The illness can be understood as the result of the constellation of these factors, and the diagnosis will fail to list all the healthy and normal aspects of the organism since they are of no importance to the diagnosis.

Similarly, in searching for the causes of the adolescent condition, a negative selectivity prevails and only those circumstances are reported that seem to explain it. We investigated the "organ" of culture and found certain characteristics that help us understand the development and persistence of the adolescent condition. Obviously, there are many cultural factors that do not contribute to this condition, but they are not our concern here since they contribute nothing to the diagnosis.

Hence, the picture that emerges from our examination is grimmer than the total reality. Not all aspects of culture work against the adolescent, and not all adolescents stand outside society's blueprint for behavior. Many American teenagers are sufficiently adjusted, and American culture is no more an ogre to the young than most other cultures. Before adolescents realize it, the vast majority of them have grown up and adjusted—and the erstwhile ogre has become a reasonably comfortable habitat.

America has many teenagers who have made a comfortable and even creative adjustment to their culture, enjoy its various institutions, and participate in its programs. A later discussion will touch on some of these aspects.

SUMMARY

American culture, as culture everywhere, is responsible for interpreting life's experiences and issuing blueprints for behavior. The blueprints of our culture contain a number of elements that add complexity to adolescence. The discussion dwelled on several major aspects.

Theories of tracing adolescent "storm and stress" to physiological maturation have largely been replaced by anthropological principles emphasizing the role of cultural relativity in perceiving such organic changes. In American society pubescent changes create adjustment problems because culture avoids giving adequate explanation for them. Youth is thus left unaided to cope with new growth patterns. Social adulthood is not synchronized with biological maturation. During the time teenagers are sexually mature but socially underprivileged, cultural interpretations cause them to feel guilty about sexual expressions.

American culture lacks a definitive rite of passage into adulthood. Transition unclarity creates maladjustments.

Americans are subject to such value dichotomies as competition and cooperation, piety and free thinking, sex and chastity, work and leisure, individuality and conformity. It is difficult for adults to decide which value applies in certain situations and even more difficult for teenagers still working on a basic orientation. Another schism of values breaks the continuity between child and adult roles. Children are kept from continuous involvement in responsibilities and decision making; they are also allowed to dwell in a fantasy world; later they are expected to relearn or unlearn many modes of thinking and behaving when entering adult positions.

Adolescents are particularly vulnerable to anomie in American life because they do not yet have access to specific positions in the productive sector that would help them derive identity and stability.

$$8$$

The Modern Family

Of the various groups to which we belong, the family has the most far-reaching impact on personality development. Quality of family interaction, and its bearing on the way the young grow into adulthood, is significantly affected by the structure of the family. A discussion of the modern family should therefore begin with a look at structural conditions.

Since the discussion focuses on aspects of the family that contribute to the formation of adolescence in American life, it must be selective and may at times appear one-sided or negative. But obviously, not all aspects of the modern family promote adolescence and not all families are the same in degree and manner of reinforcing adolescent symptoms.

As mentioned earlier, such communities as the Amish or Hutterites have succeeded in immunizing their young against adolescence by religious dogma, simple farm life, and isolation from public schools. Other minorities have curbed adolescence sufficiently so that it is different from the typical urban middle-class experience. Hence, the adolescent experience varies according to such background features as ethnicity, race, socioeconomic status, religion, and so forth.

This discussion dwells primarily on historical trends that have intensified the adolescent experience and affected most American families, especially the middle class. We have two concerns: (1) To show similarity rather than diversity among American families, and (2) to identify the new structural conditions that facilitated the rise of modern adolescence.

CHANGING STRUCTURE

Toward the Isolated Nuclear Family

In 1800, more than 90 percent of the population of the United States were farm families. This proportion consistently declined, amounting to 60 percent in 1900, 30 percent in 1930, 23 percent in 1940, 15 percent in 1950, 9 percent in 1960, 3 percent in 1980, and 2 percent in 1988.[1]

The traditional rural family often included such close relatives as grandparents, uncles, aunts, and cousins, and the child grew up in close association with them. In addition, occasionally such nonrelatives as maids and farm hands became permanent members of the household. While in 1910 almost every fourth American family included nonrelatives, in 1961 only every twentieth family included such a person.

In the traditional setting, many married children shared the household of their parents. In 1910, for example, 7.7 percent of married couples did not live in an independent household; by the 1960s this proportion had decreased to 2.1 percent. Statistics show that the average number of persons per household has decreased from about six in 1800 to 2.9 in the mid-1970s, making it the first time in American history that the average size of households has dropped below three, and to 2.7 in the mid-1980s.[2]

Factors that have reduced household size include the divorce rate, which in densely populated West Coast regions has run as high as 70 percent. About 50 percent of first marriages occurring in the 1990s end in divorce. For second marriages, the projected level is about 60 percent.[3] Estimates for the 1990s have put the proportion of American children living in one-parent households at 26 percent, amounting to a 23 percent increase over the previous decade. The estimate for black children is 57 percent, amounting to an 18 percent increase over the previous decade.[4] Living in one-parent families usually turns out to be a permanent arrangement for the children, since the remarriage rate, especially for women, is substantially lower than the rate of divorce for families involving children.

---

[1] U.S. Bureau of the Census, *Current Population Reports*, Series P–20, No. 439, Government Printing Office, Washington, DC, 1989, p. 3.

[2] U.S. Bureau of the Census, *Current Population Reports*, Series P–20, No. 398, Government Printing Office, Washington, DC, 1985, p. 8.

[3] Derived from U.S. Bureau of the Census data and compiled by Paul C. Glick, "Marriage, Divorce, and Living Arrangements. Prospective Changes," *Journal of Family Issues*, Vol. 5, March 1984, p. 23.

[4] Ibid.

An interesting component in the growth of one-parent families is the rise in the number of unwed mothers. The proportion of American children living with a mother who has never been married rose to 4.5 percent in the 1990s, up from 2.9 percent in the 1980s.[5] The mid-1980s Census Bureau figures show that over 20 percent of white births and 75 percent of black births were out of wedlock.[6] As would be expected, the overwhelming majority of single-parent families are headed by women. Because it is no longer such a stigma to be an out-of-wedlock mother, and because economic conditions make single parenthood feasible, young women are no longer rushing into wedlock once they become pregnant.

Another interesting change deals with childlessness. The women of age groups who traditionally have had children, but are childless today, roughly fall into two major categories: those who have decided to lead a childless lifestyle, and those who are postponing parenthood until they have accomplished certain other things in life, mainly an education and a career. The former, research has found, include a disproportionate number of only-children or first-borns who had to care for younger siblings and apparently were influenced by knowing the realism of child rearing.[7]

This change seems to affect college women in particular. Whereas in the 1950s only 9 percent of women of child-bearing age had no children, now 25 percent of college-educated women between 35 and 45 are childless. Apparently these changes are due to heightened individualistic expectations on the part of modern women, including education and careers, plus more stringent economic conditions. As public opinion expert Daniel Yankelovich opined: "In the 1950s a single breadwinner could support a family of five. Now it takes two breadwinners to support a family of four."[8]

More young Americans are postponing marriage to an older age. There has been a steady increase in the median age at first marriage. The average marriage age for men was 22.6 years in 1960, 23.2 in 1970, 24.7 in 1980, and 25.9 in 1988. The average age for women was 20.3 in 1950, 20.8 in 1970, 22 in 1980, and 23.6 in 1988.[9]

In addition, more Americans than ever before stay single. Based on the Census Bureau figures it has been concluded that during the 1990s "this country would be changing from one of the developed countries with the smallest proportion never marrying to a country with one of the largest proportions never marrying."[10] The percentage of Americans in their early

---

[5]Ibid.

[6]"Single Parent Heads US Families," *Arizona Republic*, November 5, 1986, p. C1,

[7]Martha Smilgis, "The Dilemmas of Childlessness," *Time*, May 2, 1988, p. 88.

[8]Quoted by Martha Smilgis, ibid.

[9]U.S. Bureau of the Census, *Current Population Reports*, Series P–20, No. 432, Government Printing Office, Washington, DC, March 1988.

[10]Glick, "Marriage," p. 13.

30s who have never married has more than doubled since 1970, increasing the probability that an increasing segment of the American population will stay single all their lives. Unmarried men 20 to 24 years old amounted to 78 percent of this age group in 1988, an increase of 23 percent over 1970. Unmarried women 20 to 24 years old amounted to 61 percent, an increase of 25 percent over 1970.[11]

These various changes have sometimes been equated with the change from an extended family, where the household included members of several generations plus other relatives and possibly also service personnel, to the nuclear family, including just parents and their offspring. This is, however, an overdrawn assumption. Excepting a few ethnic subcultures, the American family experience has had a tendency to be nuclear from the very beginning.[12]

The opportunities of this continent have always incited Americans to move on, to acquire, to seek their own "hearth," and to stake out their own physical and psychological parameters. Youthful activism, material acquisition, and individualism have never fully promoted the spirit of the classic extended family. Thus, the change in American family structure is more properly described as change from the larger nuclear family to a smaller nuclear family.

There have also been changes in the relationship between the family and the community—changes that are of equal importance in understanding the nature of the modern family. Due to growth in size of communities, resultant anonymity, increase in mobility, and retreat to individualism, the modern family has lost much of its integration into the community and has become isolated to a notable degree.

Looser integration into the community is matched by looser internal integration within the family. With today's emphasis on individualism, the family is no longer a coherent and enduring unit. A person's family used to be his or her unalterable fate, but late-twentieth-century Americans view marriage and the family as something arrangeable—just as occupations or homes are. If spouses feel disappointed, they leave; if teenagers are dissatisfied and feel shackled, they may leave, too. The reason is less often related to personal disillusionment with other family members than the simple desire to pursue one's own interests. Theologian Sam Keen encourages modern Americans to face the problem pragmatically, make mobility part of the family, and, through increased flexibility, save it. He likened the family to a gypsy caravan, which serves as a point of stability and yet, simultaneously, keeps on

---

[11]U.S. Bureau of the Census, 1988.

[12]Bernard Farber, *Family and Kinship in Modern Society* (Glenview, IL: Scott, Foresman and Co., 1973); Peter Laslett, *Household and Family in Past Time* (New York: Cambridge University Press, 1972), p. 575,

moving. Family members may leave the caravan occasionally and then again catch up with it.[13]

It is doubtful whether this vision will replace that of the family as being supposedly permanent, since the latter belief is a cherished American dream. Nonetheless, the vision may be closer to American reality than the dream, but that is usually neither recognized nor admitted.

CHANGING FUNCTIONS

The smaller and less stable family has signaled basic changes in how Americans relate to each other. The consequences of the changed structure and various other components of the new family lifestyle are discussed below.

Exit Role, Enter Individual

The traditional family can also be called the "institutional" family because institutional norms and procedures were preferred over personal attitudes and desires. Integrity of the family as a unit used to be safeguarded by the various members playing roles. Deviations were frowned on, punished by informal or formal sanctions, and made difficult by economic dependence on the family unit. Also, the role of spouse or offspring had metaphysical overtones and was commonly considered as a sacred "blueprint" not to be taken lightly. This was familism, the philosophy that the family's goals and purposes have priority over those of the individual.

The modern family, however, places a premium on interpersonal competence rather than on skill in role functioning. The traditional family with its legal rigidity and hierarchical structure has become outdated, and modern Americans seek "self-actualization." Emphasis is now on flexibility, looser integration, and greater individualism. The high divorce rate is a manifestation of these changes, indicating that we are now highly divorce-prone because of the lack of institutional coercion, the easing of economic limitations, and the acceptance of individual volition that is monitored by little other than the rewards of companionship.

This, however, should not be mistaken for abandonment of marriage and the family. On the contrary, Americans adhere to the family as an institution within which they expect fulfillment of emotional needs, which now emphasize individualism and personality functions. These functional changes call for competence in interpersonal relations. Safe but rigid role

---

[13]Reported in "American Family: Future Uncertain," *Time*, December 28, 1970, p. 39.

blueprints are replaced by a highly individualistic style of relating that requires sensitivity, increased communication, and constantly new interpretations of interactional situations.

Demands for interpersonal competence include new emphasis on sexual knowledge and sexual equality, problem-solving skill, sublimating proficiency when frustrated, willingness to resort to professional therapy, and skill in family and couple communication. Interpersonal harmony depends so heavily on improved communication that family sociologists have recommended communication theory be applied to the marital dyad.[14]

Adolescents must learn to replace old, rigid role matrixes with sensitive personal communication. This means giving up the age-old security of knowing *a priori* how to act or react in interpersonal situations, especially in the relationship between the sexes, and accepting the new freedom of being able to style uniquely and creatively every human encounter. Learning to act individualistically takes both courage and experience. While the young may have the former, they may lack the latter. Learning adequate responses to the liberalized style of human interaction constitutes an immensely difficult task—a task requiring the treatment of each social scene as a situation that presents unique problems and requires unique solutions.

Probably the change most vexing to the young is the altered female role. Increasingly, mothers fail to convey an easily predictable role model. Until recently, wives were supplementary to husbands and not expected to express a full range of capabilities. Today, women have much greater expectations— and also frustrations. Nearly 60 percent of American women are now employed, and when a woman is working, she has a new perception of herself, behaves more independently, and refuses to be cast in a cultural matrix. There are difficulties of adjustment to this derigidification process for everyone involved. Girls are thrown back on their personal identities and must become fully conscious of them. Boys, while witnessing the expanding role of the female, are still largely trapped in the rigid role of masculinity and must make concessions. Skillful communication seems to be the basic key for successfully coping with encounters between the sexes, and a family sociologist calls attention to a Family Communication Game that can be used for education and fun by high school students.[15]

Difficulties arising from the modern family situation are not to be necessarily construed as having a negative value. New equity and flexibility promise greater opportunity for creativity and identity formation and can lead to deeply rewarding relationships.

[14]Sherod Miller et al., "Recent Progress in Understanding and Facilitating Marital Communication," *The Family Coordinator*, 24 (April 1975): 143–52.

[15]William Saur, "Family Communication Game," *The Family Coordinator*, 24 (April 1975): 227–29.

From Status Ascription to Status Achievement

An individual growing up in the traditional family rarely had to be concerned with the question of social mobility, since he or she "inherited" the status of the family. A teenager at the turn of the century was exposed to considerably less intergenerational mobility than his or her counterpart of the mid-twentieth century. Familistic norms and values mitigated the problem of adolescent discontinuity, and a teenager knew his or her "place" in the family as well as in the larger society. Anxieties accompanying contemporary youth's task of determining their place and prestige in the social structure were thereby avoided.

Today, finding one's place is more individualistic. Although family background, especially if the family belongs to either extreme of the socio-economic spectrum, is still an important influence on status achievement, its influence has diminished and status differences between parents and off-spring are common. Many modern families consist of members who differ in social prestige, primarily because they pursue different careers. In short, the criterion for social status in modern society is based more on occupational achievement than on family reputation. Some family sociologists go so far as to conclude that family obligations in modern urban-industrial society tend to detract from single-minded pursuit of highly prized personal success, be the goal scholarly, commercial, or professional.[16]

The shift toward individualism is reflected in such catch phrases as "proliferation of associations," "personality market," "individuation," and "self-actualization." More and more relationships are achieved and are relatively role-free, including those cultivated at school, at work, in numerous voluntary associations, and now also in the marital dyad. Achieved relationships are essentially idiosyncratic and potentially boundless. A pessimistic interpretation is that "herein lies their threat to the family, for they, like many other aspects of contemporary life, may readily infringe upon family claims, may alienate members from the family."[17]

The modern family's loss of the placement function, and thus its loss of the status-ascription function, has direct bearing on the problem of adolescence. Teenagers cannot expect much help from home during the process of working out a status by and for themselves. Their parents' statuses do not necessarily have finality in determining their own statuses. While family background is of minimal ascriptive effect, the achievement syndrome is of maximum importance. Absence of status certainty and prospects of an uncharted journey toward some yet undefined and obscure adult status may

---

[16]Charles W. Hobart, "Commitment, Value Conflict and the Future of the American Family," *Journal of Marriage and the Family*, 25 (November 1963): 405–06.

[17]Ibid., p. 406.

create feelings that are aptly described by contemporary teenagers when they say that they feel "lost" and are "going nowhere."

Again, it must be pointed out that negative aspects can be balanced by a positive gain: Modern teenagers have an unprecedented freedom to choose among different lifestyles. There may be something to be said for "being lost" and "going nowhere" for a while, instead of knowing from the beginning where one is going, but possibly neither liking the direction nor having the chance to change the course. Factual as well as fictional accounts of a past era are replete with the tragic stories of young individuals who had to pursue a course in life they had not chosen.

Limited Adult Models

The traditional family was able to provide a number of adults who could serve as significant models. This was possible not only because there were more individuals in the family but also because their work performance was more visible. In addition, the family was integrated into the community and could bring the young in contact with neighbors and relatives whose behavior and occupational pursuits could be observed. This helped the young to learn patterns of problem solving and derive value orientation.

In the isolated nuclear family, learning from available persons is extremely limited. Normally, there is only one adult of each gender present, and if this parent is not readily observable, the young lose models. A special concern of many social scientists is the middle-class boy who frequently suffers identity problems because of father absence.[18]

Even if the male child has the opportunity to associate with his father and observe his actions, one must allow for the possibility that this model, for whatever idiosyncratic reason, may not be acceptable to the child. Rejection of a father can lead to a situation in which the father changes from a model to an object of scorn. A frequent theme underlying cases of father rejection is modern youth's refusal to accept a person as a model whose only qualification is the *position* of father. Regard for institutions and formal positions has changed from the "sacred" to the "secular." Trying to uphold reverence and obedience for a position when it is occupied by a person considered unqualified can result in serious interpersonal disharmony.

Barrington Moore expressed one of the most poignant opinions on this matter. He accused the modern nuclear family of being "obsolete and barbaric" because of the young's "obligation to give affection as a duty to a particular set of persons because of the accident of birth." Moore called

---

[18]Michael E. Lamb, "Paternal Influences and the Father's Role," in John Keating, ed., *Social Psychology*, Annual Editions (Guilford, CT: Duskhin, 1982), pp. 68–73.

attention to "the exploitation of socially sanctioned demands for gratitude when the existing social situation no longer generates any genuine feeling of warmth."[19] Most important, he considered adolescence to be the outgrowth of the modern family's incapability of stabilizing the personalities of its offspring.

While Moore's ideas may have some validity, they are only partial explanations of the variables causing adolescence. Nevertheless, it is true that deprivation of role models may develop in situations where the offspring refuse to acknowledge parental authority. When father-absenteeism is combined with rebellious attitudes, sex-role identification indeed suffers. While such dysfunctional conditions were avoided in the larger traditional family, the nuclear family fails to offer children flexibility in choosing models, thereby complicating the transition from childhood to adulthood.

Moore's contention could be expanded to include mother-absenteeism from the home. Nearly 60 percent of all women now work, including a growing percentage of women with children. While it is true that this may entail a reduction of the time and the opportunities children have to use mother as a model, there is little support for the claim that this is detrimental to the child's personality. As already indicted in Chapter 5, psychologist Bronfenbrenner found that the decisive variable regarding the fate of latchkey children is the type of activities planned for the child by the working parent.[20]

It has been found, however, that outside work by mothers may be detrimental to the marriage. Mothers who work outside the home have a notably higher divorce rate. Scott South's findings were interpreted to mean that if a woman is in a better economic position to make it on her own, she may terminate an unsatisfactory marriage.[21]

Nonfamilial Peers

In the large, traditional family the child usually grew up with peers who were of his or her family group. They were playmates with whom they shared the same sentiments. Charles H. Cooley's concept of primary group found near perfection in this arrangement. Interaction was intimate, face-to-face, and self-perception was in terms of "we" instead of in terms of "I and they."[22]

[19]Barrington Moore, "Thoughts on the Future of the Family," in *Identity and Anxiety*, eds. Maurice R. Stein, Arthur J. Vidich, and Daniel M. White (Glencoe, IL: The Free Press, 1960), pp. 393–94.

[20]Discussed by Jeff Meer, "Children—Alone but not Neglected," *Psychology Today*, August 1985, p. 11.

[21]Quoted by Vincent Bozzi, "Till Death or Economic Hardship Do Us Part," *Psychology Today*, May 1986, p. 6.

[22]Charles H. Cooley, *Social Organization* (New York: Scribner's, 1909), p. 23.

This type of family blended primary and secondary socialization into one process and prevented marginality because integration into the consanguine family group was a lifelong proposition. When the young married, they would often remain in the household of the family of orientation, or at least in the same community.

In contrast, most modern nuclear families are isolated from kin and cannot provide playmates who are relatives. Modern youth grow up seeing few, if any, of their relatives; many of them live and grow up with only one parent. Hence, children of nuclear families find their playmates outside of the kin group and commonly transform the school environment into a primary source of friends.

Recreation and leisure have been transferred from the family to commercial agencies. Commercialization aims at individuals, or individuals in certain age groups, but rarely at families as units. This is reflected in movie ratings, music festivals, concerts, and pop musicals—all being events that have become age-specific.

Parents' prime competitors seem to be their children's nonfamilial peers, who, unlike siblings and cousins growing up in the same family system, frequently have divergent attitudes and fail to share common loyalty to one family. They are a peer group independent of family life. Thus, teenagers enter a marginal status with respect to both the family of orientation and the family of procreation. They are no longer an intrinsic part of the parental home and have not yet formed their own families. They are suspended between two membership groups and compensate by temporarily joining a subculture. James S. Coleman, in his classic *The Adolescent Society*, reported large, complex "teenage societies" among high school youth, organized along lines diametrically opposed to the standards of parents.[23]

Equally powerful is the influence of the mass media, particularly television. Prime targets of the television industry are preadolescents and adolescents. By the time children reach eighteen years of age, they will have watched twice as many hours of television as they spent in the classroom. Although some of the fare is realistic and educational, most of it is violent, unrealistic, and divergent from parental values.

Responsibility for youth's peer-family conflict lies partly with parents and partly with the changing structure of the modern community, according to psychologist Urie Bronfenbrenner.[24] Through evaluation of various statistics and their integration into a trend indicator, he predicts increasing isolation of American teenagers from parents and adults. Many factors conspire to

[23]James S. Coleman, *The Adolescent Society* (Glencoe, IL: The Free Press, 1961).

[24]Urie Bronfenbrenner, "Children and Families: 1984?" *Society*, 18 (January/February 1981): 38–41; *The Ecology of Human Development: Experiments by Nature and Design* (Cambridge, MA: Harvard University Press, 1979); and "Ecology of the Family as a Context of Human Development," *Developmental Psychology* 22 (1986): 723–742.

isolate the young from the rest of society: (1) decline of the large or even extended family, (2) separation of residential and work areas, (3) impersonal neighborhoods, (4) zoning ordinances, (5) occupational mobility, (6) child labor laws, (7) consolidated schools, (8) television, (9) age-segregated patterns of social and recreational life, (10) working mothers, and (11) delegation of child care, education, and therapy to experts. Bronfenbrenner regards the trend as a manifestation of decreasing opportunity for meaningful contact between generations.

Erosion of cohesiveness of the social network has isolating effects not only on the young but also on the family as a unit. Centrifugal forces generated within the family by its increasingly isolated position have propelled its members into different directions. As parents, especially mothers, dedicate more time to outside careers, children gravitate toward nonfamilial settings, some organized and others informal. For example, the number of children enrolled in day-care centers has more than doubled in recent years, and demand far exceeds supply. The young spend increasing amounts of time in the company of agemates to fill the vacuum created by withdrawal of parents and other adults.

Bronfenbrenner refers to sources showing that today's reliance on the informal peer group, at every age and grade level, has enormously increased, and that this is particularly noticeable among children from homes in which one or both parents are frequently absent. These peer-dependent youth describe parents as less affectionate and less firm in discipline. They also display greater pessimism about the future, rate lower in responsibility and leadership, and are more likely to engage in antisocial behavior.

Social scientists have interpreted these conditions as roots of alienation. Over time, they believe, these conditions will become more prevalent, and greater peer dependency as well as more serious manifestations of alienation will evolve. This, presumably, is the major explanation for rising rates of juvenile homicide, suicide, drug abuse, and other forms of delinquency.

Parents, Peers, and Autonomy

The contrapuntal peer association vis-à-vis the family should not be dismissed as entirely dysfunctional. Excepting certain destructive by-products, the peer culture can serve a valuable function. Mannheim reminded us that affiliation with peer culture is instrumental in loosening dependence on the family and should not be sweepingly defined as a "social problem."[25] Adolescents' desire to establish distance from their family groups finds implementation through affiliation with nonfamilial peers who, in concerted rebel-

[25]Karl Mannheim, *Essays on the Sociology of Culture* (New York: Oxford University Press, 1956).

liousness, try out new norms and values and in the process obtain skill in problem solving and develop unique identities. A major function of modern adolescence is renunciation of dependence on the family and substitution of peer groups for the family group. This substitution includes fulfillment of emotional needs essential for individual growth, such as stimulation, empathy, loyalty, the opportunity for role playing, identification, and sharing of guilt and anxiety.

It can be said, then, that the peer group facilitates the young individual's autonomy process and emancipation from the family. The end result is an individual who is relatively autonomous in three respects. First, there is *emotional* autonomy as the person relaxes ties to the family and emotionally unfolds to establish bonds of love, support, and confidence elsewhere. Second, there is *behavioral* autonomy as the person acquires skill and courage to do what he or she wants to do. Third, there is *ideational* autonomy as the person thinks and struggles through basic ideas and established personal convictions.

Some researchers disagree with the conflict theory and point out that if a contrapuntal subculture does in fact exist, it has been exaggerated and that in ordinary middle-class families cooperative and mutually rewarding relationships between parents and teenagers are more in evidence than conflict.[26] Moreover, by the time children become adolescents, they have more or less achieved independence from parents. Psychologist Albert Bandura argues that establishment of autonomy of the adolescent poses more of a problem for parents than for young individuals, since parents have to adjust to the loss of a family member. Having enjoyed a relatively harmonious family relationship, teenagers tend to be discriminative in their choice of reference groups and generally establish peer associations that allow implementation of norms and values they learned in their homes. Hence, peergroup membership is usually not in opposition to family values and generates little intergenerational conflict.

Bandura tries to explain the discrepancy between his research findings and the traditional theory by pointing out the distortions present in massmedia sensationalism; questioning the validity of generalizations from biased samples (such as data based on deviant adolescents); showing the rigidity of the theoretical approach, which glosses over individual variation; and stating the self-fulfilling prophecy that if adults label adolescents as rebellious, then rebellious they will become.

Eugene Thomas' study of political attitudes between generations supports Bandura's hypothesis,[27] revealing that children of highly politicized

---

[26]Albert Bandura, "The Stormy Decade: Fact or Fiction," in *Issues in Adolescent Psychology*, ed. D. Rogers (New York: Prentice-Hall, 1972).

[27]Eugene Thomas, "Family Correlates of Student Political Activism," *Developmental Psychology*, 4 (March 1971): 206–14.

parents tend to be like their parents both in political attitudes and political behavior. This supports the conclusion that stratification theory explains political activism much better than generational theory. While the latter presupposes that the young rebel against their parents and therefore resent symbolic authority figures, the former suggests that these attitudes cut across generational lines. Reuben Hill and J. Aldous, Jr. explored attitudes and beliefs of three generations and found that while behavior concerning practical issues (for example, the division of labor in the household) has changed, fundamental values such as religious beliefs have hardly shifted at all.[28]

Additional researchers questioning the validity of the assumption that youth-parent conflict is a primary feature of adolescence are Elizabeth Douvan and her associates, whose data consistently showed a more harmonious youth-parent relationship.[29] Their findings suggest a more peaceful scene than much theory and most social comments would lead us to expect: " 'Rebellious youth' and 'the conflict between generations' are phrases that ring; but, so far as we can tell, it is not the ring of truth they carry so much as the beguiling but misleading tone of drama."[30]

However, some of these researchers' data are based on narrow samples. Just as theorists may project generalizations from too broad a base, interviewers may project generalizations from too narrow a base. For example, most of the evidence that led Douvan to make the condemning statement cited above grew out of work dealing mainly with girls. In addition, little elucidation of data was provided to give a fuller picture of developmental changes. It seems, for instance, that seriousness of conflict is progressive; that is, it increases with age within the adolescent span. In one of the few instances where inquiry was directed at age-differentiated conflict and where girls were asked what they most disagreed about with their parents, the results showed three quite distinct peaks: the younger adolescents reported narrow narcissistic issues; the middle group had interpersonal problems; and the older girls were concerned with broader social issues. Thus, in the under-fourteen group, clothing and make-up were the types of issues over which there was most disagreement; in the fourteen-to-sixteen group, whom, when, and how to date appeared major issues; in the oldest group, most disagreements dealt with basic ideas. Not only do researchers like Douvan and Gold fail to commit themselves to a certain age category when they make generalizations (usually about a harmonious youth-parent relationship), but even

[28]Reuben Hill and J. Aldous, Jr., "Socialization for Marriage and Parenthood," in *Handbook of Socialization Theory and Research*, ed. D. Goslin (Chicago: Rand McNally, 1969).

[29]Elizabeth Douvan and Joseph Adelson, *The Adolescent Experience* (New York: John Wiley, 1966), and Elizabeth Douvan and H. Gold, "Modal Patterns in American Adolescence," in *Review of Child Development Research*, vol. 2, ed. L. Hoffman and M. Hoffman (New York: Russell Sage Foundation, 1966).

[30]Douvan and Gold, "Modal Patterns in American Adolescence," p. 485.

more important, they neglect to sufficiently clarify whether boys are equally restrained in their attitudes toward parental rule as girls appear to be. The Douvan studies suffer from the major weakness of comparing a small number of boys at one stage during their adolescent development with a large number of girls throughout the age range.

In any event, the reader is advised to accept either interpretation — the "conflict" as well as the "harmonious" theory — with caution and remain open to further insight that, hopefully, will eventually accrue.

The Law and the Young: Independence, Individualism, and Isolation

American society appears to look at marital and family affiliations as essentially private relationships outside of the purview of the public's meddling, be this informal interference or legal encroachment. This is not to say that the law is indifferent to what is going on in the family, but rather that serious dysfunctions within the family system are approached as *individual* matters and not as family issues.

If the adolescent exhibits disturbed or delinquent behavior, he or she is approached as an isolated individual and not as a representative of a primary group the disturbances of which he or she is manifesting. The law's pursuit is the individual, and jurisdictional interests proceed regardless of family context. The "hands-off" policy is particularly emphatic in the case of marital dissolution. In a sense, the law concerns itself only with keeping records of who enters and who leaves marriage.

This, then, is the individual-centered legal context within which rights and obligations of American children and teenagers must be understood.

A legal landmark in clarifying the young Americans' status was the Twenty-sixth Amendment to the Constitution in 1971 which gave eighteen-year-olds the right to vote and helped them to obtain many other legal privileges. The rights that eighteen-, nineteen-, and twenty-year-olds have gained include the right to own property, make wills, sign binding contracts, sue and be sued, marry without the consent of parents, and undergo medical treatment (including treatment for venereal disease) without parental approval.[31] The majority of states have granted eighteen-year-olds the privileges they formerly had to wait until twenty-one to receive.

In fact, the states are now extending "without consent" medical rights (including pregnancy care, birth-control prescriptions, abortion, treatment for venereal disease, drug addiction, and psychiatric problems) to youths

---

[31]"Kids, Sex, and Doctors," *Time*, November 25, 1974, pp. 91–93, and Lavelle E. Saunders, "Ignorance of the Law Among Teenagers: A Barrier to the Exertion of Their Rights as Citizens?" Paper presented at the Annual Meeting of the Pacific Sociological Association, Victoria, British Columbia, April 1975.

under eighteen. In all states (except Wisconsin) younger teenagers have the right to get treatment for venereal disease without consulting their parents. California's emancipated youth laws extend this right to anyone over twelve years old. New Jersey allows minors of any age to obtain pregnancy care and abortion without parental consent but, ironically, requires parental consent for contraceptive prescriptions up to age eighteen. Oregon has dropped the age of medical consent to fifteen, and Alabama to fourteen.

The age group most conspicuously affected by the new laws are college students, who have been freed from *in loco parentis* authority. Colleges may no longer require students to live in campus dormitories; out-of-state students may find it easier to establish legal residence within a state and thus pay lower tuition fees for state-supported institutions; parents may no longer get a chance to see the grades of their adult children or be informed of any trouble they have gotten into, unless their son or daughter specifically gives the college permission; students from higher-income families, previously barred from most financial aid in college, may now claim they are independent of parents, account for only their own income, and receive financial aid; and students can sue and be sued, which enables colleges to take students to court in cases of vandalism, disruption, or cheating without involving the parents, and, likewise, students can file legal complaints.

Many parents, educators, and administrators feel that their authority is being undermined. They perceive an exaggerated emphasis on individualism that results in too much independence for the young and that alienates them from their families. This alienation is deepened by moving individual-centered legislation to the forefront of human interaction. As legalistic consciousness grows, the informal cooperation and personal trust that used to be a natural part of family life is being diminished.

The Rise of the Personality Function

Industrialization has prompted the transferral of one traditional family function after another to specialized institutional settings. The economic and production function has been relegated to the factory and office; the educational function has been entirely absorbed by schools; the religious function has been formalized and is now the exclusive domain of the church or synagogue; the recreational function has been commercialized and is dominated by profit-seeking institutions like movie theaters and sports stadiums; the medical function has been transferred to the doctor's office and the hospital. Family members usually go to these places individually, not as a family unit.

The family is left to provide psychological security for its members, but little else. In short, the trend of increasing specialization in American society has affected the family and made it a specialist. It now specializes in gratifying psychological needs. The question of whether the modern family can meet basic personality needs, in particular such needs as the feeling of belonging and security, is important for youth's physical as well as mental health. Experience of structural discontinuity between statuses of child and adult is difficult and confusing under normal and secure circumstances. If, in addition, there is lack of psychological security, youth faces an extremely difficult time.

Many sociologists have attempted to answer the question of whether the modern family is able to offer this vital security, and two main theories have emerged. Interpretations of the changes in family life have led one group to answer "no" and the other "yes" to the question of the family's psychological functionality. Besides Barrington Moore, a well-known spokesperson for the "no" group, there is Carl C. Zimmerman, whose work offers an extensive historical study of the family, draws conclusions from previous societies, applies them to the contemporary scene, and predicts the doom of the modern family.[32] The hypothesis is supported by historical data suggesting that the modern family has lost too many functions to be of further importance. Since, according to Zimmerman, the disintegration of the family heralds the disintegration of the society at large, his theory has been called the *doomsday theory.*

Opposing interpretation is offered by Talcott Parsons, who presents a more optimistic point of view.[33] Changes are interpreted as processes reforming the family into an agency specializing in the *personality function.* This specialization is the American response to the need to derive from the family psychological security to a degree heretofore unknown.

These acute psychological demands appear to be symptomatic of the problem of identity, which can be considered the prominent mental problem of the modern era. It is within the confines of the family that Americans hope to find the answer to the basic question, Who am I? This burdens the family with an immense responsibility. If people fail to find the coveted identity and feeling of security in a particular marriage or family, they are apt to terminate membership and try anew with different partners. According to Parsons, this insistence on "self-fulfillment" explains the high divorce rate in modern America. The rate, as alarming as it may seem, does not necessarily indicate the doom of the family institution but rather the need of contemporaries to succeed in gratifying psychological needs. If the need is not met with one particular partner, the partner is changed; but the same conventional institution, marriage and the family, is used, reused, and upheld.[34]

---

[32]Carl C. Zimmerman, *Family and Civilization* (New York: Harper and Row, 1947).

[33]Talcott Parsons and Robert F. Bales, *Family, Socialization and Interaction Process* (Chicago: The Free Press of Glencoe, 1955).

[34]There is a significant difference between a particular *family group* and the *institution of the family.* The two should never be confused. The former refers to a specific group of people, in this case a primary group within which the members engage in an intimate face-to-face interaction. The concept of institution is more abstract, referring to norms, values, and customs with which society regulates family life.

Without necessarily endorsing Zimmerman's negative outlook, we nonetheless must acknowledge that the nuclear family is beset with difficulties that limit the success of the personality function. The detracting conditions include (1) high divorce rate, (2) insufficient family communication, (3) increasing numbers of mothers directing their attention to outside careers, (4) continuing remoteness of fathers from the socialization process, and (5) high mobility. These conditions cause many adolescents to be inadequately involved in family communication—without a definite sense of being accepted and understood, and without a basic trust in the stability of the family group.

Some of these detracting conditions must be singled out as particularly important. For example, communication is a skill not automatically earned by merit of being a parent but must be acquired by practice. How many children grow up doubting whether they are loved and accepted by their parents, consequently suffer under these doubts, and later in life reproach a reticent parent for not having communicated love and care? As mentioned earlier, proficiency in communication is imperative for success in the modern family, where role playing is no longer the predictable form of communication. To implement the modern personality function, the communication process must be improved by greater sensitivity and by spending more time on it.

But modern parents' time schedule has not always taken the need for more communication into account. Modern fathers are known as notorious shirkers of the responsibility to equitably share in socializing the young, and excuse themselves as being absorbed by their jobs. Admittedly, this aspect of modern family life seems to be undergoing modification thanks to the protests of the women's liberation movement. But the progress made in this direction tends to be neutralized by the mothers' newly acquired taste for career pursuits. While this may connote progress to many creative mothers who heretofore were cloistered in the kitchen and nursery, it may be an obstacle to the increased communication needed by the child in order to feel secure and understood.

Communication does not merely mean "talking to each other," it means *doing things together*, using the media of common projects, work, and recreational activities. These media can be used to express thoughts and feelings to each other, to get to know each other, and to feel a belonging to each other that can rarely be established by way of abstract verbalizations. Actions speak more convincingly than words, and the young can benefit immensely by shared feeling, touch, and motion—ingredients that will generate common emotions, which form the foundation for conveying the sense of belonging and security.

Another obstacle to the personality function is mobility. Spatial mobility of Americans is truly remarkable: every five years about one-half the U.S. population moves. In the process, they increase the variety of readjustments they must make, lose the immediate support of neighborhood and friendships they had enjoyed, and decrease informal discouragement against separation or divorce they had (or could have) derived from integration into the community.

Mobility plays a prominent role in the lives of businessmen, white-collar workers, and young executives who are constantly on relocation call for the corporation and have been called "corporate nomads." The price of promotion includes a willingness to be geographically mobile. A typical example is the mobility record of a newly promoted assistant secretary at Humble Oil and Refining Co., who at the age of thirty-three had moved six times in eleven years. His nine-year-old son had never finished more than one grade in the same school. Within ten months, a young aspiring executive of Johnson Wax was moved from Wisconsin to New York and then to Chicago to become regional office manager, with his son going through kindergarten in three different schools.[35]

Young people need consistency in life patterns, including physical and social arrangements, to achieve stable reference points. Informal associations like the peer group, neighborhood, and friendships, and formal associations like school, church, and clubs, constitute social-control mechanisms, and youth's integration into them has a stabilizing influence—provided that it is consistent and continuous.

Although one could say a few things in defense of the functionality of high mobility, for example that exposure to a wide variety of stimuli can contribute to a more sophisticated outlook on life and that job contingencies require knowledge of a variety of human interactions, they seem to be neutralized by such dysfunctions as exposing the young to too many stimuli (and possibly inconsistent ones) and to more people than can be meaningfully integrated in the understanding of the young—a typical consequence of overstimulation and overexposure. Although the relationships may turn out to be expedient and efficient, they tend to remain shallow. In other words, quality of human interaction is replaced by quantity. Relationships of deep understanding and genuine loyalty require time to grow—time many mobile parents fail to provide for their children. The sense of impermanence of these relationships intensifies the need for *some* relationship that is durable. And it is, given the impersonality of the larger social system, almost invariably the family that is sought out for this important function.

Now we have arrived at a circular irony. The family seems to promise personality security, commonly fails to live up to its promise, and Americans nevertheless keep trying to make marriage and the family work. It is like Sisyphus attempting to roll a boulder uphill, and the whole situation smacks of overdependence on a limited structural arrangement.

Whether these changes will eventually bring about the downfall of the

[35]"The Job: Corporate Nomads," *Time*, September 29, 1967, p. 56.

family system as we know it today are speculations that cannot be put to an empirical test at this time. In any case, the functional changes of the modern family can be summed up in three points: (1) a number of traditional family functions have been transferred to other institutions, (2) the modern family has become a specialized agency, (3) people turn to the family to derive a sense of total psychological security.

The Question of Primary Group Quality

The socialization experience in the family is so profound that what we conceptualize as "human nature" can be traced back to this primary group. The human organism responds to the slightest variation in style of socialization, and some modes complicate the adolescent process. It appears that a child growing up in a family that fulfills the criteria of a healthy primary group will be better equipped to cope with the contingencies of adolescence than a child whose association was either in a disturbed primary group or mostly in secondary groups.

Before pursuing this argument further, the question of what a primary group is must be clarified.[36] A primary group is characterized by intimate face-to-face interaction and spontaneous cooperation. It is primary in the sense that it is instrumental in generating the social nature of the individual. The psychological result of the intimate association is a blending of several individuals into a social entity in which one's self becomes an integral part of the common life and goals of the group. The emergent sentiments involve the sort of mutual identification for which "we" is the most natural expression. The members' identities become anchored in the feeling of belonging to the whole.

This does not necessarily mean that the atmosphere of the group is always one of harmony. There is often self-assertion and passion. But these sentiments are tempered by sympathy and a sense of common fate. While an individual member may show ambition, its chief motivation is the self-esteem he or she derives from the others, and interaction will be governed by allegiance to common standards of loyalty. This is the social-psychological background that explains why a child may come to dispute with teammates his or her place on the team, but will strive toward common glory for the team.

The most compelling examples of such primary associations are the family, peer group, and, decreasingly, the neighborhood or community. Primary involvements are virtually universal and are the basis of what is universal in human nature and fundamental in human sentiments.

The definition of secondary groups consists of elements that contrast

---

[36]The statement on the primary group, paraphrased in the following passages, comes from Cooley, *Social Organization*, pp. 23–24.

with the primary group—impermanence, casualness of contact, fewer ties of deep sentiment among the members, and a lesser degree of derivation of basic values from the group's norms and goals. In reality, groups do not come neatly divided into either primary or secondary types; rather, social reality presents us with a continuum, the poles of which we define as primariness and secondariness of group quality. Groups differ from one another not categorically, but in the *degree* to which the interacting behavior of the participants reflects primariness.[37]

Has the American family shifted along the continuum of primary-secondary group relations? In other words, is the nuclear family less primary than the traditional family? To answer this question, it is helpful to examine specific elements of the criteria of primariness.

An important element of the primary group consists of *common value orientation*. Family sociologists fear that consensus within the family, especially between the generations, has been eroded by modern socialization practices that promote more nonfamilial exposure of the young to nurseries, day-care centers, peers, schools, and youth subculture than to parents and relatives. Bias for the traditional growth process in the primary group family is reflected by a number of sociologists' negative views of the changes in family functions. They regret, as Hobart put it, that "the shaping of a human life, a human personality, a future of happiness or hell, which is best accomplished in the primary group, is turned over ever earlier and for longer periods to secondary, impersonal, social agencies."[38] These agencies tend to merely "handle" children in groups, rather than care for them as individuals.

Bronfenbrenner is even more outspoken about parental failure to enforce a value orientation in the children. Reporting about his cross-cultural study of child-rearing practices in America and West Germany, he admitted that he expected German parents to be stricter than American parents. Although the hypothesis was borne out by the findings, it was also found that the German parents were more affectionate and spent more time with the children. This calls into question what exactly is meant by *permissive*; perhaps it means that parents are not paying much attention to their young. American parents have been told by experts to "let children be themselves"; that counsel has been taken to mean "let them grow up by themselves." Bronfenbrenner rejects *laissez-faire* philosophy and believes that the young "should not grow up associating only with other children because they haven't much to give to each other."[39]

Teenagers themselves have complained that parents fail to give them

<hr />

[37]Definitions like "primary" or "secondary" are ideal-type definitions; that is, they are useful—yet arbitrary—typologies. They are useful for tracing trends, comparing different systems, and facilitating communication. Ideal-type concepts are instrumental in many social analyses and can be called *heuristic* in nature.

[38]Hobart, "Commitment, Value Conflict and the Future of the American Family," p. 408.

[39]"The American Family: Future Uncertain," *Time*, December 28, 1970, p. 37.

guidance and are too permissive. It seems that they sense a need for more authoritative counsel. A national sample found that teenagers ascribe primary responsibility for excessive teenage drinking and use of "dope" to their parents' failure to wield enough authority.[40] This attitude illustrates teenagers' dissatisfaction with modern home anomie, which allows them a high degree of individual freedom but also creates uncertainty. Anomie is not characteristic of a primary-group setting; rather it offers rules and values of insuperable aid in stabilizing personality.

Common activities, another mark of the primary group, have drastically declined in the modern family. As discussed in previous chapters, the place of work is somewhere else, and children, unless they live on the farm, are not drawn into adult activities. Similarly, leisure activities are usually age-segregated because of different interest. If time is spent together, it is usually a passive gathering—watching television, traveling someplace, or being entertained—instead of doing things together.

A core trait of the primary group is that it forms the social nature of the individual. To what extent is the modern family still instrumental in carrying out this function? Is it imbuing the young with the same loyalty and empathy as the traditional family? Bronfenbrenner has found that all factors indicating growth, happiness, and effectiveness of the young are declining. Conversely, he discovered increasing isolation and evidence to anticipate impairment rather than improvement in competence and character of the next generation. His pessimistic conclusion was that the system for making human beings human in this society is breaking down and that "the destructive effects of these changes derive from the progressive segregation by age in American society, resulting in isolation of children and those responsible for their care."[41]

As a rule, parents gladly let other agencies take over socializing. Nurseries, kindergartens, schools, churches, and the various media of entertainment encounter little resistance from parents, who willingly surrender a territory that means fatiguing work, time, and often frustration. Television in particular has become a convenient baby-sitting device, changing the family circle to a semicircle.

Finally, the characteristics of the primary group include the blending of several individuals into a social entity. But in our age, the young do not defer individual goals to common goals; rather they look at the family as a pragmatic arrangement that can be useful but as only one alternative in learning values. In short, the family has changed from an end in itself to a means for individual purposes.

---

[40]Leonard Gross, "America's Mood Today," *Look*, June 29, 1965, p. 21.

[41]Urie Bronfenbrenner, "The Challenge of Social Change to Public Policy and Developmental Research." Paper presented at the President's Symposium, *Child Development and Public Policy*, Denver, CO, April 12, 1975, abstract.

This does not mean that the average family of today is of secondary-group quality. Rather, there has been a shift on the continuum toward more secondariness of group qualities, with the family playing a modified role in the process of extending identity. The proliferation of secondary-group affiliations and the impact of the mass media are to some extent replacing the socialization function of the family. It seems that both the family and the secondary influences are not meeting the needs of the young. The paradoxical result is that the young turn to the family for identity and warmth, but are confronted with its ineffectiveness in stabilizing personality and are thus driven back to the conflicting and piecemeal socialization of secondary groups.

PARENTHOOD: THE LAST STAND OF THE AMATEUR

The distress of the modern family has invited critics to blame parents for all the trouble, branding them amateurs in a world of experts. While unqualified accusations merely add insult to injury and overlook the fact that parents themselves are victims of changing times, some critical comments are well taken and should be discussed.

The need to control parenthood expresses itself most distressingly at the time of adolescence, when many of the young show evidence of inadequate parental help. Many parents did not know what the socialization process would demand of them and gullibly followed the all-American bandwagon of "parenthood as a natural and beautiful state of existence."

Regulation of, or even mere advice about, the individual's reproductive behavior is considered by most Americans as an encroachment on their "natural right" and flatly rejected. The noncooperative stance has prompted some social scientists to suggest radical measures for curbing unqualified parenthood; they believe that society must restrict the reproductive privilege. Sociologist Kingsley Davis suggested charging high fees for marriage licenses, levying a "child tax," reversing the traditional taxation of singles over persons having children, and legalizing sterilization and abortion.[42]

Anthropologist Margaret Mead recommended that Americans accept what seems to be a naturally evolving dual marriage system. One is the "individual marriage" for young couples not intending to have children; and the other is the "parental marriage" for couples planning to have children.[43]

---

[42]Kingsley Davis, "Population Policy: Will Current Programs Succeed?" *Science*, 158 (November 10, 1967): 738. A number of other sociologists have made statements basically in agreement with Davis' concern: Michael Young, Ronald Freeman, Bernard Berelson, Philip Hauser, Orville Brim, Jr., Brewster Smith, Reuben Hill, George M. Foster, Everett Rogers, Nicholas Demerath, and others, in "Meetings: Behavioral Science and Family Planning," *Science*, 158 (November 3, 1967): 677–82.

[43]"Margaret Mead Today," *Time*, March 21, 1969, p. 77.

Biologist H. Bentley Glass thinks that parenthood should be permitted only after a couple obtains a "child license."[44] The question of enforcement of such an ordinance is understandably pertinent. Glass suggests court-ordered sterilization of parents who violate the license law more than once.

Politicians also recognize the need for laws against irresponsible parenthood. For example, an Illinois state representative sponsored a bill in 1971 that would force Illinois welfare parents who had three children to be sterilized to preclude burdening the public with additional expenses.

These arguments warn that unchecked parenthood and population growth will reduce living standards and life chances for everyone and that the conventional view of parenthood as an asset to society needs drastic revision. Parenthood has become a liability, not only because of all-too-frequently poor parenting, but also because we are endangering our resources through overpopulation.

THE QUEST FOR ALTERNATIVE STRUCTURES

Disillusionment with the modern family has led to experimentation with alternative primary groups. The vast majority of experimenters are young individuals who try new arrangements that they hope will both give them the gratifications of the ideal family and spare them what they see as stifling elements of the nuclear family system.

Many of them fail to recognize, however, that frustration and sacrifice are essentially unavoidable ingredients of the universal experience of growing up and cannot always be explained by structural contingencies. Not understanding the near universality of emotional distress, they tend to blame the structure in which they find themselves at the time of self-search and during the process of growing up. Frustrating curtailment of desires and painful adjustments are hardly novel aspects of the human condition and cannot justly be blamed on the nuclear family.

This is not to say that the modern family system is faultless and could not be improved. Rather, it should remind us that there is no structural alternative that will do the soul searching, self-integrating, and growing up *for* the young. Hence, many a search for an alternative family system is really an attempt to run away from basic developmental tasks, an excuse to avoid responsibilities, and a confusion between reality and utopia. At the core of this confusion is a basic misunderstanding of what human nature is. The fact that youthful communes have an extremely short life span and an exas-

---

[44]Los Angeles Times Service (June 24, 1964); AP Report (Atlantic City, NJ, February 13, 1967).

peratingly high turnover of members bespeaks the pseudosolution that these alternatives represent. There is no support for the contention that the alternatives work better than the nuclear family.

Complaints about the modern nuclear family are legion. It has been accused of suffering from isolated structure and from atrophy of vital functions. Bronfenbrenner believes that the modern family is experiencing an unprecedented atrophy and that the all-too-frequent one-parent situation constitutes a highly unreliable structure.[45] Because of its maimed condition, the family no longer provides communion of religious belief, shared work experience, a medium through which to contact others in the community, and a source of convincing norms and values.

Additional complaints aim at the larger social system: the emptiness of organized religion, the meaninglessness of the Protestant ethic, the rigidity of Puritanical sexual mores, the anonymity of urban-industrial life, and the agonizing anomie of American culture.

These ills, many of the young feel, are not alleviated by the current family form, and they are seeking a structure that would correct its failures. Many college students admire the type of integrated environment of such groups as the Amish and Hutterites, the Israeli kibbutz system, and the type of tribal or village life of which they have learned through Margaret Mead's, Oscar Lewis', and Bronislaw Malinowski's anthropological reports. They believe that the Samoan way of growing up would be ideal since the organization of the household eliminates most of the seeds that germinate into the dysfunctional emotions and conflicts with which our nuclear-family-raised children seem to be afflicted. The Samoan child's world is composed of male and female adults, all of whom can be depended on and must be deferred to. In cases of disagreement between parent and child, or in cases where it would be useful for a child's learning of a certain skill, the child is free to move into the home of a relative. The child is not falsely protected from the realities of life: sex, pregnancy, childbirth, and death are all familiar occurrences. "Among the factors in the Samoan scheme of life which are influential in producing stable, well-adjusted, robust individuals, the organization of the family and the attitude toward sex are undoubtedly the most important."[46]

Life in the modern American family contrasts sharply with the Samoan vision. The differential fuels the dissatisfaction of modern youth who would like to revert to a type of extended family system that promises fellowship, integration, security, and all the other things they fail to find in the nuclear family.

The closest they have come to that ideal in their experimentation is the

---

[45]"A Look at the Disintegrating World of Childhood," *Psychology Today*, 9 (June 1975), 34.
[46]Margaret Mead, *Coming of Age in Samoa* (New York: Morrow, 1928), p. 228.

commune. Communes range from religious economy with sexual exclusiveness to group marriage.[47] Most communes hold property in common, but leave responsibility for other aspects of life to the nuclear units, including the care of children. Other communes have utopian or revolutionary orientations. Still others are non-ideological, the communards' chief concern being "experience"—perhaps with drugs, sex, the occult, or simply "relationships" through which they try to find intimacy and sharing.

While each commune is unique, some common traits can be discerned. To some degree they all share property, minimize competitiveness, and emphasize social concerns over utilitarian and financial gains. Commune dwellers search for meaning in life and strive toward personal growth, share the work necessary for maintaining property, dwelling, and livelihood, and share a common distaste for the Establishment.

Most experimental communes last only a short time, having an average life of two years. Individual membership lasts about eight months. Joyce Gardener, one of the founders of Cold Mountain Farm, illustrates the condition of rural and urban communes alike: ". . . empty people who had come to fill themselves, sapping our energies, needing to be taken care of and giving nothing at all—and now there were only between four and six couples and a few single people left. . . . We didn't find a way of sharing our vision . . . and we didn't have a shared vision to hold us together."[48]

Healing Waters, a commune in the desert of Arizona, demonstrated relative longevity. The commune, set around idyllic natural hot springs, attracted nomadic New Agers for nearly 10 years, and was held together by a core of, initially, idealistic leaders. Healing Waters grew food and maintained a number of New Age health practices, including vegetarianism and transcendental meditation. These activities evolved as specialties or instructional responsibilities of individual members. Presumably all property was held in common, the children brought along by some communards or born into the commune were considered the children of all, and the place welcomed people with "higher consciousness" from all over the country. Alas, in the early 1980s, disharmony erupted in the leadership clique and the New Age Mecca closed its doors to the New Age and turned into a commercial

---

[47]Saul V. Levine et al., "The Urban Commune: Fact or Fad, Promise or Pipedream?" *American Journal of Orthopsychiatry*, 43 (January 1973): 149–63; Bennett Berger et al., "The Communal Family," *The Family Coordinator*, 21 (October 1972): 419–27; Sallie Teselle, ed., *The Family, Communes, and Utopian Societies* (New York: Harper & Row, 1972); James W. Ramey, "Communes, Group Marriage, and the Upper-Middle Class," *Journal of Marriage and the Family*, 34 (November 1972): 647–55; Laurence Veysey, *The Communal Experience* (New York: Harper & Row, 1973).

[48]Joyce Gardener, "Communal Living: Economic Survival and Family Life," in *Changing Family: Adaptation and Diversity*, ed. Gordon F. Streib (Reading, MA: Addison-Wesley, 1973), pp. 117–18.

enterprise—with the decisive word spoken by the person holding legal deed to the land.[49]

Some communes make compromises with the nuclear family arrangement. An example was Lama, a commune north of Taos in New Mexico, where the members worked together growing and distributing crops, but withdrew to individual nests at nights: a tepee, an A-frame, or a tent, which they shared only with a spouse (or semipermanent companion) and the children. Most couples were married, had children, owned their own homes, maintained middle-class respect for property and work. Although the philosophy of sexual freedom was retained abstractly, it played a minor role in the actual behavior of the communards.[50]

Other communes deviated farther from the lifestyle of the American family and included such groups as the Sandstone Commune in Los Angeles, which kept varying in size between three and twelve members and usually included uneven proportions of men and women. They considered themselves an "intentional family" with sexual freedom, and as one member let it be known: "It's a smorgasbord. It's so much more exciting to have nine different dishes than just one."[51] The group hesitated to have children because it wanted to stabilize its "marriage" first.

The commune movement, then, is a quest for many dreams. It may be a quest for revolutionary restructuring of society, for economic security, for more meaningful relationships than the participants had in their parental homes, or for expanded experiences in respect to sex, drugs, and other interests.

For most, a communard role is short-lived and they fail to find the answers to their questions and the gratification of their needs. In most cases, the communal experiment fails because the members have compounded their problems through interaction with others who suffer from similar troubles of personal anomie. It resembles a situation where one blind person asks another blind person for direction. Sometimes the economic basis of the group is too weak to sustain membership. Sometimes the attempt at a common work project is sincere, but it fails because members lack experience, knowledge, and the actual physical stamina to do the work. Sometimes the animosity of neighbors causes a commune to break up. And in other cases, the commune gradually fades away because of inadequate leadership or because the participants lack the vision to formulate a common goal in the first place.

---

[49]Hans Sebald, "The Waxing and Waning of a New Age Commune—From Nudity to Business Suit," *Humboldt Journal of Social Relations*, Vol. 15, Winter 1988, pp. 1–27.

[50]"The American Family: Future Uncertain," p. 38.

[51]Ibid., p. 36.

Hence, the commune movement of the 1970s and 1980s has subsided. But it has not died. While most communes disintegrated, a few proved to have longevity. The idea of the commune is still alive and still attracts numbers of young Americans who hope to find it more rewarding than their nuclear families.

In contrast to the pessimism of Bronfenbrenner, many family sociologists believe that the companionship-type of nuclear family holds out greater promise than any other experimental arrangement, and that in spite of difficulties, it will survive as the preferred lifestyle. David and Vera Mace express this sentiment:

> The companionship marriage, based on intimacy, equity, and flexible interaction, offers a promising new lifestyle which in fact is the preferred choice of the great majority of men and women in our culture today. The other new lifestyles which have been given such prominence are by comparison of minor significance, and are best viewed as pioneering social experiments which as yet have come up with nothing that could remotely offer a viable substitute for traditional marriage.[52]

SUMMARY

Family dynamics penetrate into the individual's personality and have a decisive influence on how he or she weathers the crisis of adolescence. Family processes are complicated today because of rapid changes. The following points sum up major changes affecting the modern family and, in turn, the lives of adolescents:

1. Family structure has changed to the small nuclear family, which has relinquished integration into the larger social network and become isolated. The young have become deprived of concrete adult models, visible adult work, and familial peers. This increases the potential of associating with peers opposed to the family and stimulates the development of youth subcultures.
2. The modern family has abandoned numerous functions, now taken care of by outside specialization, and has itself become a specialized agency trying to fulfill the "personality function." With increasing isolation and anomie in the industrial environment, the individual has turned to the family to find direction. The identity quest leveled at so fragile a structure appears to be too much of a burden.
3. The family has changed from institutional to companionship interaction, minimizing role behavior and maximizing personal uniqueness. The new style calls for communicative skill.
4. Young people can no longer rely on the family's placement function, which

---

[52]David R. Mace and Vera C. Mace, "Marriage Enrichment—Wave of the Future?" *The Family Coordinator*, 24 (April 1975): 133.

used to define their standing in the community. Now they must rely on their individualism and personal decision making.

5. Modern legislation has given young people more freedom than any previous generation in America, but has done so without regard to family context. Independence from the family has increased the isolation of the individual.

6. The primary-group quality of the family has decreased. Secondary institutions have come to compete with the family. This raises questions about modern socialization's impact on "human nature."

7. Adolescence is often complicated by parents who lack insight and skill. Restricting such unqualified parenthood has become the preoccupation of a number of educators and scientists.

8. Youthful search for what may well be utopian has led to a quest for alternative structures to ameliorate certain limitations of family life. The commune, with a questionable success record, has been a limited experiment that was more common during and right after the counterculture years.

A final word. While it is true that throughout our discussion certain aspects were selected that promote adolescence and prove to be dysfunctional for literally everyone involved, these adolescence-generating effects do not exhaust all the consequences of family changes. Liberating effects have also been brought about by these changes. These include liberating captive creativity from the bondage of familistic servitude and enriching the personality market with talent, aptitude, and individualism. However, we must not forget that the human condition includes the eternal dilemma of not being able to combine two dreams of humanity: freedom and security. Normally we can enjoy only one at a time, and it seems that modern adolescents, whether they like it or not, are satiated with the former and hunger for the latter.

9

The Modern Educational Experience

TRENDS IN AMERICAN EDUCATION

The American ethos considers the right of every citizen to an education—elementary, secondary, and higher—to be as basic and undisputable as the "pursuit of happiness." But education for all was not always the conviction of the American public. Until late in the last century, education was primarily an elementary-school affair. Preparation for higher education was accomplished in private secondary schools and a few public schools. In 1870, for example, teenagers could choose from among only 800 public high schools. Those who attended institutions of secondary education usually had college in mind. Although in 1900 only 11 percent of the high-school-aged youth were in school, two-thirds of the graduates did go on to college—a proportion that has since never been equalled.

The appraisal of high school education in the United States used to be influenced by the European tradition that considered secondary education in the French *lycée*, the English grammar school, or the German *Gymnasium* as the proper experience for the "educated class." The children of farmers were usually not thought of as members of this class, and before or directly after the eighth grade they generally left school to work with the agricultural family unit. Similarly, workers' sons left school to become apprenticed for a trade.

The adulation of secondary and higher education is thus relatively new. Pragmatic reasons underlie this valuation. One involves the fruits of education and vocational training, which have increased the amenities of life. Another reason is the need to keep teenagers out of the labor force. This necessity has developed with industrialization, automation, and the rural-urban migration.

Automation has arrested the increase of blue-collar jobs while expanding the number of white-collar positions that require high school training— clerks, accountants, salespeople, and office workers. In effect, the division of labor no longer needs—or even allows—the labor of the young. Barred from the labor force as well as from free-roaming idleness, America's teenagers were "institutionalized" and delivered into the care of high schools. The institution of secondary education not only kept them out of the way, but even succeeded in preparing some of them for the new white-collar jobs. High school education ceased to be a voluntary matter chosen by the few who prepared for higher education and became an involuntary mandate for all. Statistics illustrate the trend: in 1900, 11 percent of the high-school-aged youngsters attended school; in 1920, 32 percent; in 1930, 51 percent; in 1940, 73 percent; and in the 1960s the percentage achieved a level of over 90 percent, at which it has remained ever since.

The expanding role of high school in the lives of the young is also illustrated by the percentage of young adults (twenty-five to thirty-four years old) who completed four years of high school. The proportion of white males was 36 percent in 1940, 51 percent in 1950, 59 percent in 1966, 77 percent in 1970, and over 80 percent since then. For white females, the proportion was 41 percent in 1940, 55 percent in 1950, 63 percent in 1960, 75 percent in 1970, and also over 80 percent since then. For black males, the proportion was 10 percent in 1940, 18 percent in 1950, 30 percent in 1960, 49 percent in 1970, and just under 70 percent since then. For black females, the proportion was 12 percent in 1940, 22 percent in 1950, 36 percent in 1960, 57 percent in 1970, and approximately 65 percent since then.

These figures show that over approximately the past thirty-five years the white males' and white females' high school graduation rates have nearly doubled; the black males' and the black females' more than doubled.

This upswing in educational participation by America's young modified the functions of secondary education. No longer were high school graduates destined only for college, but instead primarily for business and industry. Concomitant with the growth of the proportion of teenagers attending high school was a decline in the proportion of graduates enrolling in college. The college-entering proportion dropped from two-thirds in 1900 to about half in 1920 and finally to about one-third in 1940, indicating that the majority of teenagers preferred to go directly into jobs after graduation. This preference stimulated significant changes in secondary school curricula. Preparation became centered on immediate vocational fields rather than on extended higher education. This new emphasis gave rise, indeed often priority, to such short-range and practical goals as typing, bookkeeping, industrial arts, shop, and mechanics.

The change in the function of the high school, coupled with the coercive nature of attendance, has produced an essentially new atmosphere in the secondary school system. Academic preparation is no longer the prime objective; rather, general "life preparation" has moved to the forefront. Emphasis on seven basic principles of secondary education evolved: health, command of fundamental mental processes, mature home-membership, vocational preparation, civic education, constructive use of leisure time, and ethical character. More than academic endeavor, the pursuit of these principles constitutes a general program for "life adjustment." The responsibilities of high school teachers now include not only transmission of knowledge, but also character formation, the instillment of motivation, and the counseling of personal problems. In essence, by taking over character-forming functions from the family, secondary education became more a place of general socialization than of information service. Furthermore, this socialization experience was not optional; teenagers had to submit to it, and teachers were burdened with the extra task of convincing them that school was worthwhile.

This is not the end of the story of modern education in the United States. Industrialization and automation have progressed to the point where there is little demand for youth's labor after high school. College education has developed into another means of preventing youth from swamping the labor market, while at the same time trying to prepare them for the ever-increasing number of white-collar and other sophisticated positions. As a consequence, the steady decline of the proportion of high school graduates enrolling in college during the first half of the twentieth century has been reversed.

Since 1950, there has been a 10 percent average annual increase in the number of students entering college for the first time to work toward a degree. However, during the 1980s there has been a slowdown, with the number of those entering college increasing by only 2 percent annually. The decline is due to decreasing numbers of eighteen-to-twenty-four-year-olds in the population, not to a decreasing proportion of youth enrolling in college.

In any case, the American public is now almost as concerned about the college dropout as it is about the high school dropout. Postindustrial conditions do not require young adults in the division of labor, and their entry is delayed as long as possible after high school graduation. This expands adolescence and tends to create a population of restless youth.

EDUCATION—LARGELY A NONFAMILIAL EXPERIENCE

Although in modern societies the institutions of education and of the family have always been separate, they have never before been as unrelated as today. Values preached in school and values upheld at home are often unrelated or even contradictory; the information the child brings home from school is usually irrelevant to actual family life. In short, values and information gleaned from formal education constitute a theoretical manifesto that is more applicable to the outside world than to the family circle.

Some ethnic and religious minorities perceive this duality as a threat to their way of life. An example are the Amish, a Protestant sect living a simple rural life and attempting to survive as a religious enclave within a secular society. They often are at odds with the law, since their views on education differ from legal requirements.[1] Amish elders maintain that "worldly wisdom" taught in public schools undermines their way of life, rural simplicity, and religious values. Confrontations between the law and religious principles have repeatedly occurred in Iowa, Kansas, Ohio, Pennsylvania, and Wisconsin. When Amish farmers were fined for violating Wisconsin's compulsory school-attendance law, the issue snowballed and reached the United States Supreme Court in 1972. The court's decision upheld the Amish's right to religious freedom and restricted the state's compulsory attendance law. This minority was granted the right to maintain its own elementary schools staffed with Amish teachers and was declared exempt from having to send its youth to secular high schools.

State authorities had worried that Amish children who left school before the statutory age of sixteen might become burdens to the public. The record showed such concern to be unfounded: No Amish teenager in Wisconsin had ever been arrested for any crime, no Amish had ever had an illegitimate birth, and none had ever requested public assistance. Additional states complied with the Supreme Court's decision. For example, Iowa exempted Amish children from state education standards and allowed Amish teachers—who usually had only an eighth-grade education—to run their own schools. The Amish are reluctant to employ college-educated and certified teachers who, they fear, might steer their children away from the plain, soil-and-toil-oriented Amish faith. By adhering to this educational policy, the Amish accomplish two main objectives: to retain purity of religious faith and to preserve their young's time and interest for farm work.

By contrast, the dynamics of the urban-industrial society create com-

---

[1]Albert N. Keim, *Compulsory Education and the Amish* (Boston: Beacon Press, 1975). "In Pennsylvania: The Amish and the Law," *Time*, April 19, 1982, p. 12.

plex educational needs, which are due to at least three major conditions. First, there is rapid social change. American parents cannot mold their children in their own images, since they suffer from chronic cultural lag that may render a portion of their skills, knowledge, and attitudes obsolete. Second, the strong emphasis on individualism prevents parents from determining the occupation of the young by family rule. Rather than relying on familial norms and models for deciding on their future occupation, the young may prefer nonfamilial, formal education. This preference is related to the third condition, the high degree of specialization of modern occupational careers, which calls for vocational preparation outside of the family unit.

The effect of these three conditions has been to shift the responsibility of preparing offspring for their future "specialties" from the family to specialized institutions and to ensconce the young more and more in nonfamilial education.

The satirist Erma Bombeck, by making fun of the transfer of functions from the family to the school, may approximate reality to a valid degree when she quipped: "Barry's a discipline problem at home. What's the school doing about it?" Or: "Stan is depressed and doesn't want to go on living. Didn't the school see this coming?"[2]

An exception to this trend is, of course, found in home schooling, where parents obtain permission from the authorities to educate their child/children at home. The standards of many states are relatively lax and parents with minimum proficiency can usually qualify. In the state of Arizona the qualification requirements consist of passing the reading, grammar, and math proficiency examination for certification to teach in public schools.

IMPACT OF TECHNOLOGICAL INNOVATIONS

There has been a surprising modification of the generally nonfamilial nature of American education. It has been brought on by one of technology's most recent innovations—one that is increasingly finding its way into family life: the personal computer, commonly referred to as the PC. It is a tool for learning or entertainment—or, actually, an activity that combines both—and, for many American teenagers, it makes learning fun. How this revolutionary technological innovation would affect the young and their family integration used to be a question with an uncertain answer. The first in-depth study was completed by a New York University team in 1984 and revealed that the computer had far less impact on American family life than, for example, the

---

[2]Erma Bombeck, "Stoke the Home Hearth," *Arizona Republic*, October 4, 1988, p. 13.

automobile or TV had in previous decades.[3] And what impact it is having seems to be of a more positive nature. It appears that youngsters who work/ play with their computers at home become more integrated in existing family patterns. Reasons for this seems to be that the teenager spends more time at home, using a stimulating device that is as much a toy as a learning tool. Furthermore, the quality of their school work seems to benefit from using it and earns them the praise of the parents. In addition, the home PC can be shared by parents and offspring in joint fun and learning.

However, there was also found the peril of addiction to the new tube. Some parents, the study showed, found it necessary to limit the hours the offspring were allowed to dedicate to their new obsession. One mother complained that her teenager's complexion turned the "color of cream cheese" as a result of spending marathon hours in front of the new screen.

The impact of TV viewing on the young seems to differ significantly from the impact of the computer. First of all, TV viewing occupies an enormous portion of youth's time, a portion only second to the amount spent sleeping, and on the average accumulates by age 18 to 22,000 hours, that is two-and-a-half years, which is exactly twice as long as the 11,000 hours they have spent in the classroom. In light of this impressive investment, it is important to note that virtually all pertinent studies agree that TV viewing, even programs we usually label "educational," decreases creative thought processes. Creative thought primarily refers to coming up with unique and effective approaches to solve problems. Apparently the technological properties of TV releases the human brain from having to translate TV's visual and auditory stimuli into imaginary pictures and sounds. The screen is doing all that for the viewer; there is no need for the brain to set into action circuitries to conjure up ideas as to how things look or sound—quite unlike in the reading experience where our brain is charged with the task to translate the printed or written word into visual, auditory, and other sensory perceptions. Largely unbeknownst to the reader, the brain is stimulated to creatively imagine the setting that the reading material suggests. TV fails to stimulate; it merely saturates.

Nationwide data published by the U.S. Department of Education in 1990 focuses on American eighth-graders.[4] The findings reveal that the youngsters spend an average of 21.7 hours a week watching TV, 5.6 hours doing homework, and 1.8 hours on outside reading. Girls read more than boys—2.1 hours vs. 1.5 hours a week. Children from Asian-American homes

---

[3]See discussion in "Family Living," *Time*, October 15, 1984, p. 109.

[4]*The American Eighth-Grader*, Superintendent of Documents, U.S. Government Printing Office, Washington, DC, 1990.

top the list in doing homework with 6.77 hours a week. Topping the list in TV viewing are black youngsters with 27.6 hours a week.

There is, according to the study, one advantage that young children exposed to a lot of TV watching have over children with little exposure. Highly exposed first-graders manifest a larger and better vocabulary upon entering school than their low-exposure classmates. This advantage, however, is short-lived and after the second to third grade the difference between the two groups gradually disappears.

The side effects of so much time spent in front of the screen—whether TV or computer—may be seen in American children's inferior proficiency in basic reading and writing skills. U.S. Education Secretary Lauro Cavazos revealed studies in 1990 that showed that the already dismal state of these skills in 1970 had not improved by the late 1980s. Other intellectual skills, such as analyzing information and expressing ideas, had actually declined. "Nearly 60% of 17-year-olds cannot read at the adept level, which is defined as the ability to find, understand, summarize and explain relatively complicated material."[5] The Secretary summed up his concern: "As a nation we should be appalled that we have placed our children in such jeopardy."[6]

Among the few bright spots in the report were indications that between 1970 and 1988 some gains were accomplished by Hispanic and black children. Though, on the average, they still fall below the white children's proficiency in reading and writing, the gap has narrowed.

EDUCATION—EVER LONGER YEARS

The most conspicuous feature of American education has been its ever-lengthening duration in the lives of the young. Census Bureau data show that the average American achieved over five more years of education in the 1980s than in the 1940s.[7] The education gains applied to all regions, men and women, blacks and whites, cities and suburbs. The proportion of Americans who have had four or more years of college has tripled since 1940, going from 4.6 percent to 14 percent today. As a result of these increases, the median educational level reached twelve-and-one-half years by 1980. This means that approximately one-half of all Americans now have finished high school and have spent some time in college. How much longer today's youth spend in

---

[5]"Basic Skills Eluding Pupils," *Arizona Republic,* January 10, 1990, p. 2.
[6]Ibid.

[7]U.S. Department of Health, Education, and Welfare, *Statistical Abstract of the United States* (Washington, DC: Government Printing Office, 1980), pp. 148, 149.

educational institutions is illustrated by comparison of the median education level of twenty-to-twenty-six-year olds and the over–sixty-five age group. The former group achieved an average of 12.8 years, the latter only 9.1 years—just over a year of high school.

The typically postindustrial shift of the teenage population from work bench to school desk can be illustrated by statistics from such countries as Germany. During the 1960s about 20 percent of the thirteen- to fifteen-year-old Germans were in the labor force (usually as apprentices); by the 1970s practically no members of this age group were working. For the boys of the fifteen-to-twenty category the decline was from 81 to 59 percent; for the girls from 78 to 57 percent.[8] This shift is even more clearly demonstrated by German census data showing the proportion of the teenage population in school increasing from 17 to 35 percent between 1960 and 1970, while, conversely, the proportion of apprentices dropped from 19 to 9 percent and the proportion of unskilled teen labor from 13 to 4 percent.[9] These statistics reveal the typical correlation between increasing postindustrialism and increasing years of formal education.

Ever longer years of higher education is a phenomenon found in all modern industrialized societies. An international survey carried out by the Ministry of Education of Germany in 1989 shows that between the 1970s and the 1980s an average of half a year has been added to the educational process, so that, for example, German university students now finish on the average at age 28. At the same time, their age at the beginning of their university studies increased from 20.9 to 21.6 years. Similar trends were found in other industrialized European nations.[10]

The United States has been prototypical in setting this trend—a trend continuing unabatedly into the last decade of the twentieth century when school enrollments leveled off or even dropped. Dropping enrollment is not indicative of shortening the educational experience but rather of declining *numbers* in age groups; the *proportions* of age groups enrolled have increased. Census figures concerning eighteen-year-old Americans show that in 1950 56 percent, in 1960 72 percent, in 1970 75 percent, in 1980 77 percent, and in 1990 close to 80 percent graduated from high school. In conclusion, most American youths are involved in long years of education during which they are suspended between childhood and adulthood.

8"New Work Habits and Life-Styles," *Bulletin*, Press and Information Office of the Federal Republic of Germany, Bonn, December 20, 1971, p. 350.

9"Jugend," *Kulturbrief*, Internationes, Bonn, Vol. 5, December 1975, p. 26.

10"Studienzeit," *Mitteilungen*, Deutscher Akademischer Austauschdienst (DAAD), Bonn, October 1989, pp. 14–15.

CRITICS OF TWO SORTS

The Liberal Point of View

The assumption that the protracted sojourn in the educational institution is primarily motivated by desire to absorb knowledge and learn skills has long since been revealed as illusory. School has assumed a custodial function and tries to stem the potential flood of over-sixteen-year-olds that could inundate the labor market. Such inundation would create job scarcity and bring about a disastrous swelling of the ranks of the unemployed. Postindustrial automation simply has no use for this excess of young workers. So they end up completing high school, entering college, and establishing their ghettos and subcultures.

Since youth's stay in high school is not always motivated by free will and enthusiasm about education per se, disharmony with authorities can evolve. In its overt manifestation the discord can degenerate into vandalism and other school-related delinquency. In its more covert manifestation the problem consists of a type of psychological warfare in which the administration tries to impose "colonial treatment" on the young, and where the young counter by rejecting the moral and intellectual expectations of the authorities.

A number of writers have attempted to illuminate this side of our educational system. Many have condemned the custodial function of schools and the isolation of youth from mainstream America. John Holt, for example, suggested that schools relinquish the "jail business" and stop numbing children by overdoses of superfluous authority.[11] He assessed malfunctions of American education in five points:

1. Schools fail to promote the growth of children and substitute the custodial function for the learning function. The young are in school because they are not wanted anywhere else.
2. Schools grade and label the young. This, presumably, is contrary to the true process of education. We cannot expect young people to trust us if they know, as before long almost all of them do, that a major part of modern educators' job is compiling records that will be used to judge them for the rest of their lives.
3. Schools have adopted a missionary zeal to explicitly indoctrinate patriotism, morality (especially sexual morality), competition, and the value of the profit system. More subtle indoctrination encompasses the vast field of modern consumerism—implanting the proper consumer attitudes toward grooming norms, dress, cleaning and bath products, cosmetics, and so forth.
4. Schools divide the young into winners and losers and then train them to accept

[11]John Holt, *Freedom and Beyond* (New York: Dell, 1972) and *Escape from Childhood* (New York: Dutton, 1974).

their roles. By this process, the Establishment is assured that the winners will defend the system without guilt and the losers without rancor.

5. The most offensive aspect of modern schooling, which is closely related to the previous point, is its unrelenting attack on the dignity and self-respect of the students, who are cast into simplistic hierarchical roles of winners and losers regardless of personal uniqueness.

Another critic was Paul Goodman, who considered it absurd to grow up in a society that compelled its young to go to school when they cannot profit by it.[12] He accused American schools of ignoring the most important problems of young people, such as job prospects, sexuality, and community processes. Although failure of schools to captivate student interest is usually rationalized by authorities as "failure to communicate," the truth probably is that the message has been communicated clearly but is unacceptable to the young.

Problems of school are symptomatic of the pathologies of society. Goodman felt that youth resents what American society fails to provide:

1. Opportunities and worthwhile goals.
2. Enough and visible work positions.
3. Honest public speech.
4. People who are to be taken seriously and can serve as models to youth.
5. Opportunities for imaginative minds.[13]

Another critic of American education is Edgar Z. Friedenberg, who disapproves of compulsory school attendance, believing that such compulsion strips victims of personal autonomy and civil rights. He thinks that coercion does not serve a truly intellectual function but bows to economic pressures of a society wanting to delay youth's entry into the labor market. "A people have no right to cling to economic arrangements that can be made halfway workable only by imposing an infantile and unproductive status on adolescents and indoctrinating them with a need for trashy goods and shallow meretricious relationships that they know to be degrading."[14]

The list of this type of critic could be extended. Although some of their criticisms are well taken, many are less than pragmatic; they are romantic, if not utopian. For example, George B. Leonard believes education could be ecstasy—pure joy, involvement, and growth for both student and teacher—but that competition and bureaucratic regimens turn off the student's

[12]Paul Goodman, *Growing Up Absurd* (New York: Random House, 1960).

[13]Ibid., p. 12.

[14]Edgar Z. Friedenberg, *Coming of Age in America* (New York: Random House, 1965), p. 249.

mind.[15] To overcome such obstacles in school, Leonard recommends that we "learn delight, not aggression; sharing, not eager acquisition; uniqueness, not narrow competition."[16] In the absence of an effective plan for restructuring our educational framework and changing our cultural premises, such suggestions fall more in the category of poetry than science.

The Conservative Point of View

A new type of educational critic began to speak up during the late 1980s. This one—unlike Holt, Friedenberg, and Goodman—was critical not because our system burdens the young with too much formal education and too many prescriptions, but for exactly the opposite reasons: we are not demanding enough; we are not using our educational setup to the fullest.

Chicago University Professor Allan Bloom caused a stir in 1987 with his book, *The Closing of the American Mind,* in which he attacked the way our nation educates its young people. He felt that the intellectual standard has drastically declined because of increasingly pragmatic school curricula and the decreasing emphasis on the classics, languages, and the humanities generally. He blames the decline on the consideration accorded to various clamorous groups demanding an adjustment of educational curricula to real-life conditions in America. He identified among these groups especially the feminists, the blacks, and other minority groups. He envisioned a sort of elitist education that would restore the mastery of certain basic civilizational knowledge.

Critical reviewers were quick to brand his vision as anti-democratic, unsuited to a society as heterogeneous as America's, and neglecting the pragmatic quest of the American character.

In a similarly provocative manner, University of California scholar Russell Jacoby (*The Last Intellectuals,* 1987), University of Virginia Professor E. D. Hirsch, Jr. (*Cultural Literacy,* 1987), and Boston University President John Silber ("Free Speech and the Academy," 1990)[17] have assaulted what they feel is an inferior educational process in late-twentieth century America. They turn against the neglect of teaching our Western cultural heritage, again emphasizing the role of classic literature in this connection, and against the mind-stifling atmosphere created by bureaucracy in the academic environment. Where are, Jacoby wonders, the young intellectual heirs to carry on the bold thinking of such splendid American scholars as David Riesman, John Kenneth Galbraith, and Daniel Bell? Jacoby blames the deterioration of academe's integrity and greatness on the double-effect of young academics

---

[15]George B. Leonard, "How School Stunts your Child," in *Children's Liberation,* ed. David Gottlieb (Englewood Cliffs, NJ: Prentice-Hall, 1973), pp. 145–66.

[16]Ibid., p. 162.

[17]*The Intercollegiate Review,* 26 (Fall 1990): 33–41.

seeking security and specialization. Instead of standing up to be counted as a critic, the new university intellectual prefers the feather-bedding offered by academe and its warm but stifling tenure.

Silber thinks that the price we are paying for the barbarism that came during the 1960s and 1970s—camouflaged as "relevant" courses in university and college curricula—is the loss of a universal vision and the encapsulation of the student in anti-intellectual splinter groups. He calls for a revitalization of the study of Western culture and its plethora of classic works, pointing to the universal and timeless value of such works as the *Odyssey* and the *Iliad.* In them, he believes, we find reported the rich range of human modalities, which give us insight into our common humanity and instill a vision of human nobility.

Once More: In Loco Parentis

While most of Bloom's, Jacoby's, and Hirsch's commentaries were directed at the college and university level, the late 1980s also showed a trend toward reassertion of institutional authority on the high school level. This once more brings into focus the concept of *in loco parentis* authority. After a lapse of this type of authority during the 1960s and 1970s, where a more liberal and permissive stance prevailed, the late 1980s and early 1990s saw teachers and administrators reasserting their right to be in control in the classroom and on the campus in general.

Examples include the case where a Missouri high school principal ordered the removal of two controversial articles from the school's newspaper. The student editor and her staff thereupon filed suit in court against the ruling, claiming their First Amendment rights as student journalists had been violated. The court battles climbed all the way to the U.S. Supreme Court, which in 1988 took the side of the school principal, upholding his *in loco parentis* authority.[18]

Another case dealt with the action of a New Jersey high school principal, who insisted on opening and searching a fourteen-year-old girl's purse. The girl had been caught breaking school rules by smoking in the lavatory. She denied the accusation and claimed she never smoked. Her purse, however, contained not only cigarettes, but marijuana as well—and several notes indicating that she was selling pot to other students. The principal then turned the matter over to the police. After several years of legal battles, including three lower court proceedings, the case reached the U.S. Supreme Court, which supported the school principal's action by pronouncing that "public school is a special place wherein the usual guarantees and restrictions

---

[18]"Censorship," *State Press,* February 4, 1988, p. 5.

of the Fourth Amendment regarding search and seizure of an individual or his property do not necessarily apply."[19]

Still another teenage issue made it to West Virginia's highest court. It upheld a rule in 1990 that allows young school dropouts to be denied or stripped of the driver's license. This was the first state to aim a law at the sixteen- and seventeen-year-old dropouts.[20]

THE CASE AGAINST COLLEGE

Some critics of American education have taken a radical view and actually suggest that a noncollege education might be preferable for large numbers of American youth. Sociologist James S. Coleman argued that the focus of American schools is too limited, too competitive, and fails to develop in students the ability to manage their own lives in a responsible fashion.[21] Schools not only fail to promote these qualities, they so monopolize young people's time and energy to prevent them from acquiring these skills elsewhere. Until a few generations ago, children learned adult qualities from family models. However, segregated by age, modern youth is saturated with information but deprived of experience. Coleman suggested an alternation between study and work to introduce students to the careers they choose. Prolonged education often renders a distorted view of adult life. Many colleges have tried to correct this by bringing the outside world into the classroom and introducing careers without harnessing students to them too soon.

The best solution, according to Coleman, would be to graduate the young earlier, at about sixteen, and place them in organizations like businesses, hospitals, factories, and symphony orchestras. These establishments could make use of the youths' contribution, while training them and supervising further part-time schooling. This would be a fundamental shift from the customary American view of education as a means of secular salvation to the old way of socializing through apprenticeship. Coleman's design would provide all sixteen-year-olds with vouchers worth four years of college tuition; the vouchers could, however, also be used to join an apprenticeship program or for enrolling in a vocational school.

Implementation of Coleman's plan might diminish adolescence and its collective expression. Young people would usefully integrate themselves into society, build self-respect through meaningful work, and avoid being segre-

---

[19]"Search Rules," *Time*, January 28, 1985, p. 77.

[20]"'No School, No Drive' Law Is Upheld," *Arizona Republic*, December 1, 1990, p. A4.

[21]James S. Coleman et al. *Youth: Transition to Adulthood*, Report of the Panel on Youth of the President's Advisory Committee (Chicago: University of Chicago Press, 1974).

gated. Integration would reduce unrealistic segregation from adult respon-sibilities and limit the breeding of subcultural lifestyles.

Another argument against the pressure to attend college was raised by Caroline Bird, who believed that the majority of college students are not in college because they like it or because they want to learn. She estimated that hardly one-fourth of the students enjoy academic work and that the rest, at best, experience college as a social center and at worst as a detention center preventing them from entering adult life for several more years.[22] During these years students feel unwanted and useless. Postindustrial efficiency, with its labor-saving automation, renders them superfluous. To get them temporarily out of the way, we send them to college—where only a fraction of them are intellectually motivated and prepared to enjoy studying. According to Bird, many college students describe their time in college as if it were a sentence to be served—and yet, as unpleasant as it is, preferable to the drudgery of a boring job or to the possibility of being unemployed.[23]

AMERICAN EDUCATION IN PERSPECTIVE

The attacks on American education are legion. And they usually come from within and not from without the nation, being part of the syndrome of American self-consciousness. Hardly any other nation indulges in such merci-less self-criticism.

One cannot help but wonder how much of the criticism is based on romantic expectations and utopian fancy instead of on realistic assessment. For example, such critics of the American school system as Edgar Z. Frie-denberg, Paul Goodman, John Holt, George Leonard, and David Gottlieb have complained that schools require adolescents to surrender and/or sup-press their creativity, individuality, and identity to the demands of the skill- and information-oriented curriculum in order to qualify for "success." Schools have been accused of causing foreclosure of creative and individu-alistic potential for the sake of making children acceptable to postindustrial society in general and the school authorities in specific. The price is too high, these critics claim, and the diminishing of unique individuality and the obscuring of personal identity is a defeat not justified by the educational accomplishments gleaned from American schools. Most of all, these critics feel that the true happiness of the young is foreclosed.

Part of the argument, as in most issues in life, is correct. It is undoubt-edly true that the socialization process, be it couched in formal educational

---

[22]Caroline Bird, "College Is a Waste of Time and Money," *Psychology Today*, 8 (May 1975): 28.
[23]Ibid., p. 32.

terms or in informal familial terms, necessitates some degree of abrogation of individuality and establishes some degree of conformity. How could it be otherwise? The young everywhere must be socialized, and individuality can be tolerated only within certain limits.

Perusal of the writings of these romanticist critics creates the impression of a Rousseuan presupposition: the myth of the innocent child of nature, the innate goodness and fairmindedness of the young, and the destruction of these natural impulses by our corrupt urban-industrial society. From a sociological perspective, there is no evidence to support such wishful thinking. In fact, one could cite research showing that those young individuals who have made adjustments to school and society, thus falling in the category of the supposedly foreclosed subjects, were more comfortable than those fighting foreclosure. They were more comfortable in school and held more positive attitudes toward their educational experience, whereas the uncommitted and searching (those taking unbridled advantage of the adolescent moratorium) evaluated their educational experiences negatively.[24]

Of course, this finding could be turned around and used in favor of the romanticist critics, presumably showing the placidness of the suppressed individuals. But any style of socialization, including the formal educational process, will create problems and leave many wishes unfulfilled because of the very definition of socialization, which implies involuntary submission to the indoctrination of a culture. The American system must be viewed with these universal limitations in mind.

From a cross-cultural perspective, the American educational structure is a far greater success than many guilt-racked Americans would allow. In spite of certain limitations, it does function as an equalizer between racial, ethnic, and socioeconomic groups. If it has not shone with particular brilliance in this respect, the fault does not lie with the structure of the American school system, which probably has the soundest potential of any school system in the world. Many European systems do not offer this potential. Their educational structure is a *parallel* system whereby most children go through nine (it used to be eight) years of elementary education plus two years of part-time school and are then irrevocably finished, while a minority—usually of upper socioeconomic background—switches in the fourth grade to a radically different system that eventually allows them entry into the university. These parallel structures divide the young into elite and proletariat, into intelligentsia and passive masses. Quite differently, the American system pursues a *sequential* structure that allows the individual to continue in educational endeavor, to continue where he or she left off. It is a democratic system and the structure bears it out, permitting everyone to

---

[24]A. S. Waterman and C. K. Waterman, "The Relationship between Ego Identity, Status and Satisfaction with College," *Journal of Educational Research*, 64 (1970): 165–68.

progress, drop out, and reenter without having experienced a prohibitory bypassing of certain mandatory and absolute switching points.

Another oversight of the critics deals with the assumption that the school is not only the central instrument of education (which it certainly is), but also nearly the only one, which it certainly is not. When it is argued that the home and the mass media have more to do with the success or failure of education than do the schools themselves, such observations are received as a sort of treason against the august function of education.

But the facts indicate that the educational structure is paralleled by so many other socialization influences that shape the attitudes of the young that their success or nonsuccess in the educational structure can no longer be blamed on this structure alone. Take alone the fact that the average American child spends more hours in front of the television screen than in the classroom, and that his or her affiliations with formal and informal organizations, clubs, and groups have proliferated to the extent that school is just one of them.

Perhaps we ask too much of school. In the past we expected our schools to accomplish what in the Old World the family, the church, apprenticeship, and the guilds accomplished in concert. Today we ask that the school render the services of what their modern equivalents, plus a hundred voluntary organizations, fail or refuse to do. In short, modern American schools have become the scapegoat for the failures and shortcomings of a multiphasic and anomic society.

What parents, particularly middle-class parents, expect school to give to their offspring amounts to virtually *everything*: loving attention, advanced babysitting, academic brilliance, effective preparation for a profession, character building, skill in getting along with others, a sense of creativity as well as a sense of conformity, athletic excellence, and, most pronouncedly, psychological health (whatever that may mean). The dropout is seen as the patent failure of the school in conferring these qualities to children. With a peculiar zest for guilt feelings, many Americans, including what appear to be masochistic educators, actually believe in a simple cause-effect relationship—the cause for dropping out is the failure of the school.

Notwithstanding the enormous difficulties and the staggering demands leveled at the American educational structure, American education renders an amazingly successful service.

This is not to say that the American institution of education is free from serious problems and awful deficiencies. (Discussion will once more touch on this topic in Part V, Challenges and Outlook.)

Probably the greatest dilemma of the American high school lies in trying to do justice to a divergent population of students: to those preparing for entry into the labor market and those preparing for college. The American democratic ethos tries to safeguard the privileges of both groups, and in the process perpetuates the dilemma and makes it practically unsolvable.

This makes high school the weak link in the American educational system. But what are the alternatives? A European system that favors some sort of elite and sorts out, at a preposterously young age, the "lower" from the "higher" educational material? Most likely this would result in unspeakable, even though unintentional, hardship for masses of young people who recognize their interests and their educational potential at a later age—an age when they find themselves excluded from the trajectory of higher education.

The Europeans, incidentally, have learned from the tragedies of this arbitrary and parallel system and are trying to correct it. In the process of modifying their archaic structure, they are working out a "middle way" that presumably gives young people a second chance at higher education once they have bypassed the significant switching point at age ten. But the overall structure has become only more cumbersome and complex. Worst of all, it has failed to eliminate the socio-economic bias of the old system: West German official reports in 1982 admitted that the elite/proletariat pattern is still recognizable, with only 14 percent of all university students coming from working-class families. This statistic becomes more glaring when one considers that working-class youngsters are the largest group in the student-age population of West Germany.[25] Many European educators wish they had inherited a sequential system like the American one with its democratic simplicity rather than a structure that divides the young into categories alienated from each other by different unbridgeable educational careers.

SUMMARY

Education in postindustrial society is nonfamilial, longer, custodial, and *in loco parentis*. In addition, it has assumed a ghetto atmosphere that age-segregates the population and promotes the formation of a subculture. It is typical of modern society to shift the teen population from work bench to school desk. High school education has become not only a "basic right," but also a coercion. This reflects not merely an abstract value of the American society, but also the necessity of keeping the nation's youth from entering the labor force at an age when they are unprepared for the labor market, and when the labor market is unprepared for them.

Some critics suggest a case against the pressure to continue education on the college level. Unmotivated and unqualified youth might do better and be happier with alternative careers and vocations.

Technical innovations have left their marks on the educational process, as well as on family life. TV has been found to suppress creative thought and probably detracts from the learning process, whereas the computer seems to

---

[25]"Bildungspolitik," *Mitteilungen*, DAAD, 5, May 1982, p. 7.

supplement and even encourage learning, as well as integrates into family life.

Two types of critics should be noted. One accuses the American school system of squelching the development of individuality and creativity and goes as far as hinting that the dropout is one who tries to preserve these qualities. Much of such criticism is based on romantic visions of what some kind of hypothetical human being might be—"if the school would only give him or her a chance." The myopia of the criticism overlooks that (1) postindustrial society has spawned so many other influential media and affiliations that the blame for failing to successfully socialize the young can no longer be justifiedly laid at the doorsteps of the school; (2) socialization is not a liberating process but by definition has to some degree a suppressive function; and (3) the sequential nature of the American school system is of greater democratic value than the European system, which is based on an elite/proletariat dichotomy.

The other type aims criticism at the college and university level and largely is critical for such reasons as the neglect by the American educational system to insist on teaching the cultural heritage of Western Civilization—its history, literature, and philosophies.

10

The Role of Television and Other Mass Media

Human beings have the capacity to think in symbolic terms and need not rely on the actual presence of persons or objects to form views of themselves and the world. Humans are also inventive and have created mass media to expose vast audiences to a constant barrage of stimuli that bear significantly on personality development.

SCOPE OF EXPOSURE

Of the various media, television reaches nearly all people in this country; it is notoriously popular, easily accessible, and commands the largest share of time Americans spend on any of the mass media. Television has absorbed some of the functions of the press, radio, and movie industry. Movies, for example, have become almost synonymous with television, and it is only a matter of time before the latest productions can be seen at home. Television is probably the most influential source of common experience in the lives of American children, and, along with home and school, has come to function as a major socializing agent. Through mass media, the actual live person or group can be bypassed, and personal interaction can be replaced by the spectator–mass-media relationship, allowing an almost unlimited range of vicarious identifications.

One should not conclude that the significant other person and the concrete group have been replaced entirely. The feeling of security that a child derives from association with caring parents is still of paramount importance for personality development. But needing parents and wanting to be like them are two different processes. The first deals with the need for security and the second with the absorption of ideas, impressions, and behavior styles. Parental care is a universal imperative for survival that has rarely been successfully replaced, while identification is a process allowing alternative objects of identification. Mass media offer a vast number of such alternatives. Modern children, although depending on their parents physically, can select ego images from the characters presented by ubiquitous mass media. Through screen, radio, and print, characters of many different types are presented to youth, who cannot escape from the incessant flow of stimuli and cannot avoid incorporating some aspects of these "types" into their behavior patterns and identities.

The effects that the mass media have on the personality of the young are not yet well known. It may safely be assumed, however, that the effects are not superficial, when one considers that over 99 percent of American homes have a minimum of one television set and that among American children time spent viewing television ranks second only to sleeping.[1] By the time the American teenager reaches eighteen years of age, he or she will have watched an average of about 22,000 hours (that is approximately 2½ years) of television compared with 11,000 hours spent in the class room. The average American, both child and adult, views over six hours of television daily. By the age of fourteen, the typical viewer will have witnessed 11,000 TV murders; by the age of eighteen he or she will have been exposed to 350,000 commercials.[2]

Television viewing starts early in America, and it soon starts to reflect the symptoms of addiction. A study at Michigan State University discovered that when four- and five-year-olds are offered a hypothetical choice between giving up television or their father, one-third would rather part with father.[3] Children get up early in the morning to watch television before leaving for school, and millions of children under the age of twelve watch television as late as 10 P.M. on week nights. The peak of television viewing is reached somewhere between the sixth and the eighth grades, just before entering the

[1]Robert M. Liebert et al., *The Early Window. Effects of Television on Children and Youth* (Elmsford, NY: Pergamon, 1982), p. xv.

[2]Joan A. Wilkins, *Breaking the TV Habit* (New York: Scribners, 1982), pp. 10, 13, 32.

[3]"Getting Unplugged," *Time*, October 11, 1982, p. 99.

adolescent years, and then decreases slowly until around the twelfth grade, when the adolescent is reaching a plateau of about two and one-half hours of television viewing a day.[4]

The main reason for the heaviest period of viewing occurring between the sixth and eighth grades and then dropping off can be found in the new freedom that this age group experiences in staying up later in the evening. The gradual decrease after this age is no doubt largely due to the social involvements of the adolescent. The television set is at home, and home is not where most adolescents want to spend their time. Their process of autonomy and their increasing interest in the peer group and in dating mean less time for television.

Americans most likely hold the world record in television viewing, but other countries are not far behind. Statistics show that West German children rate television their favorite pastime, spending approximately one and one-half hours daily watching it, and list as their favorite shows (1) comics, (2) wildlife shows, (3) children's programs, and (4) Wild West movies.[5] Concern about TV's family-destructive potential has been expressed on the highest government level. For example, in 1982 West German Chancellor Helmut Schmidt called on his nation to observe a family night at least once a week—*with TV off.*

Nonetheless, television as an internationally ubiquitous medium is on the rise. Its growing magnitude in technologically advanced societies illustrates the emphasis that postindustrial systems place on the service function, including entertainment, communication, and advertisement.

PROMINENT INGREDIENTS: UNREALITY AND VIOLENCE

Television portrays a variety of values that cannot fail to have impact on the young. A number of the dominant values conflict with those that most parents would like to instill in their children:[6]

1. Violence. It is virtually impossible to watch television without seeing humans killed, tortured, or maimed, and it has been estimated that by fourteen, the average child has seen 18,000 humans killed on television.
2. Unreality. Television exposes the young to a world of unreality that not only invites escapism from real life—a function of fantasy that is often useful—but

---

[4]Wilbur Schramm, Jack Lyle, and Edwin B. Parker, *Television in the Lives of Our Children* (Stanford, CA: Stanford University Press, 1961). Also see "A Profile of the American Eighth-Grader," Superintendent of Documents, U.S. Printing Office, Washington, DC, 1990.

[5]"Fernsehen," *Kulturbrief Inter-Nations,* 2 (August 1972): 22.

[6]Most points are based on a discussion by E. E. Le Masters, *Parents in Modern America* (Homewood, IL: Dorsey Press, 1974), pp. 159–61.

seriously distorts reality. Fantasy is more honest: it openly admits that it is not reality but simply a flight of fancy.

3. Sex. Sexuality is usually presented in movies and television on a physical level, both visually and verbally, but disguised as "love."

4. Idealization of immaturity. Idols and heroes are often immature and teenage-like and seem to have achieved wealth and fame with minimal talent.

5. Materialism. Many programs imply that happiness comes with success, and success means houses, cars, vacations, and so forth.

6. Instant achievement and solution. This theme glorifies the power of technology and promises instant solutions to life's problems. Many commercials peddle chemicals assuring immediate success in problems that range from romance to insomnia. During a two-hour television period, forty-two such claims were presented in the form of commercials.[7]

In addition to these themes, there are, of course, more positive values presented, and they will be discussed later in the chapter. For the moment, we are concerned with two dimensions: unreality and violence.

Unreality

Unreality is a generic concept that can be divided into fantasy and deception. *Fantasy* identifies itself as such and is youth's favorite in the form of cartoons, fairy tales, ghost stories, comedies, and science fiction. Although the interest in the fantastic is not new in history, the recent preoccupation with it is of more than literary significance. For the first time in history, it is now possible to intensively expose children to such themes every day. Interpretations of this preoccupation have described it as symptomatic of the present anomic age—as wishful thinking, as searching for solutions, as another version of longing for magic that can solve problems, and, finally, as escape from a world that looms confusing and perilous.

Rarely, however, does fantasy lead to confusion between real and unreal, and there is speculation that television fantasy, and the vicariousness with which the young experience it, has therapeutic effects by providing an outlet for frustration and a reprieve from anxieties.[8] Fantasy may even stimulate creative thought and the ability to solve problems.[9]

However, researchers have found that exposure to television—a prolific source of fantasy—does not significantly improve the child's school performance. Studies of two samples of children, one group with and the other without a television set at home, revealed that the group exposed to televi-

---

[7]Henry L. Lennard et al., *Mystification and Drug Misuse* (San Francisco: Jossey-Bass, 1971), and Hans Sebald, "The Pursuit of Instantness in Technocratic Society and Youth's Psychedelic Drug Use," *Adolescence*, 7 (Fall 1972): 343–50.

[8]For details on the function of fantasy, see Eleanor E. Maccoby, "Why Do Children Watch TV?" *Public Opinion Quarterly*, 18 (Fall 1954): 239–44.

[9]Alfred R. Lindesmith et al., *Social Psychology* (New York: Holt-Dryden, 1977), p. 154.

sion entered school with larger vocabularies—an advantage that was of short duration. After a period of school attendance, the language proficiency of the two groups became comparable. Also, there was little difference between them in respect to interest in class work, completion of assignments, and test performance.[10]

Exposure to fantasy may lose its beneficial effects through overexposure. A child may become "addicted" to mass media fantasy, try to substitute the "safer" world of make-believe for the real world, and actually find it difficult to separate the real from the unreal. A child or teenager watching television more than four hours a day has to do an extraordinary amount of switching back and forth between the two worlds. This oscillating existence does not contribute to his or her ability to concentrate on real problems and tasks.

A chronically disturbed youth is particularly prone to experience detrimental effects from prolonged exposure to fantasy, since fantasy can reinforce escapism to the point where a youth loses touch with reality and refuses to be bound by the rules of the social environment. Maybe the greatest danger is the possibility that the young use certain mass media images and models to formulate identities that become harmful not only to themselves but to others. Many of the television crime-busters invite emulation, although imitation of their techniques would be disastrous in real life. The world of fantasy has different rules and protects the foolhardy hero, who is pictured as invincible. If children act as though they were protected by the rules of fantasy and withdraw too often from the real world into the euphoria of make-believe, they are then headed for serious adjustment problems. George Gerbner, one of the nation's foremost TV-fare analysts, concludes in his recent research that young persons may come to view themselves in the light of fantasy and acquire a pseudoidentity that would have to be changed for everyday life.[11]

It might well have been of television's fantasy and its overexposed "addict" that the poet Gibran spoke when he said, ". . . that stealthy thing that enters the house as a guest, and then becomes a host and then a master."[12]

Another aspect of unreality concerns *pretension* about the real world. No genre of the mass media is immune from portraying reality deceptively: comedy, drama, adventure, detective stories, love stories, and the news—all have their own slant. It is this type of misrepresentation that generally is more harmful than pure fantasy. While fantasy may prove to be relatively ineffectual with respect to identification and personality formation because

[10]Eleanor E. Maccoby, "The Effects of TV on Children," in *The Science of Human Communication*, ed. Wilbur Schramm (New York: Basic Books, 1963), pp. 116–27.

[11]Reported in "Life According to TV," *Newsweek*, December 6, 1982, p. 136.

[12]Kahlil Gibran, *The Prophet*, copyright © 1961, p. 32. Reprinted by permission of Alfred A. Knopf, Inc.

the average youngster knows that it is make-believe, the pseudoreal programs seriously tempt the young to identify and select models for emulation. Movies are a frequent source of such identifiable images and models. The heroes are part of plots that range from "real-life" detective thrillers and Wild West epics to the "wholesome" swim-ski-and-surf type stories.

Grant Noble speaks of the danger of projecting mass media personalities into real life:

> These characters serve as something akin to a screen community with whom the viewer regularly talks and interacts. Viewers who feel they know these characters well may indeed compare new people they meet in real life with such characters in order to predict how these new people are likely to behave later.[13]

Books are another medium through which unreality or violence can be conveyed. One of the most typical conveyors of unreality is the Gothic novel, which presents a plot in which all the heroine need do is be beautiful as she travels through mysterious adventures and ultimately finds fame, fortune, and the man of her dreams. This type of romantic reading material seems to be still popular especially with girls. The power of imagery that reading can exert over the human mind of the young is, however, minimal when seen in the light of 1990 statistics that show that on the average young teenagers spend merely 1.8 hours on outside reading (other than homework) per week compared with 22 hours of TV viewing.

These plots, whether occurring in books or on television, purport to depict real life but actually select only certain aspects of life. They convey situations, achievements, and human relationships that have little or no validity in the real world. The heroes as well as the villains of these stories display superior strength, imagination, and achievements, making the parents seem pale and unimaginative in comparison.

And the flawless beauty of the heroine, as well as her miraculously good luck in life, is extremely difficult to match in the real life of the teenager — as one look into the mirror or stepping onto the bathroom scales may well prove. At that moment, ideas of equivalence or imitative possibilities may abruptly cease and painful frustration set in.

Violence

Violence, the other major theme, is heavily laced with unreality—both in quantity and quality. The vast majority of all types of violence in real life takes place between persons who are friends or family members. In only about 10 percent of all homicides are the assailant and the victim strangers. In the television world, the majority of violent acts occurs between strangers.

---

[13]Grant Noble, *Children in Front of the Small Screen* (Beverly Hills: Sage, 1975), p. 164.

Similarly, crooks make up 17 percent of all TV characters vs. 1 percent or less in real life.[14] Gunslingers, psychopaths, and sadists have leading roles in a significant portion of television entertainment, and their behavior is shown to millions every day. The classic content analysis by Wilbur Schramm of 100 television hours of the so-called children's hours, 4:00 P.M. to 9:00 P.M., Monday through Friday, produced an impressive list of nonhumorous (as distinct from cartoons and comedies) acts of violence:

12 murders
16 major gunfights
21 persons shot (apparently not fatally)
21 other violent incidents with guns
37 hand-to-hand fights (15 fist fights, 15 incidents in which one person slugged
    another, an attempted murder with a pitchfork, 2 stranglings, a fight in the
    water, a case in which a woman was gagged and tied to a bed, and so forth)
1 stabbing in the back with a butcher knife
4 attempted suicides, three successful
4 people pushed over cliffs
2 cars running over cliffs
2 attempts made in automobiles to run over persons
A psychotic raving in a flying airliner
2 mob scenes, in one the mob hangs the wrong man
A horse grinding a man under its hooves
A great deal of miscellaneous violence, including a plane fight, a hired killer
    stalking his prey, 2 robberies, a pickpocket working, a woman killed by falling
    from a train, a tidal wave, an earthquake, and a guillotining.[15]

The reason this study can be called a "classic" is that it established an early assessment of the *nature* of violence in American TV programs during the children's hours. While the nature has hardly changed, the *quantity* with which we bombard children with violent images has increased over the years. Mid-1980s statistics by the National Coalition on TV Violence reported a notable rise since the 1960s in the use of violent images on TV and MTV, as well as in the lyrics in popular rock 'n' roll music.

Precise figures were published in 1989 by University of Pennsylvania communications professor George Gerbner in the report, *Violence Profile 1967–1989: Enduring Patterns*. The project uses a "violence index" to compare from year to year the programs offered by CBS, NBC, and ABC. Violence is defined as explicit physical acts or threats of hurting or killing in any context. The rate of violence during weekdays' prime time has increased insignificantly, from slightly under six acts per hour before 1980 to a little over six acts after 1980. During prime time 70 percent of network programs use violence, but during children's hours 90 percent of the programs show

---

[14]"Learning to Live with TV," *Time*, May 28, 1979, p. 49.
[15]Schramm et al., *Television in the Lives of Our Children*, pp. 139–40.

violence. The most significant increase in violence has been found in the weekend daytime children's programs. Whereas before 1980 there were 18 violent acts per hour, after 1980 their number increased to 26.

Simple arithmetic tells us that if we count an average of six acts of TV violence per hour's watching (basing it on the more moderate weekdays' prime time), then an eighteen-year-old American, who has on the average watched 22,000 hours, has witnessed 132,000 acts of violence.

THE QUESTION OF IMITATION

Such staggering figures justify raising the question as to how violence influences the audience, especially the malleable young.

The Controversy

Representatives of the broadcasting industry claim that television has no harmful effects on the viewer. Mental health officials, social workers, teachers, and the general public are divided over the question, some believing that exposure to violence breeds violence, and others assuming that exposure has a cathartic and pacifying effect, allowing children to identify with the aggressor and in this way rid themselves of pent-up hostile emotions without harmful acting out.

The divergence of interpretations is typically exemplified by the dispute between sociologist Paul Hirsch and communication researcher George Gerbner. Hirsch, using National Opinion Research Center data, compared heaviest and lightest viewers and concluded that heavy watchers show no negative signs. On the contrary, he thinks, TV is probably more of a solution to their problems than a cause of their problems. Gerbner rebuts by pointing to Hirsch's biased sample, which was only 6 percent of those polled by NORC, including housewives and retired folks whose TVs are almost constant companions against loneliness and not agitators intent on imitation. Hirsch's study is not representative of teenage viewers, who may watch less but more violent fare and may be affected quite differently.[16]

The controversy reached the highest echelons of the American political institution. In 1990 Congress reacted to the critics of the TV industry, ranging from religious conservatives to consumer groups like Action for Children's TV, and sent a bill that would set limits on commercial time in children's programs and increase educational fare to President Bush.[17] But the modification even as mild as the bill suggested—the question of censor-

[16]"Are TV Addicts Healthy?" *Time*, October 20, 1980, p. 81.
[17]"Is TV Ruining our Children?" *Time*, October 15, 1990, pp. 75–76.

ing violence wasn't even raised—encountered Presidential reluctance. President Bush argued that the bill would infringe on broadcasters' First Amendment rights. Two years earlier President Reagan had vetoed a similar measure. This goes to show that American TV networks enjoy nearly unchecked license.

Experiments and Studies

Insight into the nature of media violence influence is derived from the Bandura experiments at the Stanford University psychological laboratories, which evaluated the impact of televised aggression on preschool children. Experiments tested the extent to which children copy aggressive behavior when such behavior is demonstrated by models in three different situations: in real life, on film (television), or as cartoon characters on film. The typical experiment divided the children into four groups. While three groups witnessed violent behavior under the different conditions mentioned above, the control group was not shown any violence. After the children of the three groups had watched the acts of violence, they and the control-group children were individually placed in an observation room under conditions that mildly irritated them. The observation room contained a variety of toys, including a three-foot Bobo doll that could be used as an object of aggression. Each child spent twenty minutes in the room, and his or her behavior was rated by psychologists observing through a one-way mirror. The results left little doubt that exposure to violence stimulated aggressive tendencies. Children who had viewed the aggressive adult demonstrated approximately twice as much aggression as those in the control group. The researchers concluded: (1) Exposure tends to reduce inhibition to act in a violent manner. (2) Exposure tends to shape the form of aggressive behavior. While most of the children from the first three groups sat on the Bobo doll and punched its nose, beat it on the head with a mallet, tossed it in the air, and kicked it (the exact kinds of attack they had observed), the children of the control groups rarely acted that way. (3) Display of violence on film is almost as influential as a display in real life. The child exhibits a high degree of imitation in both situations. However, the children were slow to imitate cartoon characters.[18]

The weak element in the Bandura experiments is the substitution of an inanimate object, the Bobo doll, for a real human being as the target of aggression. The substitution is understandable. In spite of certain risks involved, some other studies tried to measure aggression as it was directed at actual persons. The findings were positive. For example, one study showed

---

[18]Albert Bandura, Dorothea Ross, and Sheila A. Ross, "Imitation of Film-Mediated Aggressive Models," *Journal of Abnormal and Social Psychology,* 66 (January 1963): 3–11.

that an 11-day overexposure to aggressive cartoons led preschoolers to enact violence toward peers.[19]

A large and methodologically sophisticated study by the Huesmann team followed approximately 1000 elementary school boys and girls in the United States and in Finland for three years.[20] It provided for the examination of the larger social matrix in which the children lived, with an emphasis on family conditions. The study yielded a major insight insofar as it revealed bidirectional effects. That is, watching TV violence stimulates the child to become aggressive, and the more aggressive the child becomes, the more it selects violent programs. It is, in short, a mutually stimulating process. Another significant contribution by the study showed that aggressive behavior has multiple causes. There is a complex mesh of at least seven conditions that seems to make for a positive relationship between media violence and its enactment: (1) The child's belief that the violent show portrays life as it is. (2) The child's identification with the violent hero. (3) The child having habitual aggressive fantasies. (4) The child's mother being noticeably more aggressive than would be considered normal. (5) The child's lower socioeconomic background. (6) The child doing poorly in school. (7) The child being unpopular with peers.

What this important study shows is that TV violence is not the only cause of aggression in children; rather, it is one of the conditions in a highly complex causative matrix. Nonetheless, it appears that media violence was a salient enough condition to be called a predictor of future levels of aggression for boys and girls in both cultures.

Periodic upsurges in public concern over possible negative consequences of violence-filled TV programs have prompted a number of official inquiries. The first major inquiry was the 1972 study by the Surgeon General's Scientific Advisory Committee on TV and Social Behavior, yielding five volumes of findings. Generally, the findings linked violence on TV with aggressive behavior in young people. Here are two representative studies.[21]

Monroe M. Lefkowitz studied 900 third-graders, observing them over a ten-year period. He found that children unpopular as third-graders stayed unpopular ten years later. The child unpopular in the third grade watched TV more as he or she grew older and continued to be unpopular. There was a direct correlation between degree of violent program preferred and aggressive behavior, both in the third grade and ten years later. While the re-

[19]F. B. Steuer et al., "Televised Aggression and the Interpersonal Aggression of Preschool Children," *Journal of Experimental Child Psychology*, 11 (1971): 442–47.

[20]L. R. Huesmann et al., "Intervening Variables in the TV Violence-Aggression Relation: Evidence from Two Countries," *Developmental Psychology*, 20 (1984): 746–75.

[21]Surgeon General's Scientific Advisory Committee on TV and Social Behavior, *TV and Adolescent Aggressiveness*, vol. 3 (Washington, DC: Government Printing Office, 1972).

searchers conclude that this phenomenon illustrates the impact of TV violence on personal aggressiveness as well as its cumulative effects, the study as such does not prove its contention but merely points out a correlation.

A similar study by John Robinson and Gerald Bachman completed a longitudinal study of 2,200 tenth-graders throughout the United States between 1966 and 1970. Among the boys who initially were found to be most aggressive, preference for violent TV shows was linked to their behavior. More instances of violent fights occurred among heavy viewers of TV violence than among those who had no violent shows among their favorites. Again, it is not clear whether this finding is a correlation or a causal relationship.

Predictably, the television networks reacted defensively and, reminiscent of the parallel rationalizations by the tobacco industry, tried to capitalize on the technicality that though a *correlation* was established, there was no proof of a *causal* relationship between TV violence and aggressive behavior.

The matter was more or less laid to rest until 1982 when the National Institute for Mental Health published another notable report. *Television and Behavior: Ten Years of Scientific Progress and Implications for the Eighties* derived from a two-year review of hundreds of research studies and reached an unambiguous conclusion: Television is a "violent form of entertainment" that clearly leads to aggressive behavior by children and teenagers.

Again, network reaction to the report was quick and predictable. All three networks rejected the report. NBC felt certain that many of the report's conclusions would be challenged by social scientists conducting independent research. It also announced that it would publish its own report at a later time, showing that the NIMH conclusions about the effect of viewing TV violence are not supportable. The networks' basic argument was that, based on high ratings, the programs are giving the public exactly what it desires and the networks are therefore serving the public interest.[22]

In addition to these comprehensive reports, which integrate masses of research data, there are numerous specific studies that contribute valuable insights. For example, one study's focus dealt with gender-differentiated responses to media violence. Up to about 1970, researchers had regularly found girls to be less influenced by media violence; either they did not watch TV violence in the first place or did not respond aggressively to such violence. Boys, on the other hand, were more interested in violent shows, viewed more of them, and reacted aggressively. This gender difference has changed. Psychologist Leonard Eron's latest study shows that such gender-differentiated responses to media violence has been erased.[23] His explana-

[22]"Warning from Washington," *Time*, May 17, 1982, p. 77; also AP report, Washington, May 9, 1982.
[23]"Learning to live with TV," p. 49.

tion: TV's violent female role models have dramatically proliferated and star in such regular shows as *Bionic Woman, Wonder Woman, Charlie's Angels,* and *Policewoman.*

In spite of what appears overwhelming evidence for negative influence, some social scientists continue to remain aloof from the imitation theory. They are convinced that television is a secondary cause of real-life violence and that other factors, such as the individual's background and personality, are much more causative. Some feel that television violence may actually make viewers *less* violent by allowing them to cathart their pent-up hostility. Among those who deemphasize the imitative role of media violence are Seymour Feshbach and Robert D. Singer, who experimented with several groups of boys aged nine to fifteen and varied their exposure to media violence under controlled conditions.[24] Some groups watched aggressive programs, such as *The FBI, Gunsmoke,* and *The Untouchables;* other groups watched milder ones. The experimenters kept track of the changes in aggressive attitudes and values as well as in the number of aggressive acts in which the boys engaged during their exposure to the different fare. The findings failed to support the traditional theory. The group that watched the milder programs engaged in more than twice as many fist fights as the group that watched the rougher shows; as for angry arguments, the "nonviolent" group had 859 arguments, compared with the "violent" group's 407. Criticizing or insulting others amounted to 973 versus 456 instances, respectively, manifestations of jealousy compared 254 to 87 instances, and instances of destruction of property were equal.

The researchers arrived at the conclusion that *no* group became more aggressive as a result of viewing aggressive television programs and that some subgroups actually became *less* aggressive. Astonishingly, they found that youngsters who watched the nonaggressive television programs became *more* aggressive in their behavior. In short, they concluded, the vicarious aggressive experience is therapeutic and calming.

Another reason mentioned by social scientists for nonimitation of violence is viewers' ability to discern between fiction and fact. Robert P. Snow found children capable of interpreting acts of violence on television as taking place in a "play" setting; they were rarely tempted to reenact them.[25] If seen in this light, the experiments by Bandura lose some of their significance insofar as the children may have realized that a Bobo doll is not a real person, and beating it is therefore not to be equated with any degree of violence against another human being.

[24]Seymour Feshbach and Robert D. Singer, *Television and Aggression: An Experimental Field Study* (San Francisco: Jossey-Bass, 1971).
[25]Robert P. Snow, "How Children Interpret TV Violence in Play Context," *Journalism Quarterly,* 51 (Spring 1974): 13–21.

Examples of Imitation

The argument that media violence breeds imitation in real life can be more effectively supported by reports that clearly show its existence. Some examples (from the author's "imitation" file) include:

1. Teenage girls gang-rape a San Francisco girl in imitation of a scene from the 1974 TV movie *Born Innocent* in which Linda Blair played the victim of sadistic teenage girls.
2. An inmate escapes by helicopter from a Michigan prison; the escape was planned after seeing the movie *Breakout.*
3. Teenagers commit several inventive Chicago murders, following in vivid detail the killings depicted in the TV detective series *Shaft.*
4. Teenagers immolate a woman in a Boston street forcing her to douse herself with gasoline, in imitation of a scene in the TV police story *Fuzz* presented two nights earlier. Later that year the scene was reenacted in Miami where a derelict, as in the movie, was set on fire; three young teenagers were charged with murder.
5. A seventeen-year-old boy stabs to death a young woman, imitating a scene from the Emmy-Award-winning TV movie, *The Marcus-Nelson Murders.* The boy had memorized the movie down to the last detail and arranged the crime scene to look exactly like it did in the movie.
6. A sixteen-year-old boy kicks to death an old man after he had seen it done by the "hero" in *A Clockwork Orange* and tells the police that he remembered his act "like a scene from the film."
7. Two fourteen-year-old boys commit suicide when they imitate the mock hanging they had seen performed on TV by rock music star Alice Cooper.
8. A young man extorts $500,000 from Quantas Airlines in a pressure-bomb hoax modeled after Rod Sterling's *The Doomsday Flight,* which had just been shown on Australian TV. When the movie was shown on American TV, bomb threats against airlines went up 80 percent within a week.
9. A fifteen-year-old boy shoots to death an eighty-three-year-old woman and is defended in court as a victim of "involuntary TV intoxication" and his parents in 1978 filed (unsuccessfully) a $25 million damage suit against the three major TV networks.
10. Two California youths rob a bank in imitation of an *Adam 12* story and hold twenty-four hostages against a $1 million ransom.
11. A sixteen-year-old girl sprays a crowded San Diego elementary school with rifle fire in 1979, killing and wounding several persons. The sniper told police later that she had always fantasized about being a sniper and derived idea and technique from watching *SWAT* on TV.
12. In the movie *Taxi Driver* a disturbed cabbie, played by Robert De Niro, sets out to shoot a presidential candidate in an attempt to impress a child prostitute played by Jodie Foster. John Hinckley, after seeing the movie 15 times, so identified with the film's hero that he bought an Army fatigue jacket, took to drinking peach brandy, and sent emotional messages to Foster, as did De Niro's character. Then, in 1981, he shot President Reagan.
13. Three youths, aged fifteen, nineteen, and twenty-one, sadistically murder a Florida talk-show celebrity in 1982 by reenacting a bizarre ritual patterned after the movie *The Shining* (involving ice to suffocate or freeze a person to death and the word "redrum"—murder spelled backwards). The movie had been shown on television during the week of the slaying.

Besides such spectacular imitations, making national if not international headlines, most imitations remain local news. A sampling includes numerous TV-inspired burglaries. Among them were an eleven-year-old boy and his seven-year-old accomplice, who imitated detailed techniques of breaking into homes. A Washington youth committed burglaries by skillfully forcing skylights, a method he had observed on TV. An *Ironside* script had Jackie Cooper playing a scientist who was locked in an explosive belt by a criminal. Ten days later a young man was arrested when he tried the same method to kidnap a Hartford businessman's daughter. A four-year-old Brooklyn boy died in 1979 when he fell seven stories from a building ledge while imitating Superman. Inmates of the Florida State Hospital in 1980 armed themselves with sharp metal objects and makeshift clubs for a three-hour rebellion minutes after they had watched the TV movie *Attica*, which depicted a similar situation. Teenagers affected by the 1979 movie *The Warriors* went on a rampage and caused several thousand dollars worth of damage at a Scottsdale, Arizona elementary school.

Imitation of media violence has crossed national borders and shaken the public in other countries. For instance, a fourteen-year-old London boy committed self-immolation in 1979 in exactly the same manner as he had seen on TV the night before; the diary he left behind attested to his carefully planned imitation. This case, and others, dramatically illustrate the findings by William A. Belson, sociologist at the London School of Economics' Survey Research Center, whose six-year study of nearly 1,600 London teenage boys disclosed that long exposure to TV steeply increased their acts of violence (smashing cars, damaging phone booths, setting fires, etc.).[26]

Imitation of a peculiar form of violence took place in 1976 in the diocese of Würzburg in Germany. A 22-year-old university student, Anneliese Michel, exhibited the classic symptoms of Satanic possession after the movie *The Exorcist* had made its rounds in the local theaters. Ensconced in a Catholic environment of true believers, she attracted wide attention by what finally was officially diagnosed by the Church as genuine possession. Two priests were charged by the archbishop with the responsibility to perform the appropriate rituals—as specified in the *Rituale Romanum*—to drive out the Devil. Anneliese, unbeknownst to the priests and the family, did a splendid imitation of Linda Blair's notorious role in *The Exorcist*. Only the outcome took on a particularly macabre twist: the priests starved the girl to death. That's when the D.A. and the courts took over. Psychiatric experts posthumously diagnosed that the young woman's affliction had been a mixture of role playing and epileptic symptoms.[27]

[26]William A. Belson, *Television Violence and the Adolescent Boy* (Lexington, MA: Heath, 1978).

[27]Hans Sebald, *Witchcraft—the Heritage of a Heresy*, (New York: Elsevier North Holland, 1978), p. 233–34.

"Disturbance" Theory

Many researchers warn, however, against overgeneralizing the impact of media violence. They think that imitation occurs only under certain circumstances, as in cases where disturbed adolescents are exposed to violent fare. While this assumption has the ring of plausibility, it raises questions of definition. What is disturbed; what is normal? These definitions are not yet clear and they differ among researchers. For example, if we equate what Freud called "moral anxiety"—the entirely normal control emotions that accompany the conscience and without which a person would be a sociopath—with being "disturbed," then normal would mean being occasionally anxious and disturbed. Most research concentrating on imitators indeed finds many of them disturbed to some degree. But it would be difficult to prove that all nonimitating viewers then must be "normal." It is possible that the amount of violence imitated by viewers definable as disturbed is not significantly larger than that imitated by viewers definable as nondisturbed. We don't really know how they compare. At this time, equating disturbance with receptiveness to violence imitation remains a hypothesis.

THE DESENSITIZATION EFFECT

Another possible effect of exposure to media violence is desensitization toward violence. Habitual viewing of violence may lead to the viewer thinking and feeling that violence is a normal, everyday phenomenon. Such interpretation may ultimately induce endorsement of violence as an acceptable, tolerable, and perhaps unavoidable way of solving problems—and studies have borne out that this attitude has been engendered in children.[28] Desensitization has also been measured through physiological indicators. Comparison of boys with different histories of exposure to media violence showed that autonomous nervous system responses (blood pressure and galvanic skin response) to violent scenes were significantly stronger in the low-exposure boys than in their TV-tempered peers.[29] This simply means that boys who were overexposed to media violence were no longer upset by it.

Concern that TV-induced insensitivity may spread and become a normal part of the American lifestyle has been voiced by a number of notable writers and public figures. Barbara Ehrenreich put her finger on a tragic

[28]Joseph Dominick and Bradley Greenberg, "Attitudes Toward Violence: Interaction of TV Exposure, Family Attitudes, and Social Class," in *TV and Adolescent Aggressiveness*, vol. 3 (Washington, DC: Government Printing Office, 1972).

[29]Victor B. Cline et al., "Desensitization of Children to TV Violence," *Journal of Personality and Social Psychology*, 27 (September 1973), 360–66.

element in American civilization when she called it the "warrior culture." She thinks that "our collective fantasies center on mayhem, cruelty and violent death. Loving images of the human body—especially of bodies seeking pleasure or expressing love—inspire us with the urge to censor."[30] Norman Cousins feared that "the ability to react instinctively to suffering seems to be atrophying. Youngsters sit transfixed in front of television or motion-picture screens, munching popcorn while human beings are battered or mutilated."[31] Marie Winn felt that among the characteristics of a new breed of juvenile delinquents is their heavy exposure to violent media programs. The common strain running through these youthful criminals—many have mugged, murdered, and raped—"seems to be a form of emotional detachment that allows them to commit unspeakable crimes with a complete absence of normal feeling such as guilt or remorse. It is as if they were dealing with inanimate objects, not with human beings at all."[32]

It is difficult to determine whether or to what degree a dulling of the Americans' capacity for empathy has progressed. We can only try and interpret certain symptoms. This brings to mind a large, quarter-page picture of an adorable little boy smiling at us from the front page of Arizona State University's student paper, *The State Press* (November 14, 1985). He is holding a toy revolver in his hand and is whiling his time away on the main mall of the campus by "shooting people." The reporter and the editor apparently found this a cute pose. The caption informs us that while the child's sitter, a graduate student, was busy with paper work, "Adam spent his time shooting people." The fact that a picture of fake killing was found to be an acceptable and entertaining feature and that not one letter to the editor (from a student population of over 40,000) protested it may well document insensitivity to the dignity of human life in an environment where presumably the better values of humanity are to be protected and furthered.

CONTROL ASPECTS

Most research suggests that televised models are important sources of social behavior and can no longer be ignored as influences on personality formation. However, one must distinguish between learning and acting out. Although children readily learn patterns of social behavior, including violent acts, from television programs, their imitative behavior may be limited by at least three factors:

[30]Barbara Ehrenreich, "The Warrior Culture," *Time*, October 15, 1990, p. 100.
[31]Norman Cousins, "The Decline of Neatness," *Time*, April 2, 1990, p. 78.
[32]Marie Winn, *The Plug-in Drug* (New York: The Viking Press, 1977), p. 73.

1. Children ordinarily do not have access to the weapons necessary for duplicating what they have observed. If, however, they had switchblades, blackjacks, brass knuckles, and six-shooters, it is safe to predict that the incidence of harmful imitative aggression, patterned according to television stories, would rise sharply.
2. Normally, parents suppress any learning that conflicts with what they consider "proper" conduct. Often such television-produced conflicts are merely on the verbal level, and parents have no particular difficulty in correcting them. The influence of television is ordinarily checked by the standards of parents and other adults, and the full impact of television can be measured precisely only when parental supervision is removed and the children are given the instruments they need to reproduce the aggressive behavior.
3. It is often assumed that an ethical ending to a story, in which the villain is punished, will serve to extinguish what a child has learned from exposure to antisocial models and therefore keep him or her from imitating the violent behavior.

What can be said in response to these control expectations?

First, the nonavailability of instruments is a weak argument, since consumption-oriented postindustrial society provides just about any instrument, including guns and knives, that a young American desires. The public debate about curbing the sale of handguns, especially the so-called Saturday-night specials, is testimony to the concern of many citizens about the easy availability of deadly instruments.

Second, with rising employment of mothers, children increasingly associate with peers who do not necessarily endorse parental standards. It is interesting to note the paucity of concrete suggestions in the professional literature telling parents how they can curb excessive television exposure, neutralize its negative effects, and, if necessary, substitute more creative activities. One of the best methods might be to encourage the young to take up a constructive hobby rather than spend all their time in front of the television set. But for such suggestions to be effective, parents would have to apply more than verbalization: they would have to guide and join the offspring in such projects—something they often find too time-consuming. The majority of parents find it more convenient to turn their children over to the babysitting function of television and even leave the program selection up to them. Research found that 53 percent of 600 parents studied who had eleven-year-old children did not prohibit their offspring from watching any program.[33]

Third, research seems to indicate that the "ethical ending" (or the "happy ending") is a weak safeguard against imitation.

This point can be illustrated by some of Bandura's experiments. A group of nursery school children watched a television movie in which Rocky,

---

[33]P. Musgrave, "How Children Use TV," *New Society,* 13 (1969): 277–78.

the villain, took all of Johnny's toys. Clearly, the story showed that aggression pays off. Another group of children saw the same program with a different ending: as Rocky tried to seize the toys, Johnny overpowered him and gave him a sound beating. The two groups of children were then tested. As might have been expected, children in the first group, who witnessed that Rocky's aggression was rewarded, readily imitated his physical violence and his hostile remarks, while children in the second group, who saw him punished, showed little imitative aggression. Further inquiry, however, presented the researchers with a surprise: all the children were highly critical of the way Rocky behaved and called his action "mean" and children who imitated him did so because his aggression "paid off" or "worked."[34]

Another experiment testing this question found that when a fantasy sequence in a comic strip pictured a villain as relatively successful, children were more likely to identify with him or her and wanted "to be like him or her," while they were reluctant to identify with a weak hero. The children tended to admire and copy "what works" and preferred to be like the character who was successful, regardless of the method used.[35]

These studies suggest that when children see an individual punished, they are not likely to spontaneously imitate his or her behavior. However, they seem to retain information concerning the method of aggression, regardless of the punishment of the villain. There is no denying the possibility that they may put this knowledge into practice on future occasions if they are provoked, obtain access to the necessary weapons, or anticipate a sufficiently attractive reward. The ethical ending of a story functions merely as a *suppressor* of violence, but not as an *extinguisher*.

Despite ominous correlations between TV and violence, the influence of television is obviously somehow limited. The majority of adolescents grow up without ever engaging in violence, let alone the type of violence they have viewed for so many years. Apparently elements of the American ethos proclaiming fair play, kindness, and cooperation somehow become part of their personality makeup. Once internalized, they are safeguarded by the universal control emotions of guilt and shame, which in normal human beings (exceptions are sociopaths) will be aroused when one violates one's standards of right and wrong.

When television suggests values and models inconsistent with principles parents have demonstrated, there is no evidence that the influence of television is paramount. When children have internalized values on a given subject and are not suffering from anomic blanks, television models seem to

[34]Bandura et al., "Imitation of Film-Mediated Aggressive Models," pp. 3–11.

[35]Robert Zajonc, "Some Effects of the 'Space' Serials," *Public Opinion Quarterly*, 18 (November 1954): 367–74.

have relatively little effect.[36] "It is in the area of the unfamiliar, where parents have not yet made clear their own point of view and where the child has little real-life experience to use as a guideline, that TV influences beliefs and attitudes."[37]

OTHER FARE AND FUNCTIONS

It must be stated in all fairness that not all television material thrives on violence and unreality, and that many programs convey other images and values. In fact, some of the other ingredients may help to control or balance violence and unreality.

The Information Function

The mass media have the potential of adding to the emotional and intellectual growth of children. Selective exposure to television constitutes a liberal education: available are samplings of history, music, the arts, political science, anthropology, the behavioral sciences, and various physical and biological sciences. This encounter with the world of knowledge stimulates curiosity, communication, and verbal skills. Probably the main reason such positive effects have not been sufficiently researched is their nonproblematic nature. Positive effects are relatively inconspicuous because they are acceptable and do not arouse public concern.

The information function of television for children should not be underestimated. While children, like adults, watch television primarily for entertainment rather than for education and edification, they absorb much "incidental" information about society and the world. They become electronic cosmopolites and acquire a plethora of detailed knowledge, albeit not necessarily integrated in a meaningful manner. For example, the young television pundit may know the finer points of docking in outer space, can distinguish Picasso from Michelangelo, can become a connoisseur of styles and fashions, may understand the principle of biofeedback, and may know the latest in the world of sports. In addition, these stationary tourists become storehouses of such miscellany and trivia as the facts that whales' backs get sunburned and peel, you do not tip the stewardess on an airplane, Japan is

[36]The relative ineffectualness of television in trying to change a person's perception once definite images have been established was illustrated by a study with college students on election day in 1960. It was found that students with a definite image of and preference for a presidential candidate were hardly affected by the so-called Great Debate, the public television confrontation of the candidates. See Hans Sebald, "Limitations of Communication: Mechanisms of Image Maintenance in Form of Selective Perception, Selective Memory, and Selective Distortion," *Journal of Communication*, 12 (September 1962): 347–51.

[37]Maccoby, "The Effects of TV on Children," p. 125.

the size of California and has a population of over 100 million, and no one knows the cause or cure of arthritis.

One of the classic learning programs, *Sesame Street,* has had a particularly valuable function for children who are relatively isolated or culturally deprived.[38] Its entertaining format achieved success in learning complex cognitive processes as well as verbalizing them. The product of collaboration among educators, psychologists, writers, and artists, *Sesame Street* became a fast-paced variety show with humor, intelligence, and artistry. It became an international hit, winning youthful audiences the world over.

Through television, children learn about our society's division of labor and various types of occupations. The medium's "homogenization effect" breaks down complex occupational responsibilities into images children can understand. Sociologists Melvin and Lois DeFleur warn, however, that in the process of homogenization the world of work becomes stereotyped and oversimplified with superficial and even misleading cues.[39]

Promoting Social Change and Generational Conflict

Television also functions as a force for social change, since it makes social events so vivid and immediate that it creates a sense of involvement not experienced with other media. It can bring the Mideast conflict, the energy crisis, ecological disasters, and racial injustices into the living room as no other medium can. This tangible immediacy of current problems has contributed to the rise and perpetuation of youthful activism.

In fact, some media analysts believe that the power of American movies and TV programs played a primary role in bringing down the Iron Curtain and toppling Communism in Eastern Europe. People under Communist rule were able to tune into American programs and became inspired by the images that showed America radiating with freedom, democracy, and prosperity; they consequently demanded changes in their own societies.[40]

However, while the information function of TV has made youth keenly aware of social issues, it has underplayed the tedious and time-consuming inner workings of the democratic process and, instead, presented the "show business" side of the political apparatus. This reinforces the youthful activist's tendency to embark on political projects by direct intervention, demonstrations, and a variety of "the-voice-of-the-people" proclamations. Simplistic as this approach may appear, it has rendered useful functions by speeding the

[38]Gerald S. Lesser, *Children and Television: Lessons from Sesame Street* (New York: Random House, 1974).

[39]Melvin L. DeFleur and Lois B. DeFleur, "The Relative Contribution of TV as a Learning Source for Children's Occupational Knowledge," *American Sociological Review,* 32 (October 1967), 777–89.

[40]Carl Bernstein, "The Leisure Empire," *Time,* December 24, 1990, p. 56.

completion of long-overdue work on the part of legislators and politicians. The popularity of direct confrontation with the Establishment is reinforced by constant television exposure to shows of action and emotion, not words. Such conditioning leads more to action than logic or abstract negotiation.

Some social scientists are certain that the generation gap is in part perpetuated by the nature of television fare. Margaret Mead believed that television, more than anything else, brought about the confrontation between the generations by bringing actuality into the home and destroying many myths and half-truths adhered to by parents and teachers.[41] She assumed that television's reporting of reality gives youth a glimpse of the world and an orientation different from that of the parents.

In other words, children, by merit of more extensive exposure to the mass media, often are a step ahead of their parents when it comes to instantaneous information, though it may amount to mere trivia. This once more brings into focus the concept of the *halo effect*—that is, the youngster's tendency to engage in the arguable, inductive logic of starting with an isolated instance of parental ignorance and expanding it to arrive at general parental ignorance and backwardness.

There is a related dimension to this argument that should be mentioned. Realistic and often quite graphic reporting of the legions of cases of adult immaturity and incompetence—in the context of crime, drug abuse, infidelity, child abuse, and so forth—have exposed adult behavior patterns that adults have tried to hide from children since time immemorial. TV has broken up a tacit adult conspiracy to keep children in the dark about a certain range of adult behavior. This exposure is a new feature of our age. Although Margaret Mead may have overdrawn TV's role as the cause of the generation conflict, TV's contribution to the conflict is significant.

The Identification Function

Television fare can also serve as a medium for identification. While this has obvious psychological risks and can lead to aberrations of personal identity, it can also be of temporary comfort until concrete and more suitable models are found. This may be of special aid to children whose parents fail to function as adequate models. A primary task of adolescence is to consolidate one's identity and substantially answer the question "Who am I?" In order to accomplish this, the adolescent must learn something about the adult world and the appropriate roles in that world. He or she often turns to television for help.

One of the dangers of selecting models from television fare is that they are culturally stereotyped. Women on Words and Images, a special interest

---

[41]Margaret Mead, "Our Leaders Do Not Understand TV," *TV Guide*, December 6, 1969, pp. 10–15.

group of the women's liberation movement, completed a content analysis of 1974 prime-time television and found a surfeit of men among the major characters: in situation comedies, 55 percent of the characters were male; in adventure shows, men played 85 percent of the parts.[42] The diversity of male occupations portrayed was nearly twice that of females'. While men were more often depicted as confident, independent, worldly, and decisive—in short, competent—women were more than twice as likely as men to be incompetent, bungling opportunities, and making serious mistakes. In fact, approximately 20 percent of women's behavior consisted of such incompetent acts.

The study included the analysis of over 200 commercials during these shows. The stereotypes conveyed showed men working more, playing more, eating more, and getting sick more often. Women were shown to be primarily concerned with their appearance; after that, they did housework, shopped, cooked, and cared for others—including their sick males.

The "Contrast Effect"

Another imposition of TV on the female image deals with influencing the viewers' perception of physical attractiveness. Most actresses starring in movies and shows exhibit a physical beauty that—because of a highly selective process, the help of modern make-up, and skillful photographic techniques—can rarely be matched in everyday life and hence carry an element of unrealism. How do teenagers respond to this type of unrealistic beauty? For example, can the boys' normal, everyday girlfriends live up to these images? Do these images become expectations in the minds of the teenagers? Do the images inflict inferiority feelings on the girls? The question could, of course, be turned around to focus on unrealistically attractive male images. But, it seems, in American culture the burden to be beautiful weighs heavier on the female.

Psychologists at Arizona State University examined some of these questions by conducting experiments in which males were asked to rate a picture of a moderately attractive female as to dating desirability and attractiveness. Two groups of college men, depending whether or not they were watching *Charlie's Angels*, were selected in their dorms. The perceptions of the two groups were compared and it was found that the males viewing the highly attractive females on the *Charlie's Angels* series rated the photo of the moderately attractive females significantly less attractive than those who were not watching the program.[43]

---

[42]Women on Words and Images, *Channeling Children: Sex Stereotyping in Prime-Time TV* (Princeton, NJ, 1975).

[43]Douglas T. Kenrick and S. E. Gutierres, "Contrast Effect and Judgments of Physical Attractiveness: When Beauty becomes a Social Problem," *Journal of Personality and Social Psychology*, 38 (1980): 131–40.

The Arizona State University research series included situations where the experimental variable was the nude centerfold of such erotic magazines as *Playboy* and *Penthouse*. The findings showed that after having viewed the pictures college men subsequently downgraded the appearance of their girlfriends or mates. Experiments with groups of college women who were exposed to *Playgirl* centerfolds reacted similarly toward their boyfriends or mates, though not quite as strongly. Overall, psychologist Douglas Kendrick concluded, this type of mass media fare "spoils our perception of the 'average' looking person."[44]

In today's world where media exposure is at an all-time high, it seems possible that the "contrast effect," even with a limited span of effectiveness, could pose serious problems. It becomes a real possibility that an individual might reject or be less satisfied with a normally acceptable date or mate if the relationship is influenced by media exposure that conveys unrealistic levels of physical attractiveness—and possibly makes such levels the norm for everyone. This would be particularly crucial for adolescents, who are forming criteria for date and mate selection; they might confuse artificial media images with reality, seeking the former and rejecting the latter.

Similarly unrealistic are the standards of living depicted on the screen. Usually they are unrealistically high (or unrealistically low to provide contrast), and myriads of commercials are trying to engrain this as a fact in the child's perception. The basic question of "Who am I?" becomes tied to ephemeral and superficial commercialism that guarantees the viewer a front seat in the social-status circus if he or she just uses the right deodorant, mouthwash, toothpaste, flashy clothes, and stylish car. Any serious attempt to gain prestige and sincere recognition by peers on the basis of such commercial goading would most likely end in mental and social disasters of the person gullible enough to try. Fortunately, most adolescents have the ability to discern fake from fact. Nevertheless, as mentioned earlier, disappointments, inferiority complexes, and the constant effort of sorting out reality from fiction keep the young busy, while they could be spending their time more creatively.

The Modeling Function

A good deal of television fare is couched in stereotypes that suggest formulas to be emulated. This is particularly true of commercials, which advise youngsters to equate sugar with health and snacks with happiness, ignoring the lack of nutrition in most of these edibles. The television viewer is persuaded to consider him- or herself primarily as a consumer and is promised such rewards as being or looking like the glamorous, sexy female or

[44]Reported and quoted by Rob Kelton, "Skin," *State Press*, November 1, 1990, p. 3.

popular he-man who uses the product in the ads. But stereotypes presented on television lack empirical referents or are unavailable to the vast majority of viewers. While idealization can serve as a temporary comfort and an object of identification, in the long run there is the danger of frustration, especially for the adolescent who is generally hypersensitive about his or her appearance.

Reinforcing the Self-fulfilling Prophecy

One particularly insidious stereotype reinforced by television is the equation of "good looks" with "good personality." It is simple to figure out who's who in the movies and on television at one glance. The good guys are handsome, while the bad guys range from plain to ugly, and the same holds true for female counterparts. Unfortunately, the habit does not stop with the mass media—there is evidence that people tend to make the same judgments in real life. Studies by psychologist Karen K. Dion reveal that attractive children were judged less likely to commit offenses, or if they had, to repeat them in the future, and less likely to have antisocial dispositions.[45] Unattractive children, however, were regarded as more dishonest and unpleasant than their good-looking counterparts in similar circumstances. Transgressions committed by attractive children were considered less undesirable than the same acts committed by unattractive children. This prejudiced association has serious implications. First, good-looking children get away with more than plain-looking children; there is a tendency to punish and reprimand unequally. Second, reinforced stereotypes may become self-fulfilling prophecies, with the children assuming the roles ascribed to them. Evaluation by others ultimately tends to become self-evaluation: the unattractive child may grow up with an antisocial disposition simply because adults expect it.

Suppressing Creativity

Although television may be of some benefit to the culturally deprived child for whom it is a window to the outside world, it is better at contributing to existing interests than in stimulating intellectual activity. It is interesting to note that the upper-third IQ children in a study by Wilbur Schramm spent over an hour per day less watching television than the lower-third group.[46] Interviews with the more intelligent children disclosed that by the time they entered high school, television had ceased being a challenge to them and they therefore appropriated less time to viewing. Whether bright children are bright because they do not watch television, or whether they do not watch

[45]Karen K. Dion, "Physical Attractiveness and Evaluation of Children's Transgressions," *Journal of Personality and Social Psychology*, 24 (November 1972): 207–13.
[46]Schramm et al., *Television in the Lives of Our Children.*

television because they are bright, is, of course, an open question. At this time, it is simply stated as a correlation.

However, researchers are in agreement that TV viewing suppresses creativity, the ability to see new, effective solutions to problem situations, and the knack for the unique patterning of mental, physical, and artistic tasks. And this may be one of the most significant points that can be made about the nature of TV viewing. All studies that have touched on this topic have come to the same conclusion, not even exempting those programs acclaimed to be educational. Even if we allow for TV's role in enriching knowledge and vocabulary, the special quality of creativity remains negatively affected.

Why? The answer seems to lie in the fact that TV leaves strangely unstimulated the brain's capability for imagination; it fails to set into action the brain's synergetic activities, because all the action is completed on the screen: visual and auditory information complement the scene. These are information elements that must be imagined in a situation where the person reads: the printed word supplies the script, but the brain is called upon to supply the rest—the sound, the vision, the color. These demands constitute a bundle of challenging stimuli, revving up myriads of brain circuitries that now must do the job of imagining and completing the setting. Compared with this massive brain stimulation, mostly unconsciously processed by the reader, TV viewing is a dulling, ready-made, instantly consumed package that leaves no room for personal imagination and bypasses our creative faculties.

A number of dimensions that are usually thought to be related to creativity have been found affected negatively.

Critical thinking.   When persons become habituated to looking at a medium that is as anti-intellectual as television largely is, they develop a noncritical attitude and a disposition to "look without seeing."[47] Stanley Stern completed experiments with 250 intellectually gifted grade schoolers, dividing them into seven groups, and exposing six of them for several weeks to cartoons, educational television, sports, comedies, and dramas.[48] The seventh group was not exposed to television. The children took a battery of creativity tests before and after the experimental periods. Only the seventh group registered consistent improvement, while the other six showed a notable decline in all areas of creativity except verbal skill. Cartoons had the worst effect, but even educational programs decreased creativity scores.

---

    [47]Vigo A. Demant, "The Unintentional Influences of TV," *Cross Currents,* 5 (1955): 220–25.

    [48]Stanley Stern, "Creativity and TV—A Depressing Picture," *Psychology Today,* 7 (November 1973): 14–16.

Attention span. Yale psychologist Jerome Singer found that children who are heavy TV watchers tend to be more restless and poorer students. Apparently they expect all of life, including the educational process, to be an instantaneous and entertaining experience. "A teacher who is going into a lengthy explanation of an arithmetic problem will begin to lose the audience after a while. Children are expecting some kind of show."[49] Neil Postman, communications professor at New York University and the author of *Amusing Ourselves to Death,* concurs by pointing out that even the beloved *Sesame Street* has reinforced the TV-inspired notion that education must be fast-paced and entertaining. As a consequence, many children like school only if school is like *Sesame Street.*[50]

Logic. A good portion of TV programs exposes children to simplistic, faulty, or no logic at all. Since TV's orientation is primarily geared toward entertainment, logical elements are of minor importance, and what few such elements there are must not burden the viewer with too much brain work, for that would violate show business's definition of entertainment.

Literacy and articulation. TV fails to exercise our capability to articulate thought and sentiment. Whatever has to be said is being said on the screen and is usually said in the simplest and most superficial language. It would be difficult to derive from it any measure of sophistication usable for articulate speech, let alone writing. This explains the seeming paradox whereby high exposure may provide a better vocabulary but still fails to inspire articulateness: processing words and putting them into intelligible sentence structures is a task that demands skill beyond merely accumulating words. Norman Cousins put it this way: "Clean, precise writing or speaking requires systematic, sequential thought. Words have to be crafted, not sprayed. They need to be fitted together with infinite care."[51]

The suppression of this skill led Pico Iyer and others to use the adjective "postliterate" to describe the modern American population steeped in TV fare.[52] According to these scholars, by means of the TV set we have reverted in our culture to becoming a population using pictographs instead of thought-sculpting language. We increasingly resemble the habit of prehistoric tribes who scratched signs and rough pictures onto rocks. But even they had a revered place for the word—in an oral tradition that called for skill in telling and listening. Thomas Dooling summed up the point:

---

[49]Quoted by Richard Zoglin, "Is TV Ruining Our Children," *Time,* October 15, 1990, p. 75.

[50]Ibid.

[51]Norman Cousins, "The Communication Collapse," *Time,* December 17, 1990, p. 114.

[52]Pico Iyer, "History? Education?" *Time,* May 14, 1990, p. 75.

And why should young people be inspired to be articulate? In their steady fare of TV "drama," they see thought expressed, not in words, but by action— usually direct and brutal—accompanied by musical conventions. No wonder they are not verbal! They often communicate in shared visual experience: they watched the same TV show in which any words that may have been spoken are entirely eclipsed by the power of the visual image.[53]

Time Away from Real Social Interaction

One of the concerns voiced by a few social scientists is not so much what television does to the young but what the young are *not* doing while viewing. Semanticist S. I. Hayakawa pointed out that the average eighteen-year-old American has lost 22,000 hours of potential interaction with other human beings, and that, for all the value television may have, it cannot teach human interaction.[54] The loss may be reflected by lack of skill in social interaction later in life when many of them "express their thoughts in form of tantrums." There simply is no substitute for human interaction, which includes misunderstandings, expressing and solving problems, and getting to know people. Excessive television viewing detracts from this experience, precludes this experience. Vigo A. Demant supported this notion, saying that a group watching television "can no more be called a social interaction than a number of monologues in the same room is a conversation."[55] Additional views and studies demonstrate that television seriously inhibits family communication. An interesting study of Australian adolescents by W. J. Campbell found that they spent less time entertaining, dancing, visiting, playing, and talking to friends three years after television was introduced into their homes compared to before they had television.[56] The interpretation here again expresses concern that teenagers misappropriate time and miss out on interaction with family and peers.

Other researchers, however, disagree with the negative interpretation and believe that teenagers learn appropriate ways of social interaction by viewing television. Self-reports by teenagers indicate that they feel they learned appropriate behavior modes from watching dating, playing football, and family stories.[57] Whether the images accepted as adequate and realistic will turn out as real and dependable in life is, of course, a question that still has to be answered.

---

[53]Thomas Dooling, "Glory," *Parabola*, 8 (Summer 1983): 61.

[54]S. I. Hayakawa, "Image and Reality," *The Bulletin of the National Association of Secondary School Principals*, 53 (May 1969): 35–48.

[55]Demant, "The Unintentional Influences of TV," p. 223.

[56]W. J. Campbell, *TV and the Australian Adolescent* (Sydney: Angus and Robertson, 1966).

[57]Schramm et al., *Television in the Lives of Our Children.*

SUMMARY

Exposure of American children and adolescents to television is enormous. Among the themes and values projected are violence and unreality. Unreality can be divided into straightforward fantasy and deceptive description of reality. Most experts believe that fantasy is not harmful and, on the contrary, can be beneficial by stimulating creative thought. Pseudoreality, however, can mislead the young in their search for models.

Opinions on the effects of violence are divided between those who believe that violence serves a cathartic function and those who believe that it leads to imitation. Both camps present logical thought and empirical findings in defense of their interpretations. A point accepted by both is the susceptibility to imitative violence on the part of the disturbed child or adolescent. Also, high-exposure children lose sensitivity to violence and show no or greatly reduced reactions when viewing it.

The fact that the vast majority of American adolescents, in spite of growing up with violence-laced television, fail to engage in any violence indicates that control mechanisms are operative. They may include non-availability of necessary instruments of violence, parental indoctrination, fear of an unsuccessful ending, and effects of the general American ethos of decency and fair play. Yet, there is evidence that children are tempted to imitate the villain if they profit from it and "get away with it."

To more fully understand the impact of TV on the lives of our young, we must take into consideration the total social matrix in which they are enmeshed. Few studies have achieved such completeness. Where they have approximated it, they have found that media impact is significantly modified, positively or negatively, by such family background features as mothers' disposition, education, socioeconomic background, academic achievement, and other features.

TV viewing has been found to have multifarious functions: providing information, promoting social change and stimulating generational conflict, selecting models, causing a "contrast effect," reinforcing the self-fulfilling prophecy, ushering in a "postliterate" population with minimal ability for linguistic articulation, stealing time away from social interaction, and, perhaps most importantly, suppressing creativity.

11

Etiology and Dimensions
of Subculture

With this chapter we begin to shift the focus of our discussion from the individual adolescent to the youthful collectivity. The term collectivity is broad, nonspecific, and can refer to a subculture or to a counterculture or to anything in between. The following three chapters describe, first, the subculture, as it primarily pertains to mainstream-American high school youth, and, second, the counterculture, as a largely historical phenomenon of American culture that used to be carried by mostly older and politically oriented young adults.

Both are forms of youth collectivities and can be understood, at least to a large extent, as natural consequences of the adolescent experience in a postindustrial society. These collectivities provide the young with an environment in which they find fellowship, a sense of belonging, and a haven away from the world of the adults. The most important function of such belonging, temporary as it might be, consists of members dropping an emotional anchor and deriving an identity from it. Hence the youthful collectivity functions as a compensation for an adolescent experience that otherwise might be unbearably anomic.

This chapter is a general and theoretical treatment of the question of how subcultures evolve and are sustained. The dimensions that are suggested as generic to the rise of a subculture can be applied to the general teen subculture as well as to specific youth movements. To start, we present a theoretical exploration of the development and dimensions of subculture.

DEFINITIONS AND DIMENSIONS

The conceptualization of subculture is beset with at least two major problems. First, sociologists are unclear as to the specific dimensions that characterize a subculture. Although the literature reflects suggestions concerning some subcultural elements, the notions are not followed up by a concerted effort to integrate, systematize, and apply them. The second problem deals with the frustrating fact that the suggested definitions are too general and lack operationability. An example is the definition stating that subculture "refers to norms that set a group apart from, not those that integrate a group with, the total society."[1] This definition is so general that, while it cannot fail to be theoretically correct, it is practically unusable in actual research. Another example is the proposal to combine a number of factors, such as "ethnic group, social class, region, occupation, religion, and urban and rural residence."[2] Again, these factors lack operational specifications. Finally, to epitomize the sociological disregard for the concept, Fairchild's *Dictionary of Sociology* did not even have the word *subculture* as a listing.[3]

Since *culture* refers to a blueprint of behavior for an entire society, the largest human grouping, *subculture* refers to the blueprint for behavior of a smaller group within the society. This subsidiary blueprint is frequently formed without the encouragement, acceptability, or full cognizance of the "parent culture." It is a special blueprint that accommodates a number of people whose needs and desires are not provided for by the main blueprint of society. Thus, there are subcultures for narcotic addicts, longshoremen, inmates in prison, Texas oilmen, those in the world of fashion, jazz musicians — and adolescents.

A subculture can be defined by its *functions*. As noted above, the general function of the subculture is to compensate for the failure of the main culture to provide a definite status, a feeling of acceptance, and need-satisfactions unique to a certain group of people. To accomplish these functions and to make the subculture a viable process, a number of prerequisites must be met.

Eight dimensions are proposed as basic elements of subculture: (1) Relatively unique (or uniquely accentuated) values and norms. (2) In-group lingo

[1]Milton J. Yinger, "Contraculture and Subculture," *American Sociological Review*, 25 (October 1960): 628.

[2]Milton M. Gordon, "The Concept of the Subculture and its Application," *Social Forces*, 25 (October 1947): 41.

[3]H. P. Fairchild, ed., *Dictionary of Sociology* (Totowa, NJ: Littlefield, Adams & Co., 1968).

not shared with the larger society. (3) Distinct channels of (mass) communication not shared with or dependent on "outsiders." (4) Unique styles and fads (including grooming, dress, gesture, and other behavioral patterns) often resulting in subcultural ritual. (5) A sense of solidarity and *esprit de corps* manifested by thinking in terms of "we" instead of "me and them" (or simply the cogency of in-group versus out-group sentiments). (6) Status criteria in terms of cognizing them and adhering to them in actual peer relationships. In other words, existence of a working order of social positions—at a minimum, clarifying what makes for prestige, leadership, and follower. (7) Influence and power of leaders enhancing the identity and *esprit de corps* of the collectivity. This is the dimension of *charisma*. (8) Gratification of specific needs that the larger social structure fails to provide. The significance of this item is the subcultural institutionalization of need fulfillment.

A methodological paradigm has been proposed for consistent use of the eight dimensions in examining collectivities concerning their degree of subcultureness.[4] This design provides a tool that, if consistently applied, would promote comparability of different research findings, greater reliability in following the fluctuations of a subculture over its lifetime, and, most important, a measurement in terms of *degree of subcultural quality*. It was customary to dichotomously answer the question whether a certain collectivity is a subculture with either "yes" or "no"—a method totally inconsistent with reality and with most procedures in other matters of sociological endeavor. Qualities always exist in terms of degree, and methods of analysis must be responsive to this fact. Therefore, a paradigm measuring collectivities as to their degree of subcultural quality is necessary.

The above mentioned definitional dimensions, enumerating major functions of the subculture, must be checked against the youth subculture to see whether there is enough empirical evidence to bear out some degree of subcultural salience:

1. Young people have derived from their interaction a peculiar set of *norms and values* that no longer consists of child standards nor is part of the adult world.
2. They speak an *argot* that is not shared with adults. In fact, it is only partially understood by outsiders and is often unacceptable to the Establishment.
3. Youth's channels of *mass communication* consist of mingling in youth "ghettos" (the high schools), various "underground" media (youth newspapers), and their own programs via general mass media (radio, television, etc.).
4. Young Americans cultivate their own independent *styles and fads*, and are unwilling to share them with adults. For example, teenage grooming and hair

---

[4]The technical aspects of the subcultural paradigm are discussed in Hans Sebald, "Subculture: Problems of Definition and Measurement," *International Review of Modern Sociology*, 5 (Spring 1975): 82–89.

styles led to vehement confrontations during the late 1960s and early 1970s. The young tend to change a style as soon as adults imitate it.

5. Adolescents acquire a *primary-group belonging* in which they are accepted as total individuals. Peer involvement functions as a partial substitute for the teenagers' families, which they leave gradually to establish personal autonomy. The adolescent peer group helps young individuals in their emancipation from parental control.

6. Youths derive *status relationships* that make them predictable in peer interaction. Status criteria help to ameliorate the lack of social status during the transition from child to adult. The peer group also provides criteria and models that allow emulation during a time when such models in the adult society are either lacking or too frightening.

7. They are receptive to *charismatic leadership*. The world of the American teenager includes outstanding and famous personalities who, if not precisely leaders, function as heroes. The charismatic aura of such heroes is entirely a function of teenage hero worship.

8. Adolescents have needs, problems, and anxieties for which the adult social structure makes only partial allowance. Hence, young Americans have come to work out their own substructures over the years. This *institutionalization of patterns of need-fulfillment* is probably the most powerful indicator of how far a given collectivity has matured into a subculture—or even a counterculture. (Here we approach the study of social movements and of social change.) The highly subculturized—or counterculturized—activities of American youth during the tumultuous late 1960s and early 1970s can serve as an example. The collective behavior of youth during that period indicated a high degree of social structure. Among the behavior patterns—patterns consistent and recurring enough to justify the application of the concept of subcultural institutionalization—were how food was supplied and distributed, legal aid, entertainment, psychiatric first aid, business, education, and literature.

The most salient of the dimensions deals with the establishment of social institutions within a collectivity markedly separate from the main society. I call these internal structures—dedicated to specific need fulfillment—*subcultural institutionalization*. It is this enmeshing of persons in their own segregated social structure that is of utmost importance to sociology, since structural arrangements result in regular patterns of human behavior and relationships.

It should be added that subcultural institutionalization usually arises only when a sense of solidarity prevails. Conversely, a latent function of the new specialized substructure that fulfills needs is a reinforcement of the *esprit de corps*. Subinstitutionalization often allows for behavior that would not be permitted within the structure of the larger society. In so doing, subinstitutionalization enables relatively new forms of behavior, of which drug use is an example. Some subinstitutionalizations, however, merely establish counterparts to already available avenues in the larger society. Many forms of dating, entertainment, and recreational activities are examples. In general, the desire for exclusivity, freedom from adult supervision, and unique styling determines the contours of subinstitutionalization.

THE QUESTION OF ETIOLOGY

What are the conditions and processes that make for the emergence of a subculture? It seems that the *necessary condition* for the emergence of a subculture is the existence of a *number of persons* in society who seek solutions to common problems and who *effectively interact* with one another.

It might be added that every collective segment of society has its own problems. Certain social categories, determined, for example, by age, sex, race, ethnicity, or occupation, exhibit unique problems. "The structure of society generates, at each position within the system, characteristic combinations of personality and situation and therefore characteristic problems of adjustment."[5]

The early formative stage of subculture, before the in-group structure and the norms and values become firmly established, includes a process of "exploratory gestures." This process consists of mutual explorations and joint elaborations of possible solutions, often accompanied by mass-communicative and/or physical (crowds, mobs) interchanges during which a set of common sentiments is recognized and subsequently reinforced.

The *sufficient conditions* for the establishment of a subculture lie in the acceptance of common norms and values specifying the "proper" way of doing things. When a sufficiently elaborate corollary of symbols has become the unique property of the persons involved, a collective identity has been born. One can then speak of a subcultural or a new cultural form "because each actor's participation in this system is influenced by his perception of the same norms in fellow actors."[6]

Membership in such a group or category ordinarily functions not merely as a problem-solving device in a narrow and technical sense, but also as a source of values, which ultimately has formative influence on the individual's self-perception. The price for gaining a clearly defined frame of reference is conformity to the norms of the group. In return, the member has access to ready-made conclusions, solutions, and peer-approved actions that help to solve a number of conflicts and ambiguities. There are compelling incentives not to deviate from the established ways of the group: fear of disapproval or even ostracism by the peers and fear of an inhospitable larger culture combine to keep the member within the confines of the subculture.

A collectivity of individuals becomes subcultural only when its system of norms and values is significantly different from the main culture. The solutions to the problems of the given collectivity are embodied in the larger society neither in terms of structural provision nor, frequently, in terms of

---

[5]Albert K. Cohen, *Delinquent Boys: The Culture of the Gang* (New York: Free Press, 1955), p. 55.

[6]Ibid., p. 65.

cultural acceptability. The new solutions may conflict with society's traditions and may result in the collectivity being labeled deviant, thereby generating antagonism and mistrust between the larger and the smaller social systems. From the subcultural point of view, the so-called deviant-solution approach may more effectively ameliorate needs and problems than the existing solutions institutionalized in the larger society. In addition, members of the subculture frequently do not feel that their activities could harm individuals inside or outside of their group and thus see no reason to change their patterns. As a result, they tend to perceive their activities not only as effective but also as justified.

New solution approaches and the symbols of subcultural membership may, from the outsider's point of view, be perceived as relatively haphazard and undefined behavior. For the in-group members, however, it is structured and well defined. This misconception on the part of outside observers arises because of a tendency to judge unfamiliar behavior in terms of one's own values, not realizing that the seemingly nonconformist behavior actually conforms to subcultural expectations.

One of the aspects most often ignored by observers is the subculture's different criteria for ascribing prestige. Frequently the members of the subculture, prior to their joining, have encountered serious obstacles in the path of achieving status in the larger society—a condition certainly true of adolescents. Within the confines of a subculture there are opportunities for achieving status and respect. The solution for teenagers who share this predicament of unclear status in the adult world is, therefore, to gravitate toward one another and jointly establish new criteria of status that describe as meritorious those characteristics they *do* possess and the kinds of activities of which they *are* capable. This, quite obviously, is a group approach to an individual problem. If an individual adolescent tried to establish such criteria alone, he or she would probably not only fail to achieve status in the larger society, but would suffer total isolation.

The usual side effect of joining a new status system that encourages behavior frowned on by the larger social system is an inverse correlation: the more the individual gains status in the new group, the more he or she will lose status outside the group.

Belonging to and depending on a subculture usually has far-reaching effects on the personality of its follower. The influence may be strong enough to provide the nature of one's identity. Indeed, the decision to join a subculture is normally indicative of the person's need for a clear identity. The subculture, then, comes to function as an important psychological refuge.

A chapter on the development of subcultures is not complete unless it describes, at least briefly, pertinent etiological theories. Among the models purporting to explain the origin of subcultures are the psychogenic, culture-transmission, and behavioristic. Familiarity with these theoretical frameworks aids in understanding specific elements in the complex process of subcultural development. Although they represent different ways of looking at the empirical phenomenon, they are not incompatible but rather complementary, emphasizing different aspects of the process.

The Psychogenic Model

The basic assumption of this theory is that a subculture evolves from problems of adjustment that are common to a large number of persons. Emphasis is on the independence with which individuals contrive solutions. The individual is depicted as a creative innovator. Although the role of the social milieu as the genesis of the problem is recognized, its role in determining the solution is minimized. New cultural forms emerge as a *parallel* development of individual solutions, which, more or less unaccountably, merge into a collective entity. The aspect of the subcultural development that is unaccounted for in this framework is the process of social interaction as a necessary condition during the incipient phase.

The psychogenic approach views teenage behavior as an effort to solve the problems characteristic of the frustrating sojourn in adolescence. The adolescent, standing between child and adult statuses and being devoid of a clearly structured social position, may frequently ponder the agonizing question of who he or she really is and come face to face with the issue of identity. Erik Erikson, Gordon Bronson, Margaret Mead,[7] and others maintain that the major task facing the adolescent is the search for meaningful identity. This task is more difficult in the modern urban-industrial setting than in smaller folk or tribal societies. The rapid pace of social change, exposure to a confusing variety of secular and religious value systems, and revolutionary technological innovations make the world appear too relativistic and unpredictable to provide the teenager with a stable frame of reference.

Modern teenagers experience an abstract introduction to life, which results in the perception of the world as complex and ambiguous. They have difficulties in seeing just where and how they fit in. Their escape attempt leads them to other teenagers, and this subculture offers them a subcultural identity. In the process of maintaining this identity, special clothes, language, and attitudes toward the world play an important role in symbolizing belonging.

While the psychogenic model appears to accurately reflect empirical processes, it is limited in its explanatory *range*, unable to give an explanation of the exact nature of the *formative* process of the collectivity. One of the more unexplored areas in sociology remains the analysis of the bridging

---

[7]Erik H. Erikson, *Childhood and Society* (New York: W. W. Norton & Co., 1963); Gordon W. Bronson, "Identity Diffusion in Late Adolescence," *Journal of Abnormal and Social Psychology*, 59 (November 1959): 414–17; and Margaret Mead, "The Young Adult," in *Values and Ideals of American Youth*, ed. E. Ginzberg (New York: Columbia University Press, 1961), pp. 37–51.

process that leads from individual problems to the actual beginnings of subculture.

The Culture-transmission Model

This theory is concerned with the perpetuation of an already established subculture by transmission of its values and unique behavior patterns from one generation to the next. It is interested more in understanding the *learning process* whereby, for example, the younger teenagers acquire their older peers' modes of thought and actions than in understanding the *prime* origin of these subcultural patterns. The limited scope of the approach often excludes from consideration those crucial problems that render each new generation susceptible to the established subcultural form. At the most, this theory suggests a number of plausible mechanisms of subcultural transmission, such as the learning of rules that lend orientation and direction to the life of the teenager and the role of the mass media in disseminating these rules and ideas.

Mass media, especially television and teen magazines,[8] are probably the most effective mechanisms for perpetuating the teenage subculture. Mass media offer ready-made solutions to teenagers and promise to save them the effort of searching for new forms. David L. Altheide makes this point forcefully: "Youth culture is both a product and a target of the media . . . The development of youth as an idea was a by-product of media culture and the discovery that young people could consume."[9]

A specific example of this process was the rise of rock music. It actually *changed* American youth, helped to create a self-conscious teen generation, and perpetuated this self-consciousness from generation to generation of teenagers. Before the 1950s there was no music, or any other medium, that enveloped so powerfully the feelings and behavior of young Americans. Rock music spoke clearly to the interests and needs of adolescents. "It defined the correct behavior . . . and noted the irrelevance of school routines as compared with the realities of fast cars, surfing, and the exhilaration of dancing. Throughout rock lyrics there were pointed contrasts between the teen way of life and the behavioral norms imposed by adults."[10]

The idea that rock music was a significant carrier of youth culture is further developed by Bernice Martin. Rock music evolved into what became probably the most truculent vehicle, telling, as it were, the epic story of

---

[8]Charles H. Brown, "Self-Portrait: The Teen-Type Magazine," *Annals of the American Academy of Political and Social Sciences*, 338 (November 1961): 20.

[9]David L. Altheide, "Mass Media and Youth Culture," *Urban Education*, 2 (July 1979): 224.

[10]R. A. Peterson and D. G. Berger, "Three Eras in the Manufacture of Popular Music Lyrics," in Denisoff and Peterson, eds., *The Sounds of Social Change* (Chicago: Rand McNally, 1972), p. 296.

American adolescence. Rock music became a sacrament; it interpreted agonies, joys, the holy and the unholy in the lives of teenagers. Martin visualized the role of rock music as symbolizing the "sacred" in youth culture, not unlike the need to symbolize the "sacred" in primitive tribal society. The feeling of *Communitas,* belonging together, is expressed by "ritualized symbols of group identity particularly in the beat of music, in common fashions and through the star performer who acts as sacred 'totem.' "[11]

In summary, the media facilitate connections between adolescents and perpetuate certain themes. These themes dwell on solving problems of loneliness, confusion, and alienation from adult society. They are embodied in songs, the beat of rock music, TV programs, movies, teen magazines (particularly those with "Letter" departments), and the actual physical mingling of teenagers in their ghettos—the school campuses, gangs, dance places, and rock concerts. These lyrics, rhythms, programs, stories, statements, and places are the media for communicating and transmitting subcultural thought and behavior. Needless to say, these media are powerful conditioners, often commercially exploiting the need of teenagers to communicate with other teenagers.

The Behavioristic Model

Although behaviorism has neglected to apply its framework to the question of subcultural formation and to formulate a precise etiological theory, it is capable of pointing out significant steps in the process of converting adolescents into members of teenage subcultures. It would be presumptuous to attempt to present a complete picture of the behavioristic approach in this limited context; a few remarks must suffice.

Behavioristic principles to explain the rise of a subculture resemble the psychogenic model. The point of departure again is the frustrations that youths experience during adolescence. If tensions and frustrations are equated with pain, one finds American teenagers frequently exposed to it when interacting with adults who technically would be called *aversive stimuli.* To carry the process to its logical conclusion, it follows that teenagers try to avoid this type of stimulus and hence tend to withdraw from the adult world. This type of behavior is defined as *escape behavior.*[12] The reaction is common to most adolescents since the same *hedonistic principle* applies to all. On the escape route the adolescent meets other adolescents who have similar problems. Through interaction among themselves, adolescents discover that they

---

[11]Bernice Martin, "The Sacralization of Disorder: Symbolism in Rock Music," *Sociological Analysis,* 40, 2 (1979): 87.

[12]See, for technical treatment and definition, Arthur W. Staats and Carolyn K. Staats, *Complex Human Behavior: A Systematic Extension of Learning Principles* (New York: Holt, Rinehart & Winston, 1964), p. 44.

are free of stringent adult expectations, which they have found difficult to meet and accept. As a result, they experience a lessening of tension and frustration. Interaction among peers consists of stimuli that are gratifying to teenagers and can be called *positive reinforcers*, which are usually more powerful than negative reinforcers because they allow enjoyment of common activities and interests. Thus, independently from adolescent problems, normal gregarious activities help to sustain the peer culture.

In the final analysis, these two types of reinforcers, the negative (escape from frustration) and the positive (finding security and the gratification), effectively establish and perpetuate the subcultural milieu.

There is still another aspect of the adolescent phenomenon that can effectively be explained by behavioristic principles. It deals with the consequences of *inconsistent stimuli*. In one instance adolescents are told to be responsible and independent, while in another instance they may be prevented from showing responsibility. In many cases, they are expected to show responsibility and independence concerning vocational preparation, but must obtain their parents' permission in questions of finances, dating, and marriage.

Such inconsistent stimuli are also definable as inconsistent and ambivalent role expectations, as mixing a number of elements from the adult and the child roles.

Inconsistent stimuli due to such unclear role expectations tend to produce ambivalent behavior—sometimes defined as neurosis.[13] The initial reactions to such ambivalent conditioning include frustration and tension. Eventually, this frustration makes the adolescent choose the less frustrating conditioning system of the peer culture with its simpler and more consistent processes.

DISAGREEMENTS ON THE EXISTENCE OF THE TEENAGE SUBCULTURE

Although this book relies on the assumption that the teenage subculture is a real fact in life, some academics hold different views. As has been pointed out in the discussion on peer-parent conflict and the autonomy process (Chapter 8), opinions range from affirmative to negative.

Clarity of the argument is impaired by lack of a consensual definition of subculture, illustrating the dilemma mentioned in the first section of this chapter.

---

[13]Behavioristically inclined psychologists have demonstrated the effect of ambivalent conditioning in laboratory situations using animals as their subjects. They found that inconsistent conditioning can result in neurotic disturbances, possibly to the extent of a so-called nervous breakdown. See, for example, Jules H. Masserman, *Behavior and Neurosis* (Chicago: University of Chicago Press, 1943).

The criterion of subculture that appears of pivotal significance to the discussants is "unique values and norms." The proponents who assume a youth subculture feel that there is substantial indication for the existence of this dimension; on the other side, there are some academics who think that there is not enough evidence for the existence of a youth/adult rift in values.

The argument of the *proponents* can be summed up by three related assumptions:

1. The typical adolescent is characterized by symptoms that can be described as socially caused "storm and stress." These expressions stem primarily from the adolescent's uncertain position in the social structure. Some of the confusions and insecurities typical of the American adolescent arise from uncertainty of occupational choice, difficulties in identifying with adult models, inconsistencies in authority relationships, conflicts between generations, sexual frustrations because of conflict between physiological maturation and social prohibitions, and discontinuity in socialization patterns.

2. A teenage subculture exists and is powerful and widespread. The youth subculture is a social reaction to the young individuals' uncertain statuses in the adult world and eases the transition from childhood to adulthood. The subculture is particularly dominant in metropolitan areas, exerting far-reaching demands on its followers, creating a feeling of belonging and a status system that judges behavior by subcultural standards. James S. Coleman's large-scale surveys concluded that the American adolescent is progressively becoming more ensconced in secondary institutions, from nursery school through college:

> He is "cut off" from the rest of society, forced inward toward his own age group, made to carry out his whole social life with others his own age. With his fellows, he comes to constitute a small society, one that has most of its important interactions *within* itself, and maintains only a few threads of connection with the outside adult society. In our modern world of mass communication and rapid diffusion of ideas and knowledge, it is hard to realize that subcultures can exist right under the very noses of adults—subcultures with languages all their own, with special symbols, and, most important, with value systems that may differ from adults.[14]

Talcott Parsons thinks that the characteristics of the adolescent subculture include three main aspects: (a) the rebelliousness of youth against adult expectations and authority; (b) the tendency toward peer conformity, guarded by considerable in-group intolerance of differences; and (c) a romantic adherence to emotionally significant objects.[15] Robin M. Williams, Jr., contends that the social distance between generations is sometimes so great

---

[14]James S. Coleman, *The Adolescent Society* (New York: Free Press, 1963), p. 3.

[15]Talcott Parsons, "Psychoanalysis and the Social Structure," *Psychoanalytic Quarterly*, 19 (July 1950): 378–79.

that parents and children confront each other as members of vastly different subcultures.[16] Arnold W. Green believes in the existence of a teenage subculture and calls it a "world of irresponsibility, specialized lingo, dating, athleticism, and the like, which rather sharply cuts off adolescent experience from that of the child and from that of the adult."[17]

3. The concluding assumption suggests a causal relationship between "storm and stress" and the teenage subculture, implying that affiliation with peers provides a structured social environment and personal identity. The subcultural arrangement is reinforced and its survival guaranteed by the satisfaction the teenagers derive from having found status among peers.

Most of the opponents to the subculture theory have completed studies—mostly small in scale—from which they concluded that the difference in values between adolescents and adults is not large enough to call the young's attitudes a separate value system. In fact, these researchers conclude that parental values are socially inherited by the offspring and manifested in the youngsters' choices of peer affiliation and value orientation. They concede, however, that there may be differences in norms, the rules and the means of doing things and achieving certain goals (goals that are synonymous with values and presumably coincide with those of the parents). The young, hence, may sometimes resort to deviant means to achieve such basic goals as status, success, and material gains. While it is an essential purpose of the socialization process to teach the young the proper means, some researchers feel that the basic goals are "naturally" learned and imitated.

It is possible that these researchers mistakenly equate basic human needs, such as seeking security, acceptance, expression, and new experience within the peer environment, with the cultural values of American society. In other words, the equation of seeking acceptance among peers (by cooperation and sporting material accessories) with the cultural values of cooperation and materialism of the adult world is spurious. The young's seeming imitation of cultural goals is really nothing more than their way of coping with a peer situation.

Also, much of the research findings meant to deflate the subculture theory are based on highly specific and nongeneralizable samples. For example, Frederich Elkin and William A. Westley's mid-1950s study resulted in a widely publicized and often quoted dissent from the subculture theory, since they found the teenagers of a Montreal suburb more integrated in the adult society—its customs, norms, and values—than was generally thought.[18] Family ties were close, and the degree of family consensus was high. The adoles-

---

[16]Robin M. Williams, Jr., *American Society: A Sociological Interpretation* (New York: Knopf, 1960), p. 80.

[17]Arnold W. Green, *Sociology* (New York: McGraw-Hill, 1968), p. 113.

[18]Frederich Elkin and William A. Westley, "The Myth of Adolescent Culture," *American Sociological Review*, 20 (December 1955): 680–84.

cents acknowledged their parents' right to guide them and set rules concerning dating practices, discussed their choice of school courses and vacation plans with parents, and often engaged in joint parent-child activities, such as parties, dances, and community sports events. Parents expressed few complaints about socialization problems or peer group activities of their teenage children, and the continuities of socialization were more striking than the discontinuities. In short, the patterns of the adolescents' social lives were not significantly different from those of the older generation, and adolescents demonstrated "adult" perspectives.

Despite the highly specific character of the study the findings were widely generalized, disregarding the fact that the data were derived from interviews of a sample of only twenty adolescents and their parents and from life-history material of another twenty teenagers. This selection is by no means an adequate sample from which to safely draw conclusions about American teenagers in general—especially when the researchers themselves admitted that the sample may not have been completely representative even of the community from which it was taken. Also, allowance should be made for possible differences between Canadian and American teenagers. Montreal, heavily influenced by English and French traditions, may have a different type of teenager than most cities in the United States. Moreover, the locale of the research was a well-to-do suburb, classified by the authors as upper-middle-class, where "typically, when a girl gives a party, she sends out formal invitations, and her guest list includes those she *should* invite as well as those she wants to invite. The girls take great pains to play their hostess roles properly, and the boys strongly recognize their escort responsibilities."[19]

The formal manner of social interaction in this suburb seems to be more typical of the United States upper class than of the broad middle class. Since the present focus is more on adolescents of the broad American middle class, Elkin and Westley's study has minimal relevance.

Other advocates of nondifferentiated youth-adult culture include psychologist Albert Bandura, who has argued that the "storm and stress" of adolescents has been exaggerated and that parents and teenagers are more in agreement than in conflict.[20] L. Eugene Thomas revealed that children of highly politicized parents tend to be like their parents both in political attitude and political behavior.[21] Elizabeth Douvan and her coworkers consistently discovered harmonious youth-parent relationships.[22] Reuben Hill and

[19]Ibid., p. 682.

[20]Albert Bandura, "The Stormy Decade: Fact or Fiction," in *Issues in Adolescent Psychology*, ed. D. Rogers (New York: Prentice-Hall, 1972).

[21]L. Eugene Thomas, "Family Correlates of Student Political Activism," *Developmental Psychology*, 4 (March 1971): 206–14.

[22]Elizabeth Douvan and Joseph Adelson, *The Adolescent Experience* (New York: John Wiley, 1966), and Elizabeth Douvan and H. Gold, "Modal Patterns in American Adolescence," in *Review of Child Development Research*, vol. 2, ed. L. Hoffman and M. Hoffman (New York: Russell Sage Foundation, 1966).

J. Aldous, Jr. found that religious beliefs remain relatively stable between generations.[23] Daniel Offer et al. try to explain adults' concern about a teen subculture as a misconceived view of their offspring's growth of independence. That is, parents overemphasize the influence of the peer group and "use the peer group as an externalized object and influence that provides a reference group for expressions of dissatisfaction with their offspring."[24]

What the latter authors are trying to say is, more plainly, that parents have invented a teen subculture to use it as a scapegoat for the complaints they have about their kids. This is a surprising psychoanalytic exercise for writers who, throughout their work, vehemently dispute the validity of any psychoanalytic notion. The Offer team ostensibly relies directly on the responses they have collected from their surveys and claims that "data collected directly from normal adolescents are often significantly different from what many adults assume teenagers feel about themselves."[25] That may well be so, but what the data mean becomes a matter of *interpretation*. By taking teenagers' statements verbatim, they actually fail to make an interpretation at all. What teenagers say may not adequately reveal what they really feel and experience. To conclude that if teenagers don't verbalize turmoil (and the subcultural compensation for it), then such a phenomenon does not exist is less than insightful. In sum, it appears, the Offer team holds an a priori bias according to which there is no subculture.

THE DIVERSITY OF TEENAGE SUBCULTURES

One of the more justified criticisms of the portrayal of the youth subculture deals not so much with the basic question of whether it does or does not exist, but how diversified it is. This criticism calls attention to the fact that there is no uniform subculture for all teenagers, but a number of significantly different versions. Many sociologists deplore the blanket application of the concept "teenage subculture" because it implies a monolithic membership group for all teenagers. They remind us of important differences in peer culture based on such variables as socioeconomic class, age, race, ethnicity, and rural or urban residence. For example, a black inner-city teenager living in the slums exhibits different values, has a different outlook on life, and belongs to a different type of peer culture than a white middle-class teenager growing up in suburbia.

For the purpose of communication, subcultural diversity must be sim-

[23]Reuben Hill and J. Aldous, Jr., "Socialization for Marriage and Parenthood," in *Handbook of Socialization Theory and Research*, ed. D. Goslin (Chicago: Rand McNally, 1969).

[24]Daniel Offer, Eric Ostrov, and Kenneth I. Howard, *The Adolescent: A Psychological Self-Portrait* (New York: Basic Books, 1981), p. 122.

[25]Ibid., p. 121. Also see Daniel Offer et al., *The Teenage World. Adolescents' Self-Image in Ten Countries* (New York: Plenum, 1988).

plified by some arbitrary guidelines: when the unqualified terms *youth subculture* or *teenage peer culture* or a synonymous phrase appears, reference is made to the nondelinquent middle class, reaching over into the upper-lower socioeconomic stratum. The teenage groups, cliques, campus crowds, and so on of this socioeconomic range are characterized by their independence from and usually nonviolent rejection of many adult standards, their conformity to peer-group patterns, their observance of teenage fads and fashions, their romanticism, and their participation in hedonistic activities. Specific expressions may include distinct ways of dressing, grooming, and talking. Their argot, representing a relatively exclusive communication system, is not shared with adults.

The upper socioeconomic class of the American population can hardly be said to have a youth subculture. In that social stratum one would most likely encounter the type of nonadolescent youth who is integrated in his or her family and special community and who suffers little status uncertainty— often to the point where there is no need for a compensating teenage subculture.

On the other side, lower-class youths live a subcultural life that has its own ethos. Anthropologist Walter B. Miller suggested a culturistic etiology of delinquency and tried to explain youthful offenses by a particular lower-class set of values and problems that increase the probability of law violations.[26] Over years of observing and analyzing lower-class street-corner groups, Miller discovered a number of "focal concerns" of lower-class culture that set it distinctly apart from other positions in the social order. These focal concerns include "trouble," "toughness," "smartness," "excitement," "fate," and "autonomy." They should not be understood as being in opposition to the law, but rather as helping to bring about the circumstances that invite criminal behavior. For example, the search for excitement may lead to auto theft, and the stress on toughness may encourage not only verbal insult, but physical violence as a retribution for it.

Other criminologists feel, however, that a youngster's membership in a delinquent subculture is better explained by "differential opportunities." Richard A. Cloward and Lloyd E. Ohlin, for example, think that there is more than one delinquent subculture among working-class youth and that a main goal of research should be to detect how selections of delinquency adaptations are made.[27] According to the theory, these selections depend more on characteristics of community organization than on psychological differences among delinquents. In other words, types of delinquency depend on types of illegitimate opportunities which, in turn, are primarily dependent on features

---

[26]Walter B. Miller, "Lower-Class Culture As a Generating Milieu of Gang Delinquency," *Journal of Social Issues,* 14 (1958): 5–19.

[27]Richard A. Cloward and Lloyd E. Ohlin, *Delinquency and Opportunity: A Theory of Delinquent Gangs* (Glencoe, IL: The Free Press, 1960).

of the community. Cloward and Ohlin specified three major types of delinquent subculture adaptations and called them *criminal-oriented, conflict-oriented,* and *retreatist-oriented.* These types differ in activity patterns as well as in etiological conditions. In terms of behavior, the criminalistic form concentrates on systematic theft as a way of life and a major avenue for upward social mobility into the world of organized crime. The conflict form is the result of disorganized communities in which traditional institutions of control have been rendered ineffective by high population mobility or diversity. The retreatist form provides isolation from conventional values and persons, and focuses on "kicks" through drugs, alcohol, and sex. In this form, steady work is eschewed in preference to "getting by," and the art of being "cool" is practiced.

A special type of delinquency has become notorious over the past few decades: youth-ghetto delinquency in the form of school vandalism. A 1980 report shows that 110,000 teachers, 5 percent of the U.S. total, were assaulted by students, an increase of more than 50 percent over the annual rate of the late 1970s. For example, school muggings, lawsuits, thefts, and vandalism in 1980 cost Los Angeles schools over $100 million while city and school officials were stymied over jurisdictional problems.[28]

The diversity of juvenile subcultures has been summed up:[29]

The "parent" male subculture.   This is the small gang, described as non-utilitarian, malicious, negativistic, versatile, and characterized by short-run hedonism. It is referred to as "parent" subculture because it is the most common and generic collective delinquency form.

The conflict-oriented subculture.   This is usually a highly developed form of collective delinquency, exhibited in large gangs, the membership of which may run into the hundreds. They have an elaborate organization that often includes such roles as president, vice-president, war-chief, and armorer. They have a territorial base, a name, a strong sense of corporate identity, and a public personality or "rep" in the gang world.

The drug-addict subculture.   There is usually a correlation between drug addiction and delinquency. In most cases, the addicts were already delinquent before grouping themselves into subcultures. Their delinquency is almost always of the nonviolent and income-producing type that makes their drug habit possible.

[28]"Help! Teacher Can't Teach!" *Time,* June 16, 1980, p. 63.
[29]Albert K. Cohen and James F. Short, Jr., "Research in Delinquent Subcultures," *Journal of Social Issues,* 14 (1958): 20–37.

Semiprofessional theft. This is a loosely integrated forerunner of the subculture of professional adult thieves proficient in ordinarily nonviolent thievery. In a sense, it is a stage in the life history, a specialized delinquency before ascending to the elite thievery of the adult professionals.

The middle-class delinquent subculture. Cohen and Short anticipate empirical exploration of a phenomenon not yet clearly developed. The traditional form of middle-class delinquency is usually of the "parent" type, but it may evolve into other forms. For example, the above-mentioned youth-ghetto delinquency (school violence and vandalism) could possibly be placed into this category. Generally, however, the middle-class delinquent subculture may not be clearly defined simply because it largely lacks empirical representation.

The female delinquent subcultures. A female's status is largely dependent on the status of the males with whom she is identified. There are some exceptions, however, for example, when girls organize in gangs for sexual pursuits (usually prostitution), drug addiction, or as counterparts of the male hoodlum gang. Though research literature on female delinquency is sparse, there are indications that the traditional double standard has also declined in respect to delinquent activities and that girls are catching up with boys in the arena of law violations.

But, of course, not all teenage subcultures are of a delinquent nature. Many of them rally around relatively harmless and recreational fads and styles, such as the subcultures of the surfers, bikers, backpackers, athletes, punkers, religious groups, cults, and movements. Delinquent subcultures have been dwelled on primarily because they are clearly discernible as subcultures and illustrate some of the principles of the three explanatory models of subculture etiology, particularly those of the psychogenic approach in which common problems become shared problems for which the conspirators invent a delinquent solution.

ADOLESCENT NONSTATUS AND TEENAGE STATUS: A PARADOX?

Classification of certain adolescent activities as subcultural behavior introduces a theoretical problem: how can the portrayal of teenagers as confused and uncertain adolescents be reconciled with their portrayal as members of the teenage subculture, within which they have found role security and certainty? This seeming paradox is not easily resolved, since teenagers are actually characterized by *both*. The decision as to which of the two characterizations is more applicable depends entirely on the *specific teenager-other* relationship that is to be analyzed. When examining the teenager's relationship with adults, a multitude of problems are detectable that in their sum total substantiate the claim of the existence of adolescent uncertainty. Problems intrinsic to this *teenage-adult* relationship include confused communication, unclear authority definitions, generalist-specialist discontinuity, incongruous standards, and many other problems that have been discussed in previous chapters.

However, the *teenager-teenager* relationship is characterized by few, if any, such confusions and uncertainties. Among themselves, teenagers have created a relatively stable, though temporary, social structure. They know that they belong together and observe norms and values not necessarily consistent with the adult world's folkways and mores. In others words, there is a subcultural arrangement that compensates for the experience of adolescence in the adult world.

In summary, the seeming paradox must be understood as a problem of *differential analysis*. Most modern teenagers are *both* typically confused adolescents in the adult world and relatively self-assured and status-conscious members of their peer groups—depending on the interaction being analyzed.

A final word of modification should be added. Allowance must be made for the fact that not *all* teenagers are adolescents and members of teenage subcultures. It is possible to be an adolescent and not a member of some discernible peer culture. This would be the case of a youth who is socially isolated from peers and suffers from adolescent symptoms without recourse to an agemate subculture. Such a youth might lack opportunity to communicate with peers and be unaware of the commonality of adolescent problems. However, such a socially isolated adolescent would be a rarity, because almost any degree of social interaction would provide enough opportunities to communicate, meet, and share problems with peers. In general, for American teenagers the adolescent condition constitutes an ever-present latent force whose dynamics are restlessly at work to form and maintain a compensating subculture.

It is also possible to be a member of the teenage subculture and suffer minimally from adolescent tension and confusion. This relatively conflict-free situation may be due to either one or both of two circumstances. First, the teenager may be so deeply involved in the peer subculture, may carry out peer commitments and follow peer standards to such a degree that he or she derives a sense of total belonging from the subculture. Adult standards affect him or her only minimally, and he or she suffers little or no ambiguity and confusion as to where to place loyalty. Second, a teenager may be a member of the peer culture not because of basic psychological needs but rather because of proximity or coincidental acquaintances, such as neighborhood friends and school environment. This nonadolescent may be integrated in the family, have clear perceptions of a future occupation, satisfactory access to adult models that he or she emulates, and may freely adhere to the value orientation of adults. Participation in the teenage subculture is therefore merely perfunctory and of superficial significance to personality development. This type of youth is in the minority. It is safe to assume that the majority of American teenagers are both adolescents and members of peer cultures.

SUMMARY

Many social scientists agree on the existence of the teenage subculture as an empirical reality. Numerous studies and a multitude of daily manifestations seem to support the assumption.

Care must be taken in defining subculture to specify *which* type of teenage subculture is to be discussed. Generally speaking, the present discussion refers to the teenage culture within the broad American middle class.

The seeming paradox that a teenager can be both an adolescent and a status-conscious member of the peer culture can be resolved by *differential analysis*, by focusing, respectively, on the adolescent-adult or the teenager-teenager interaction.

The functions of the teenage subculture that meet the needs of the participants and enable the subculture to become a continuous process include a number of "services": (1) common norms and values, (2) a subcultural argot, (3) channels of communication not shared with outsiders, (4) unique styles and fads, (5) a sense of solidarity, (6) a status structure, (7) the charisma of leaders or heroes, and (8) gratification of specific needs through subcultural institutionalization.

Three etiological theories complement each other in explaining subcultural formation. The *psychogenic* and *behavioristic* models focus on the prime origin of subcultural evolvement and start with the problems a number of persons have in common. *Behaviorism*, with its premise of human nature as hedonistic, explains the attraction of teenagers to their peer culture as escape from confrontation with adult culture and as gravitation toward common interests. The *culture-transmission* model deals with learning and communicating. Television, movies, radio, and magazines perpetuate subcultural ways of thinking and acting.

It must be emphasized that motivation to join and maintain a normally nondelinquent teenage subculture does not stem entirely from the need to alleviate adolescent frustration and confusion. Motivation also stems from gregariousness and the enjoyment of fellowship. Teenagers enjoy engaging in activities (for example, dating) and in sharing interests that are neither entirely child nor adult. This enjoyment of peer companionship positively reinforces the subculture and operates in conjunction with the more negatively reinforcing influence of adolescent insecurity. In fact, even for teenagers relatively unaffected by adolescent disturbances, the gregarious enjoyment alone is a sufficiently powerful positive reinforcer to attract them to the subculture of peers.

12

Inside the Teen Subculture, Part I

While the preceding chapter was theory-oriented, this chapter and the next one are graphic and draw more from popular than from theoretical sources. Inclusion of popular material sharpens the illustrations of actual behavior and events in the teen subculture. The material in these two chapters is ordered into eight dimensions that are elemental to the nature of subculture. Since there is more material on the first dimension, values and attitudes of young people, this entire chapter is on this topic; the next chapter discusses the remaining seven dimensions.

These two chapters are oriented toward the general American teenage collectivity, high school students and the younger college students, rather than the older or more activistic segment of American youth. In spite of some overlap of these collectivities, the distinction may prove helpful in ordering the immense amount of material available from the overall youth scene.

The chapter following the two subculture chapters addresses itself to the question of counterculture, mostly a historical event in American civilization. It included, rather loosely integrated, a number of youth factions, such as the young intelligentsia, radical political groups, liberation phalanxes, and cultic movements.

IN-GROUP VALUES

Any group of individuals interacting over a period of time will sooner or later come to agree on a blueprint that creates predictable behavior patterns. These patterns include norms, rules concerning *how* to achieve certain values and do certain things, and values, the goals and basic attitudes concerning *what* is important.

Teen groups hold norms and values that, though not always entirely different from those of the adult community, at least reflect a unique accent. We will now explore some teen in-group standards, such as popularity, prestige, friendship, and sex.

Researchers have repeatedly noted that popularity is the most emphasized value among teenagers. The dynamics of popularity are complex and involve such features as admiration and recognition by peers. The data of the National Norms for Entering College Freshmen show that "obtaining recognition from peers" is essential to about 40 percent of beginning college students and that this proportion varies little from year to year.[1]

James S. Coleman, in his famous survey of American high schools, likewise found a strong desire to be popular. Interestingly, the desire is more intense among girls than boys.[2] The Purdue Opinion Panel supported this and showed that 60 percent of the teenage girls answered affirmatively to "want people to like me more," while 47 percent of the boys answered in the affirmative. Of the girls, 47 percent affirmed "wish I were more popular," while 36 percent of the boys did.[3] Still another study corroborated the sex-differentiated emphasis and found that girls with middle-class background showed persistent preoccupation with popularity and social success.[4]

The most pronounced emphasis on popularity was found among girls whose fathers occupied managerial, business, and professional positions commonly referred to as upper middle class. These girls daydreamed of popularity and often cited it as a source of worry. They indicated that they would like to have more social skills, be more popular, and be more accepted by peers. This preoccupation was not exclusively a result of the standards of the high school crowd, but was reinforced by the middle-class parents. Lower-class girls and boys, regardless of specific family circumstances, were markedly less concerned about popularity.

[1]National Norms for Entering College Freshmen, annual reports for 1966, 1967, 1968, 1969, 1970, 1971, 1972 (Washington, DC: Office of Research, American Council on Education).

[2]James S. Coleman, *The Adolescent Society* (New York: Free Press, 1963), p. 30.

[3]H. H. Remmers and D. H. Radler, *The American Teenager* (New York: Bobbs-Merrill, 1962), p. 85.

[4]Elizabeth Douvan and Joseph Adelson, *The Adolescent Experience* (New York: John Wiley, 1966), p. 406.

A longitudinal study shows that the importance attached to being popular in the high school crowd has changed only slightly over the years.[5] Samples taken from the same suburban high school in the Phoenix metropolitan area were surveyed in 1976 and in 1982. The 1976 responses to the question "How important is it to be liked and accepted by other teenagers?" showed that 47 percent felt it to be of "very great importance," 37 percent of "great importance," 14 percent of "some importance," and 2 percent of "no importance." The 1982 distribution was, respectively, 17, 37, 41, and 4 percent (1 percent no response). The 1982 proportions show a marked increase of the "some-importance" category. However, the "no-importance" category changed little, showing an increase of only 2 percent. When combining all categories that report "importance," comparison between 1976 and 1982 shows an insignificant decrease from 98 to 95 percent.

Likewise, the respondents in both surveys chose very similar *criteria* of popularity. Both distributions of answers to the question "What is expected of a teenager by his or her friends in order to be popular with them?" ranked the conformity principle first (doing, speaking, thinking, dressing, etc., "our way"). Second was what could be summed up as "good personality" (being friendly, cheerful, getting along with others, etc.). Third was "being yourself" or a similar reference to individualism. Fourth was taking an interest in others and helping them. And fifth was being honest and trustworthy. The rank order of these major categories did not change between 1976 and 1982.

There were, however, some changes in the gender-differentiated responses. The 1980s responses showed a diminishing of the girls' previously extremely high emphasis on conformity and now approached the proportion of the boys (roughly a third) who felt conformity was a criterion of popularity. Shifts of gender-differentiated responses were also noticeable in some of the minor categories: While anti-Establishment behavior as a criterion of popularity elicited 2 percent of the boys' and none of the girls' responses in 1976, the responses were reversed in 1982. A shift in the same direction occurred in regard to "having money": The 1970s responses showed 4 percent of the boys and none of the girls considering it a means to be popular. The 1980s responses showed 3 percent of the boys and 2 percent of the girls considering it so. "Helping and caring," previously an almost exclusive female response, attracted 8 percent of the boys and only 4 percent of the girls. Several of these changes seem to suggest a shift away from the traditional feminine role.

Nonetheless, conformity still seems to be the main price of popularity for both sexes. Other studies have corroborated this and discovered a consistent age correlation: While conformity is not particularly characteristic of

[5]Hans Sebald, *A Longitudinal Study of Popularity among Adolescents*, unpublished survey study, Department of Sociology, Arizona State University, 1982.

children below seven to nine years of age, it increases thereafter, reaches a peak during early adolescence (around thirteen), and then declines. Young teenagers are therefore more vulnerable to the influence of peers than older adolescents.[6]

What qualities do teenagers seek in a friend? The Douvan and Adelson research found that boys and girls have somewhat different expectations, with the former seeking someone who is first "amiable and nice" and secondly "supporting in trouble," and the latter seeking a friend who first of all is "not a gossip," secondly is "amiable and nice," and thirdly is "supporting in trouble."[7]

Another quality, considered most important in a friend, emerged in a survey by psychologist Vivian Seltzer: cleanliness. Sixty percent of the teenagers in the sample said that this was a quality to which they were particularly sensitive in their peers.[8]

Sometimes a teenager's prestige determines desirability as a friend; for a minority, it is a primary criterion for choosing a friend. It is more common, however, that such choices are made on the basis of a combination, such as desirable personality traits and prestige in the group.

The prestige of a friend can cause complications—especially among girls. There is frequent rivalry among girls for popularity with boys. A girl-girl friendship must recognize the problem of differential popularity—that is, popularity sought among boys and popularity sought among girls—and make protective adjustments. This problem has generated an interesting value orientation among girls in general. In order to avoid hostility and envy from her female peer group, the girl who is popular must learn to accept her good fortune modestly. In fact, the adolescent girl ordinarily is far more concerned about her acceptance by other girls and often uses her popularity with boys for its effect on her appraisal by her own sex-peer group.

ANTI-INTELLECTUALISM

Another teenager in-group attitude deals with anti-intellectualism. Learnedness has always been the nemesis of popularity and friendship, and it usually is laid down on the altar of peer acceptance as the sacrificial offering for "belonging." Nothing has changed in this respect, and various studies have borne this out—from the early Purdue Opinion Panel (60 percent disdained intellectualism and preferred to be popular rather than brilliant) to the

[6]Jane E. Brownstone and Richard H. Willis, "Conformity in Early and Late Adolescence," *Developmental Psychology*, 4 (May 1971): 334–37.

[7]Douvan and Adelson, *The Adolescent Experience*, p. 406.

[8]Vivian Seltzer, *The Psychosocial Worlds of the Adolescent* (New York: Wiley & Sons, 1989).

Goertzel survey that showed an even further increase in anti-intellectualism.[9] What are the social psychological dynamics behind this almost invariable pattern?

The young teenager must be understood in terms of *subcultural* involvement. The individual reaches adolescence conditioned in the skills of group membership, having learned how to get along with peers and to do the accepted things. Naturally other-directed and with little self-consciousness, he or she is attuned to behave in concert with others. As an adolescent, he or she enters a life phase that increasingly calls for independence. But at the same time he or she becomes even more sensitive to the security he or she has enjoyed among peers. It is now that he or she relies on the subculture most heavily—and this subculture demands conformity. Deviation from group norms would incur alienation—a dreadful punishment for any youngster. For the most part, idiosyncratic qualities among members are suppressed. Intellectual pursuits constitute such idiosyncrasies and are immediately suspect. Researchers have shown that this attitude runs through the core of secondary schooling and that "friendliness, popularity, and mediocrity" are more highly regarded than being a "good student."

Modern education often employs the self-defeating *individual* approach when learning problems arise, overlooking the fact that the teenager is essentially other-directed and marches to the drumbeat of peers. Learning problems are frequently not individual problems but are *social* problems with the intellectually negating power structure of the adolescent peer group being the hostile background. Some sociologists have suggested that we seriously explore ways of moving adolescent peer groups collectively toward intellectual interests, rather than continue the futile piecemeal attempts to correct individual students in the hope of diverting them from identifying with their peers.

REFERENCE GROUPS AND VALUES

It would be misleading to assume that teenagers look exclusively to their peer group for value orientation. There is no such uniform reference group. In some areas of decision making they align their values with peer standards and in other areas with the views and advice of adults, particularly parents. An Arizona study (Table 12-1) indicates that adolescents are selective in their conformity and in some matters are guided by the opinions of the peer group and in other matters by their parents. In still other matters they listen to both sides, and in some sectors of life they seem uncertain, lacking a definite reference group. For example, in matters of money, choosing courses at

[9]Ted Goertzel, "Changes in the Values of College Students 1958 to 1970/71," *Pacific Sociological Review*, 15 (April 1972): 235–44.

TABLE 12-1   1982 percent distribution of boys' and girls' responses to the question: If you had to decide between your friends' and your parents' opinion and feeling in the following situations, whose opinion would you consider more important?

	Friends'*		Uncertain**		Parents'*	
	Boys	Girls	Boys	Girls	Boys	Girls
1. On what you spend your money	19	2	27	38	54	60
2. Whom to date	41	47	46	40	14	13
3. Clubs you join	54	60	38	33	8	7
4. Advice on personal problems	27	53	24	29	49	18
5. How to dress	43	53	46	44	11	2
6. Courses you take in school	8	16	35	20	57	64
7. Hobbies	46	36	41	56	14	9
8. Choosing your future occupation	0	2	35	42	65	56
9. Social events you attend	65	60	27	29	8	11
10. College or not	0	0	35	36	65	64
11. Books you read other than those requested by school	38	40	49	53	14	7
12. Magazines you buy	46	51	46	47	8	2
13. How often you date	35	24	51	49	14	27
14. Whether you participate in drinking parties	46	40	35	42	19	18
15. Choosing your future spouse	8	9	57	67	35	24
16. Going steady or not	30	29	57	56	14	16
17. Intimacy on a date	35	24	54	67	11	9
18. Whom to go for information about sex	30	44	32	16	38	40

Source: Hans Sebald, "Adolescents' Peer Orientation: Changes in the Support System During the Past Three Decades," *Adolescence* 24 (Winter 1989):937–46.

*Categories include responses of "definitely" and "probably" friends or parents, respectively.

**24% of the boys and 35% of the girls modified the label of this category by writing in "myself," "own opinion," or something to that effect.

school, deciding on future careers and plans to go to college, they tend to consult their parents more than their peers. However, in matters of dating, clothing, hobbies, attending social affairs, choice of magazines, and joining clubs, they follow the opinion and advice of their peers.[10]

[10]Hans Sebald, "Adolescents' Peer Orientation: Changes in the Support System During the Past Three Decades," *Adolescence* 24 (Winter 1989): 937–46.

The teenagers express uncertainty (or, as some specified, self-reliance) in certain areas. Roughly half of both girls and boys are uncertain whose advice they would follow when it comes to reading books other than school texts (maybe the explanation is the majority's failure to read outside books in the first place), buying magazines, selecting a spouse, going steady, how intimate to be on a date, and how often to date. Uncertainties in exactly these areas prevailed among the high schoolers of six years earlier. (See Table 12–2.) But a serendipitous finding revealed that one thing had changed: In 1976 17 percent of the boys and 16 percent of the girls had amended their "uncertain" responses by saying that he or she was guided by "myself" or "own opinion." The proportions of "uncertain" responses increased in 1982 to 24 percent of the boys and an astounding 33 percent of the girls. This was purely the initiative of the respondents, since this option had not been listed on the questionnaire.

GENDER-DIFFERENTIATED VALUES

Such a response possibly signals increasing individualism and, conversely, decreasing familism of teenagers of the 1980s. It may specifically signal increasing female liberation, since many more girls than boys shifted from parent orientation to "uncertain" or self-reliant. While the 1976 girls sought significantly more parental advice than boys in seventeen out of the eighteen areas, the 1982 girls sought more parental advice in only six out of the eighteen areas. On the other side, the 1976 girls were more "uncertain" than boys in eight of the eighteen areas, while in 1982 they were more "uncertain" (or self-reliant) in eleven of the eighteen areas. (See Table 12–2.)

Sex-differentiated responses are clearly visible in a number of items. In the 1976 as well as the 1982 survey, boys significantly more often than girls, turn to friends' opinions in regard to how to spend money, whereas girls more often listen to their parents in this respect. "Advice on personal problems" has always elicited a more peer-oriented response from girls. This might be explained by the possibility that girls understand "personal problems" to include matters of feminine hygiene, a realm where girls tend to consult girlfriends more often than parents. This tendency may also be reflected by the 44 percent of girls vs. 30 percent of the boys who go to friends for information about sex. Generally, however, the 1982 survey suggests a far less gender-differentiated picture than the earlier survey.

TREND ANALYSIS

The identical eighteen questions were asked in a 1960 survey in a suburban high school of Columbus, Ohio, a school socioeconomically (largely middle class), religiously, and ethnically (largely Protestant and white) comparable to

TABLE 12-2 Comparison of 1976 survey with 1982 survey in terms of percent distribution of boys' and girls' responses to the question: If you had to decide between your friends' and your parents' opinion and your parents' opinion and feeling in the following situations, whose opinion would you consider more important?

Survey Questions	1976: Friends'		1982: Friends'		1976: Uncertain*		1982: Uncertain**		1976: Parents'		1982: Parents'	
	Boys	Girls	Boys	Girls	Boys	Girls	Boys	Girls	Boys	Girls	Boys	Girls
1. On what you spend your money	45	22	19	2	24	23	27	38	31	55	54	60
2. Whom to date	64	54	41	47	32	29	46	40	4	17	14	13
3. Clubs you join	71	66	54	60	23	25	38	2	6	7	8	7
4. Advice on personal problems	40	60	27	53	23	5	24	29	37	35	49	18
5. How to dress	63	62	43	53	31	29	46	44	6	9	11	2
6. Courses you take in school	42	22	8	16	26	34	35	20	33	44	57	64
7. Hobbies	66	54	46	36	28	36	41	56	6	10	14	9
8. Choosing your future occupation	10	4	0	2	47	31	35	42	43	64	65	56
9. Social events you attend	76	77	65	60	20	13	27	29	4	10	8	11
10. College or not	11	7	0	0	38	23	35	36	51	70	65	64
11. Books you read other than those requested by school	52	50	38	40	41	42	49	53	8	8	14	7
12. Magazines you buy	62	54	46	51	34	40	46	47	4	6	8	2
13. How often you date	62	19	35	24	26	24	51	49	12	57	14	27
14. Whether you participate in drinking parties	62	54	46	40	20	20	35	42	18	26	19	18
15. Choosing future spouse	27	9	8	9	47	49	57	67	27	42	35	24
16. Going steady or not	54	21	30	29	32	47	57	56	14	32	14	16
17. Intimacy on a date	53	33	35	24	39	50	54	67	8	17	11	9
18. Whom to go for information about sex	46	34	30	44	30	23	32	16	24	43	38	40

Source: Hans Sebald, combined material from: "Adolescents' Shifting Orientation toward Parents and Peers: A Curvilinear Trend over Recent Decades," *Journal of Marriage and the Family* 48 (February 1986): 5–13; and "Adolescents' Peer Orientation: Changes in Support System During the Past Three Decades," *Adolescence* 24 (Winter 1989):937–46.

*17% of the boys and 16% of the girls amended this category by writing in "myself," or "own opinion."

**24% of the boys and 33% of the girls amended this category by writing in "myself," or "own opinion."

the Phoenix metropolitan school.[11] Adding data from that survey to the longitudinal view introduced above enables us to compare the responses of 1960, 1976, and 1982. Scrutiny of the responses reveals that certain changes have occurred over this period and that these changes indicate how the role of parents in the lives of teenagers has fluctuated. We can generalize that 1960 was characterized by conservative, parent-oriented attitudes, 1976 by powerful peer orientation, and 1982 by a balancing of the peer and parental reference groups.

Comparing 1960 and 1976 reveals a loss of parental influence and shows a sweeping shift toward peer orientation in *all* areas. Some of the more radical shifts (amounting to at least 20 percent) away from parent orientation affected the areas of how to spend money, whom and how often to date, going steady, clothes, which courses to take at school, which social events to attend, and participation at drinking parties. However, other decreases are just as significant, especially when considering that the time-honored tradition of consulting parents in matters of personal problems and troubles declined by 15 percent. There were also declines in following parental advice in career plans, going to parents for sex information, and seeking parental advice about mate selection. (See details in Table 12–3.)

Comparing 1976 and 1982 reveals that by the 1980s parents had partly recovered the territory they had lost during the 1960s and 1970s to peer influence or to the "uncertain/self-reliant" attitude. Perhaps the pressure of the economic slump of the early 1980s prompted increases in reliance on parents: 15 percent in money spending, 23 percent in course selections, 7 percent in career questions, 5 percent in college decision, and 2 percent in book purchases. In most areas the increases were minor, and in seven areas the changes were negative, though not as drastic as in 1976. Most of the decreases took place in the social realm, including how to dress, whom and how often to date, and in the private realm, such as advice in personal or sexual problems.

From the vantage point of the 1980s, reliance on parental advice has not recovered its 1960 standing. With the sole exception of consulting parents on college plans (only 2 percent increase over 1960), all eighteen areas have experienced decreases in parental consultation. The sharpest decreases exist in social and personal affairs, with decisions about dating, dressing, and partying now being more "uncertain" or dependent on the teenager's own taste and opinion.

The generalizations of the Ohio-Arizona surveys could be refined by controlling a number of variables, among them, for example, dropout-proneness and graduation-orientation. Identifying respondents by one of the two

[11]Hans Sebald, *The Crisis of Adolescent Discontinuity*, mimeographed research report. The Ohio State University, Columbus, Ohio, 1960.

TABLE 12-3   Changes of proportions of teenagers seeking parental advice in 18 areas between 1960, 1976, and 1982. (Boys and girls combined.)

Areas	Percent of Teenagers Seeking Parental Advice			Percent Change		
	1960	1976	1982	1960–1976	1976–1982	1960–1982
1. On what you spend your money	62	42	57	−20	+15	− 5
2. Whom to date	31	10	13	−21	+ 3	−18
3. Clubs you join	23	6	7	−17	+ 1	−16
4. Advice on personal problems	51	36	32	−15	− 4	−19
5. How to dress	35	7	6	−28	− 1	−29
6. Courses you take in school	69	38	61	−31	+23	− 8
7. Hobbies	14	8	11	− 6	+ 3	− 3
8. Choosing your future occupation	64	53	60	−11	+ 7	− 4
9. Social events you attend	30	6	10	−24	+ 4	−20
10. College or not	63	60	65	− 3	+ 5	+ 2
11. Books you read other than those requested by school	20	8	10	−12	+ 2	−10
12. Magazines you buy	21	5	5	−16	none	−16
13. How often you date	58	33	21	−25	−12	−37
14. Whether you participate in drinking parties	64	23	18	−41	− 5	−46
15. Choosing future spouse	39	34	29	− 5	− 5	−10
16. Going steady or not	41	21	15	−20	− 6	−26
17. Intimacy on a date	23	12	10	−11	− 2	−13
18. Whom to go for information about sex	48	32	39	−16	+ 7	− 9

Source: Hans Sebald, based on data in "Adolescents' Shifting Orientation toward Parents and Peers."

categories might result in a polarized picture, showing the former type of student more aligned with the peer culture and the latter with parental values. Lucius F. Cervantes' study found a sharp cleavage between the two types, establishing that dropout-prone students indeed have their own peer culture.[12] This finding deserves to be verified in future studies. In the meantime we accept the Ohio-Arizona findings as showing that teenagers in general cultivate divided reference groups, selectively looking to peers and parents for advice and guidance.

[12]Lucius F. Cervantes, *American Youth Culture: Independent or Dependent?* Paper read at the Annual Convention of the American Sociological Association, Chicago, 1965.

DECISION MAKING: PARENT-TEEN CLASHES

The demand of the parents to be taken seriously as a reference group is not always obeyed. Gallup Polls found that teenager-parent arguments erupt over a number of issues. Asking parents of teenage children "What do you argue about most with your teenager(s)?," the poll found a number of major clashes: 18 percent about chores/housework, 15 percent about freedom/responsibilities, 12 percent about evening curfew, 9 percent about homework, 8 percent about money, 6 percent about where the teenagers go, and 5 percent about choice of friends and dates.[13] In general, 30 percent of the parents felt that they were not strict enough with their teenage offspring, 11 percent felt they were too strict, 54 percent thought they were just about right, and the rest qualified their responses or had no opinion.[14]

When 13-to-17-year-old teenagers were asked about the areas of conflict with parents, a somewhat different rank order emerged: (1) what clothes to wear, (2) staying out late, (3) quitting school, (4) sexual activities, and (5) drinking. The percentages of the teenagers who felt that they themselves should have the right to make decisions in these areas were, respectively: (1) 99%, (2) 85% (3) 82%, (4) 73%, and (5) 55%.[15]

VALUES AND TEENAGE SEXUALITY

Important attitudes held by teenagers deal with their sexual activities. However, these attitudes, like just about any attitude or value orientation, fluctuate and are greatly affected by sociocultural changes. During the counterculture years of the 1960s and 1970s the prevailing sexual standards were labeled the New Sexuality, evidently characterized by liberated attitudes and equally unrestrained behavior, and can be summed up by a number of characteristics:

1. *Noncommittal sexuality.* Sex was accepted as pleasure, and the fulfillment of it was not seen as requiring a commitment stipulating exclusivity, loyalty, or continuous personal care and concern. The New Sexuality implied the intention of the young to preserve as much independence and individualism as possible—and yet to enjoy sexual intimacy.

2. *Tolerance or acceptance of varying sexuality.* Sexual liberation included many of the sexual expressions previously considered deviant. It was largely to the credit of the vocal counterculture and the women's movement

[13]*Gallup Opinion Index 1978*, #156, pp. 22–23.
[14]Ibid., p. 24.
[15]Public Opinion Survey, "Big Decisions for Teens," *USA Today*, July 13, 1987, p. D1.

that homosexuality and lesbianism were looked upon as relatively acceptable alternatives and no longer as pathological aberrations.

3. *Female sexual liberation.* The most important aspect of the New Sexuality was the changing role of women. Young women became more aware of their own sexuality and sought equal satisfaction. The aspect of pleasure was possibly the most revolutionary feature in the Sexual Revolution: the female now openly regarded sex as enjoyable.

4. *Medical and technological innovations.* Probably nothing decreased inhibition and fear of sexual activities for the woman more than the availability of contraceptives. A woman freed from the old moral compunctions did not imperil her future by unwanted pregnancy and could enjoy with impunity the physical and psychological pleasures of sex.

5. *Credo of instantness of fulfillment.* Postindustrial conditions markedly fostered a belief in instant fulfillment of needs. Insistence on an instant remedy was the response to any slackening of society's ability to come to the individual's aid and provide an effective and immediate answer to any desire that was defined as a need. Frustration was blamed on society's failure to prevent such unpleasantness. Individual sexual frustrations entered the list of such societal failures. The Sexual Revolution was strongly supported by the demand for instantness and, conversely, by the rejection of the old Protestant ethic that included deference of gratification. This new credo became a part of the new psychology of entitlement. Accordingly, young Americans assumed that they had a right (not merely a chance) to self-actualization, economic security, and general comfort.

During the late 1970s the New Sexuality ran out of steam and a new tenor became noticeable. Several conditions were responsible for the decline of the liberal sexual orientation:

1. *Disillusionment.* On the basis of books, movies, talks, rumors, and pseudoacademic promises, adolescents were faced with sexually superhuman promises that sooner or later led to frustration and disappointment. From the author's counseling experiences with college students, it appeared that many young persons were disappointed by their initial sexual experience. The failure of sex to be as glamorous as expected tended to downgrade the value of sexuality. This disillusionment became crucial when it was combined with the failure to establish a secure human relationship. Inexperienced teenage lovers were left deeply disillusioned with sex as a cure for alienation and loneliness.

Such disillusionment had manifold results. Those who had been hurt sought other routes of escape from isolation and turned to drugs, suicide, creative sublimation, or a new Victorianism. The last reaction rejected the New Sexuality and turned toward a New Asceticism which was expected to heal disappointment, solve confusion, and supply missing psychological security.

This reversal pattern may actually be a *generational* experience in which most young people go through the liberated, disappointed, and finally puritanical stages, ultimately becoming relatively conservative adults. Such a pattern may well explain in large part why there always exists a mass of conservative parents who just a few years prior were rebellious youngsters. It may also explain why each adult generation continues to view premarital sex as deviant behavior.

2. *The quest for romanticism.* The New Sexuality was inimical to a sense of romanticism. Sexual realism deprived the young of the mystery of sexuality that used to include the reverent ritual, passion-amplifying delay, pulse-raising awe, ideal-inspiring imagination, and every sort of sublimation. The New Sexuality had branded these mental gyrations as dishonest and fallacious. Shooting down romantic pathos also killed the mystique of sex, and the survivors found themselves with banal physical lovemaking that soon conveyed a feeling of relative deprivation.

Combined with the heady sense of freedom was a sometimes uneasy feeling of pressure to take advantage of the new freedom. As Dustin Hoffman said in *The Graduate*: "I'm starting to feel the same way about getting laid as I did about getting into college."

When circumstances are created that are so realistic that they allow complete insight into the everyday life of the other sex, romantic feelings go out the window. Surveys found that men and women sharing coed dorms prefer to bring in sex partners from outside.

The desire for romanticism is strong and a constant in human life. Our Western civilization is permeated with romantic attitudes and promises waiting to be called upon to embellish human relationships that otherwise appear too sober and unexciting. Crass realism, in any realm of life, usually is surprisingly short-lived.

3. *The quest for psychological security.* Though the New Sexuality had fulfilled some heretofore frustrated needs and desires, new needs and problems arose. Although, for example, sexual tension was released and a source of fun and pleasure tapped, the lack of personal commitment endangered psychological security and led to anxiety. The prevalent emotional repercussion to adolescent sexuality during the era of repressive mores had been feelings of guilt and shame; the new emotional response was anxiety and a vague feeling of meaninglessness. This anomic version of the sexual relationship seemed to weigh heavily on the minds of the young. Humans display a natural need for norms and predictability—especially when it comes to sexual relationships—and a phase of liberal excursion is usually followed by a phase of reconsideration and conservatism.

4. *The tenacity of traditional values.* The old sexual mores were by no means forgotten. The liberation had not totally obscured the old "rights and wrongs," and though many young Americans spoke—and perhaps even acted —as if liberated from them, they still responded to them on an emotional, albeit unconscious level. Though it may be true that the more prevalent

modern reaction to premarital sex is anxiety (the typical reaction to normlessness), there are still many young people who react with the traditional "control emotions"—such as guilt and shame—to their violations of social standards.

5. *The academic fabrication of the New Sexuality.* There was exaggeration in the accounts of social scientists when they interpreted changes in sexual behavior. For example, Herbert H. Otto, chairperson of the National Center for the Exploration of Human Potential, forecast in 1971 that "there are 12,000 communes in the U.S. and I foresee that within five years, 20 percent of American families will be involved in them."[16] Such misextrapolation gave the impression that modern marriage, family, and sexual patterns were changing radically.

Another example of possible misinterpretation was the high premarital pregnancy rate, which was attributed to a higher premarital coitus rate. While this may have been so, this rate was not an accurate indicator since it may merely have been a function of fewer young people feeling obliged to marry because of the pressure that pregnancy exerts.

Tenuous interpretations led some social scientists to predict and even recommend changes in lifestyles. For example, well-known humanistic psychologists suggested exploring the many dimensions of monogamy, reinventing marriage by "engaging in serial polygamy" (Sidney Jourard), and trying out an "intimate network of families" for collective problem solving (Frederick Stoller).[17]

Sexologist Albert Ellis interpreted cohabitation as an intelligent decision to learn whom not to marry. It is not a "copping out" of human responsibilities. Ellis' opinion is that "anybody who marries without living with someone for at least six months is copping out."[18] He also foresaw a change in the family structure that would allow "legalized adultery"; that is, two people will marry mostly for each other but will have casual sexual experiences with others. Lawrence Casler, in *Is Marriage Necessary?*, proposed a similar restructuring of traditional marriage, allowing for "permissive matrimony."[19] The list of academics who supported the New Sexuality could be expanded.

Though many academic suggestions were based on valid insight, some were unduly generalized and gave an exaggerated picture of changed social and sexual mores. Social scientists were heavily influenced by their immediate social environment, which is relatively isolated in academia. Their students live in an artificial hothouse climate that is significantly different from

[16]"Marriage and Family," *Arizona Republic*, December 1971, p. 47.
[17]Herbert A. Otto, "Has Monogamy Failed?" *Saturday Review*, April 26, 1970, p. 25.
[18]"Noted Psychologist Is Seminar Speaker," *Arizona Republic*, June 24, 1972, p. 51.
[19]Lawrence Casler, *Is Marriage Necessary?* (New York: Human Sciences Press, 1974).

the world of working people. Their attitudes and behavior patterns tend to influence the interpretations of sociology and psychology professors, whose research more often than not samples this population, leading them to believe that what their students say and do is what *American youth* says and does.

For example, the mostly theoretical tolerance of sexual practices previously defined as deviant is not only not shared by nonacademic Americans but is often abandoned by college graduates when they enter the world of employment and family life. Much of their professed tolerance adds up to verbiage merely deemed sophisticated and liberated among college peers.

The academic factor has been discussed in order to show the intrusion of bias into the formulation of the New Sexuality. To some extent its formulation was inspired by academicians who were overimpressed by the immediacy and vociferousness of students.

These, in sum, were the main psychological, social, and cultural conditions that bore on the decline of the New Sexuality during the late 1970s. And then, during the 1980s came the final condition that sealed the debacle of the New Sexuality: AIDS, the new plague.

This fatal peril has added an entirely new perspective on human sexuality. It is too early, however, to know the extent to which it is changing sexual behavior. Again there is the danger of overassessing its actual impact. With every New Sexuality or New Peril comes the New Verbiage, the way people talk about the new phenomenon. But does this "talk" relate directly to actual behavior? Most likely not. It seems that in spite of AIDS, relatively liberal sexual practices continue—as testified by the unabated rate of premarital pregnancies of American teenagers. Rather than initiating a new asceticism or new chastity in the moral sense, the primary reaction may be limited to a new caution, as the increased sale of condoms across the nation seems to indicate.

POLITICAL ATTITUDES

The beginning of the last decade of the twentieth century saw American youth, more or less youth of Western Civilization generally, in a calmer mood and relatively well integrated into their society. No great causes or battles were being fought. The counterculture had become a historical phenomenon and young people seemed primarily directed toward work and the completion of an education so they could make it through hard economic times.

Even the war in the Persian Gulf fought during January and February of 1991 did little to alter this mood, though a rise in patriotism could be observed, especially at the victorious conclusion of the war. Compared to American youth's reaction to the Vietnam War, factionalism was at a low key. There were some relatively minor demonstrations by the "doves"; but the "hawks" carried the day. The overwhelming majority of American youth supported the Bush Administration's war effort, elated by the low casualty rate of the American forces and the short duration of the fighting.

It is worthwhile to recall that America's youth responded radically differently to the military involvement in Vietnam. Militant opposition was shown by a significant proportion of the young. A study took the Vietnam War as a test case to examine an important question about human behavior: Does knowledge about a certain issue influence or determine the attitude toward the same issue?[20] Over 400 college students were quizzed on their knowledge of Southeast Asia, the war, and their attitude toward the American involvement. The responses showed that the sample was divided into 110 antiwar demonstrators, 50 prowar partisans, and 276 students whose non-committal attitude put them within the purview of the so-called silent majority. All of the students were given identical sets of questions relating to political, geographic, military, and historical conditions of Vietnam and adjacent areas. The "doves" did best, getting 55 percent correct; the "hawks" scored 47 percent, and the silent majority only 45 percent. Higher scores among the activists had been expected since they were the ones who had to defend their dissent, but all scores were surprisingly low. Also, the differences between the groups were not significant.

The lack of knowledge of a vital national as well as international issue was astounding: 25 percent of the students could not identify North and South Vietnam on an unmarked map; 33 percent were unable to name a single ally fighting with the United States; less than 10 percent could name a single North Vietnamese leader; and 25 percent could not even name Saigon as the capital of South Vietnam. This was at the height of the war (1970), when over 40,000 young American men had lost their lives!

The conclusion is that there is hardly a correlation between knowledge and attitude, and that emotionality about a given issue is relatively *independent* of knowledge about the issue. It seems that the genesis of an attitude does not lie at the root of knowledge or ignorance, but at the root of emotional predisposition and basic orientation—a condition to be remembered when we look at the variously expressed attitudes of youth.

ECONOMIC ATTITUDES

For generations, Americans have modeled their ideas of success after the Protestant ethic, with occupational status, money, investment, and possessions as focal points. The new generation seems to have shifted its preoc-

[20]Hans Sebald and Rudolfo N. Gallegos, "Voices of War and Peace—What do They Know? Attitudes and Knowledge About the War in Southeast Asia," *Pacific Sociological Review*, 14 (October 1971): 487-510.

cupation to various forms of self-fulfillment, moving psychological demands to the forefront. The new emphasis has effected corresponding changes in their sense of obligation to friends, family, employer, and community. Materialistic-competitive attitudes of old have given way to a privatism that cultivates social and political isolationism and aims at the satisfaction of personal psychological needs. The genesis of this attitude must be sought not merely in temporary reactions to political events, but in postindustrial conditions that encourage and allow exactly this type of self-service.

The nadir of the work ethic was reached during the late 1960s and early 1970s, when only about half of young Americans believed that "hard work always pays off."[21] In the meantime, with economic hardship providing motivation, the work ethic has made a modest comeback.

Nevertheless, it is surprising that young Americans remain relatively unimpressed by the economic crisis and somehow seem to assume that some satisfactory economic security will materialize for them. This is not so much personal optimism as it is a new *philosophy of entitlement*. This evolution of "social rights" feelings manifests itself in such attitudes as students assuming that they are entitled to codetermine how to run a university. The desire "I'd like a creative and enjoyable career" becomes the righteous demand that "I am entitled to a creative and enjoyable career." The desire "I'd like a secure income" becomes "I am entitled to a secure income." While the tendency to feel righteous about one's desires is natural and has been with us for a long time, the equation of desire with right has grown significantly in the current generation. Whether the equation can be solved is of course another question.

Notwithstanding the new philosophy of entitlement, careerism is as strong as ever. Concentrating on a career is a natural function of privatism, which is typical of modern youth. Careerism is particularly evident among modern young women. Increasing numbers of them put the career first and having a family second; while wanting both, they want them in this sequence.[22]

RELIGIOUS ATTITUDES

While many American teenagers have declined in traditional religiosity with and since the counterculture, a new religiosity has evolved over the past fifteen to twenty years. The new form is a synthesis of Oriental and Western beliefs. From a historical perspective, the extent to which it has reached masses of young people in virtually all Western societies is an unprecedented

---

[21]Daniel Yankelovich, *The New Morality: A Profile of American Youth in the '70s* (New York: McGraw-Hill, 1974), p. 26.

[22]"Youth on the Move," *U.S. News and World Report*, January 5, 1981, p. 76.

development. Theodore Roszak, the chronicler of the counterculture, emphasizes in his book, *The Making of a Counter Culture*, that the infusion of Oriental philosophy was the unique benchmark of the twentieth-century counterculture.

One of the bizarre outcomes of the new religious-mystic synthesis is that teenagers who think of themselves as Christians now innocuously add the belief in reincarnation to their personal belief system—notwithstanding the lack of logic or compatibility. Survey data collected and currently analyzed by this author shows that up to 20 percent of college students classifying themselves as Catholics, Protestants, or nonspecific "Christians" believe in reincarnation, karma, and other Oriental or occult notions. The most interesting aspect of this development is that the young synthetic believers fail to be aware of the disparate cultural origins of the components of their beliefs and, in the process of trying to integrate the components, create a religious credo that is neither Christian nor Oriental. The making of this religious synthesis was an integral part of the counterculture and thus will be mentioned once more in Chapter 14.

These, then, constitute some aspects of the new cultural values as they are emerging with the young generation. One of the most noteworthy discoveries of the nationwide surveys was the involvement of working noncollege youth in the new cultural trends. In many instances, the traditional and almost customary distinction in attitudes and values between noncollege and college youth has been erased. This is a new development.

This large group (seven out of ten American youths are not college educated) may experience feelings of relative deprivation. Having absorbed the new cultural values of self-fulfillment, enjoyable careers, and the liberated work ethic, they may experience difficulties implementing them in their work life. Here is an example of the disharmony between cultural promises and social-structural limitations. Their comparatively less independent work life will offer fewer psychological rewards than that of college-educated people and is bound to exacerbate feelings of deprivation. This, indeed, may lead to a split within the youth population that may be more severe and may prove to be more dangerous to American society than the split between generations. American society may soon be confronted with demands on the part of young noncollege-educated workers for the same enjoyment and privileges as the college-educated workers, and the demands may aim at earlier retirement, shorter work weeks, more generous vacations, greater participation in industrial planning and management, and other methods of reducing the traditional monotony and powerlessness of the industrial worker. The future will most likely bring clashes between the new cultural attitudes and the built-in rigidities and limitations of the industrial work place.

It is interesting that most of the new values had their genesis in the counterculture of the late 1960s, traveled the customary route through the student population, and have now reached working-class youth. The legacy of the counterculture is now becoming visible in the form of pervasive new cultural attitudes and feelings that affect nearly all segments of the young generation.

COMMITMENTS TO THE AMERICAN WAY OF LIFE

A portion of the teenage population manifests values that are harmonious with adult standards. These values are not indigenous to the teen subculture but are expressions of motivation transcending the circle of peers. Justification for discussion of nonsubcultural behavior is twofold: (1) to render a more complete picture of youth in contemporary America and (2) to provide a contrast to subcultural behavior and values.

Student volunteerism manifests itself in civic concern, political interests, and various social services all across the nation. The commitments include a wide range of voluntary public service programs: tutoring disadvantaged children, assisting the poor with tax returns, entertaining and nursing patients in hospitals, clearing slums, cleaning up ecological disasters, and offering health care for the underprivileged.

Many volunteers work through such organizations as Candy Stripers, 4-H Clubs, Boys' Clubs of America, Tri-Hi-Y, Scout and Camp Fire groups, student governments, and various school clubs. Also, many of the service programs of the religious communities have been supported by young people, including Catholic, Protestant, Jewish, Mormon, and other religious organizations. Additional examples of value commitment include teams of medical, dental, and special-education students who go into impoverished Appalachia, giving and teaching badly needed health care; architecture students in many states who design playgrounds and summer camps for underprivileged children; law students in several states who give advice to consumers and teach ghetto children to use the law rather than to fear or despise it; language students at New York high schools who tutor Spanish-speaking people; and young people in many cities who help to maintain "hot line" telephones.

Federal organizations have attracted thousands of young Americans who seek fellowship and the experience to serve others. Thousands of young Americans have served as Peace Corps volunteers in many parts of the world to bring about technological innovations, and at the same time have respected the customs and mores of the natives. The success of the Peace Corps can be attributed to volunteers who (1) put into practice the American value of helpfulness; (2) feel enthusiastic about performing vital tasks, and (3) want to learn more about others and themselves.

Participation in VISTA (Volunteers in Service to America) has been widespread and constructive. A study by sociologist David Gottlieb showed that more than 50 percent of the participating youths felt VISTA had changed their career decisions, and 76 percent said their experience had increased their commitment to solve the nation's problems.[23]

Another federal organization is the Youth Conservation Corps, which pays young Americans a minimum salary and teaches them conservation techniques, often pitching them against forest fires and other disasters. Again, the participants accrue tremendous personal benefits, learn to get along with coworkers of varying ethnic, racial, and socioeconomic backgrounds, and often develop a lasting interest in a conservation career (forestry, fish and game administration, construction, and reclamation work).

The California Conservation Corps is a successful example. Its twenty-five work centers are sworn to the work ethic and are home to nearly 2000 men and women between the ages of eighteen and twenty-three. The CCC members work all day and then, if their literacy is poor, take classes at night — 35 percent do because they cannot read beyond a third-grade level. There are no alcohol, drugs, violence, or refusals to work. A member breaking the rules is discharged immediately. For respecting the rules corps members receive $580 a month (minimum wage), but must return $135 for room and board. The skills they learn include sandbagging hillsides to stem floods, smashing boulders to repair High Sierra trails, building recreational facilities, battling forest fires, erecting solar panels, and planting trees. In the early 1980s the CCC had a nine-month backlog of requests from all over California to do work that cities and counties could not afford. According to a study, for every dollar invested in the CCC, the state benefited $1.20. As a result, several other states are considering initiating similar projects of their own.[24]

The American Red Cross attracted four million unpaid youth volunteers during the early 1980s. Young people were found to work longer hours, had more energy, and were willing to take physical risks for helping people in need.[25] Tornado-devastated Grand Island, Nebraska, benefited from youth volunteers, some of whom put in 90 hours a week. A 1980 Washington, DC, fire left 140 people homeless, and youth volunteers helped set up shelter with food, blankets, and other needs. Blood-donor centers, hospitals, homes for the elderly, and recreation centers are regular recipients of youth volunteer help.

It would burst the frame of this chapter to try and enumerate all the service projects that young people make possible all over the nation. The above examples, showing American high school and college youth lending more than a token hand in many vital services, must suffice as illustrations.

Every experience has a variety of consequences. Some of the results

[23]New York Times Service (May 24, 1971).
[24]"The CCC," *National Wildlife*, 20 (February/March 1982): 17–18.
[25]"Youth on the Move," p. 76.

may simply be the achievement of material goals that projects set out to accomplish, but there are also unanticipated consequences, which involve psychological by-products. In the case of youth volunteerism, these by-products include:

Integration into society.   Service work is an integral part of society and provides a status rooted in the Establishment. This bonds youth to society and alleviates youth's feelings of alienation, showing them a side of society with which they can identify.

Self-testing.   The service experience is an example of the welcome respite that Erik Erikson called a psychosocial moratorium. Not only is the youths' delay in choosing a vocation socially accepted while they are serving in voluntary agencies, but there is a simultaneous opportunity to assess one's own resources, capabilities, and interests, and thereby apply a valid test to one's identity.

Independence.   Meaningful service is a constructive expression of independence from parents and provides a sound resolution of the adolescent conflict. Peace Corps returnees reported that they appreciated the high degree of responsibility given and the extent to which they could exercise their own initiative. It seems that volunteer service helps young individuals achieve social maturity, which otherwise might be delayed or not achieved at all.

Solidification of values.   Joining volunteer service is often a symptom of experimentation with alternative values. While many choose to pursue more competitive and materialistic values, those who focus on humanitarian values are able to test their chosen values through service projects. The outcome of the test often reinforces these values, and the person achieves greater certainty and self-assurance. This last point has been supported by a survey of returning Peace Corps volunteers who overwhelmingly (75 percent of the men and nearly 90 percent of the women) reported great satisfaction with their experience. While both sexes thought they had gained in self-assurance and outgoingness, the young women were especially convinced of having gained in the area of self-determination, greater curiosity in life, and effectiveness.[26]

The reasons American youth participate in service in the adult world involve a complex mixture of motivations. While the desire for service probably is a prevalent motive, healthy self-seeking, curiosity, interest in travel and

[26]Norma Haan, "Changes in Young Adults After Peace Corps Experiences," *Journal of Youth and Adolescence*, 3 (1974), 177–93.

other people, and a patriotic desire to improve the image of the United States are other elements.

SUMMARY

This chapter started the discussion on the dimensions of the subculture, focusing on the first one: unique values and attitudes. This dimension is so important and yields so much material with which to describe the teen subculture that an entire chapter was needed to discuss it.

The various aspects included (1) in-group values and concerns, especially as they reflect teenagers' needs for popularity and status among peers; (2) anti-intellectualism as a particularly significant attitude, for it bears heavily on the outcome of teens' educational experience; (3) the different roles that reference groups play in guiding teens' preferences in life, especially as they differ between the parental and the peer reference groups; (4) distinctions between girls' and boys' attitudes, with the former holding noticeably more emancipated attitudes than during previous years; (5) the curvilinear trend of parent-orientation on the part of teenagers over the past few decades, with high degree of parent-orientation during the 1960s, extremely low orientation during the 1970s, and again moderately high during the 1980s; (6) the clashes between parents' and teens' assumptions as to who may make the decisions in a number of realms; (7) the rise and decline of the New Sexuality, with AIDS as the new great peril; (8) some political attitudes that reflect unrelatedness between knowledgeability and basic emotional disposition concerning such important national issues as war and peace; (9) the new philosophy of entitlement, departing from the old Protestant Ethic and demanding economic security and psychological gratification as a "right" that society should guarantee; (10) the new religious synthesis between Christian and Oriental ideas, as a spiritual heritage, though mostly unawarely so, of the counterculture; and (11) various commitments in the form of volunteerism that are indicative that American youth is not suffering total isolation or alienation from the traditional American way of life.

The next chapter continues discussion of teenage subcultural dimensions.

13

Inside the Teen Subculture, Part II

This chapter continues the discussion on the basic dimensions of subculture, examining how teenage behavior expresses itself through them. The first dimension examined deals with argot, the linguistic quality of a subculture or a peer group, a quality which linguists and many sociologists consider of much deeper significance to the human mind than merely being a vehicle of in-group communication; in its most significant function it conditions the mind to think in certain ways and perceive the world through linguistically predetermined categories and nuances.

ARGOT

Argot is a "special language" reflecting the idiom of a particular group or social class. It is used by persons who interact over a considerable period and share special circumstances. One example of an argot is the language of the law. In the course of their professional associations, lawyers employ a language markedly different from ordinary speech. Other examples are the ecclesiastical language, the argot of thieves, the military establishment, miners, and medical doctors.

These sublanguages are adaptations to particular circumstances; most people speak only a few of them well and have little knowledge of others. The common characteristic is the function of adapting communication to the particular needs and interests of the group. Medical students have to learn a medical vocabulary; students of this textbook must be familiar with some sociological and psychological terminology.

Acquisition of an argot means more than just learning a new vocabulary. It signifies membership in the subculture to which the lingo is indigenous. It promotes group cohesiveness and insures privacy. It also stands for new knowledge and insights, both cognitive and affective.

Teen lingo is a special language. An adult listening to typical teenagers talk is aware of being a stranger to their ways of thinking. Iona and Peter Opie, in their study of several thousand English schoolchildren and their lingo *outside of the school,* discovered a lore and terminology of the children's argot that was largely unknown to the adult population.[1] Adults in England or the United States are not familiar with many of the terms and idioms of teenagers, and consequently not capable of cognizing and reacting in the same way. Usually, the only way to acquire the meaning is to join teenagers and participate in their activities — provided they accept the adult. Of course, many adults recall their own teenage days and may be able to roughly equate terms of today's argot with similar terms they used themselves, since many of the experiences, conditions, and circumstances of the adolescent phase have remained similar throughout recent generations.

The reason teenage argots evolve and are tenaciously maintained must be sought in their functions. At least six major functions can be discerned:

Shorthand device.   Many of the terms of teenage argot are designed to save time when referring to complex processes in which teens are involved. For example, to spell out the fine details and connotations of what is meant when referring to a person or an event as "cool" would take considerable time and would slow down communication. The word evokes a clear concept for teenagers, saves time and effort, and preserves their unique style of communication.

Precise reference.   In conjunction with the exposure to unique adolescent circumstances and conditions, the teenager finds that adult standard language does not include a sufficient reservoir of expressions to describe many of the ensuing experiences. Teenagers meet their need by modifying the general language with a battery of subcultural words that, in effect, lead to an argot. As a result, teenagers use words that are literally untranslatable into adult language because the empirical referents are unknown in the normal adult environment.

Teenage lingo can be vivid and clever. It can be sly enough to fool the

---

[1] Iona Opie and Peter Opie, *The Lore and Language of School Children* (Oxford: The Clarendon Press, 1959).

uninitiated, occasionally describing the diminutive without bothering to use the diminutive grammatical form. Many teenagers play their lingo like virtuosos, skillfully hitting just the right nuance of pronunciation and accompanying it with studied body language.

Not all experts credit teenage slang with discriminatory acuity. Dissenting opinions fail to take seriously the claim that teenage talk is profoundly discriminatory between nuances of meaning. For example, Cleveland Amory in one of his classic columns in *Saturday Review* dissected a number of frequently, if not ubiquitously, used teenage expressions. He concluded that they were practically interchangeable since their meanings hardly differed. What differed was merely the sound between the phrases as "with it," "far out," and "right on."[2] Similarly, Norman Cousins abhorred "slovenly speech . . . drained of color and distinction; [and] chopped-up phrases, relying on grunts and chants of 'you know' or 'I mean' to cover up a damnable incoherence."[3]

Status criterion. Ardent and masterly use of argot functions as a prestige gauge among peers. Symbolic bluffs can be played out by clever use of argot, and the degree of their skillfulness often determines leader or follower status. Not unlike other species, it is not necessarily the physically strongest of the group (or pride, flock, covey, or herd) who assumes the leadership position, but the one who impresses most. This may be the lion in a pride who consistently roars loudest and most ferociously, or the teenager who uses subcultural lingo most cleverly. In both instances, no physical test of strength is necessary; status differentiation is accomplished through the use of signs or symbols.

Group solidarity. When teenagers use or hear their "own" words, they are strongly reminded of their peer membership. Hence the use of lingo functions as a phonetic banner proclaiming association with the peer group.

Value statement. Argot reflects what is important to members of the subculture. The index of argot is such a sensitive indicator of peer values that it can be used to determine the type of association of a given individual. Research found that although argot, peer values, self-reports, and police contacts measure different referents, they are so highly correlated that measuring argot by itself is sufficient to determine the nature (delinquent or nondelinquent) of a teenager's peer involvement.[4] The high correlation is due to the unity of argot, values, and behavior.

[2]Cleveland Amory, "Curmudgeon-at-Large," *Saturday Review*, October 2, 1976, p. 51.

[3]Norman Cousins, "The Decline of Neatness," *Time*, April 2, 1990, p. 78.

[4]Paul Lerman, "Argot, Symbolic Deviance and Subcultural Delinquency," *American Sociological Review*, 32 (April 1967): 209–24.

Linguists discovered that the significance to a group or a society of a given thing is indicated by the number of words they use to refer to it. The classic example is Benjamin Whorf's oft-cited observation that Eskimos have various terms referring to snow, while standard English has only one.[5]

Linguistic conditioner. Once firmly entrenched, value-laden argot greatly influences (if not determines) the way members of a group perceive their social environment and, most significantly, the way it patterns their behavior.[6] It is through this linguistic process that habitual and distinctive ways of thinking and behaving of the typical teenager can be explained to a significant extent.

Teenage argot, as based on the above six major elements, does not consist of a uniform body of linguistic expression for the American teen population. Rather, it is divided into sublingos, bearing out the principle that different environments and different needs call for different vocabularies. It is therefore no surprise to hear the teenage surfers of the West Coast use a set of expressions of their own. The psychedelic drug users have developed their own lofty vocabulary. So have reborn Christians. Inner-city and black youths cultivate a version of argot closely related to racial and ethnic lingos. The lingo of athletes illuminates another side of the youth scene. And the vocabulary of cross-country skiing would excite only the aficionado of SNS (Salomon Nordic System): "tail" (rear portion of the ski), "base" (running surface), "ultra tuning" (base preparation), "waist" (midsection of the ski), "camber" (the arc in the midsection), and so forth. Some of these vocabularies overlap and are understood, although not spoken, by most teenagers; they are like different dialects of one language.

Research discovered that familiarity with subcultural phrases also varied according to age and sex.[7] Frequency of argot use increases during childhood and reaches a peak during adolescence. Some topics prompt greater increases than others, with relatively small increases used in referring to money, cigarettes and smoking, and clothes and styles. These, apparently, are issues that do not change much in significance between the years of childhood and adolescence; thus no significant changes in style of references take place. However, there were large increases for topics concerning alcohol and drinking, popularity, and (particularly among males) for cars, motorbikes, and girls. Girls tended to use more argot references concerning clothes, styles, appearance, and being popular or unpopular. Boys and girls lin-

---

[5]Benjamin Whorf, *Language, Thought, and Reality* (New York: John Wiley, 1956).

[6]Gary Schwartz and Don Merten, "The Language of Adolescence: An Anthropological Approach to the Youth Culture," *American Journal of Sociology*, 72 (March 1967): 453–68.

[7]Edward A. Nelsen and Edward Rosenbaum, "Language Patterns Within the Youth Subculture: Development of Slang Vocabularies," *Merrill-Palmer Quarterly of Behavior and Development*, 18 (July 1972): 273–84.

guistically accentuate those aspects of their lives in which they are more involved and interested.

Although every generation of teenagers seems to adhere to an argot, its specific content, such as particular expressions, changes from one generation to the next. What was "keen" twenty years ago changed to "tough," "boss," or "dapper," and finally back to "keen"—all referring to roughly the same phenomenon. It would therefore be futile to present a glossary of current teenage lingo, since it would rapidly become outdated. The linguist Jacques Barzun reminds us of the ephemeral lifespan of argot and slang expressions: "Only 50 years ago, in a representative novel of college life called *The Plastic Age*, the young men and women say: isn't it the darb!, that's the bean!, pike along, pash, razz, bughouse, simp, smack for him, and other mysterious remarks. The very word *plastic* in the title of that book has almost lost its original meaning thanks to the chemical industry."[8]

How do certain teenage expressions spread and become part of the argot of the national teenage subculture? Often it is the entertainment media that are responsible. The argot of the "valley girls" of Los Angeles' San Fernando Valley suburbs went national when, in 1982, parody-rocker Frank Zappa and his fourteen-year-old daughter created a record with "Val-speak."[9] Teen slang, up to that time not heard in any other part of the country, suddenly was imitated by teenagers everywhere.

On a more local scene, teen expressions spread as a result of imitating the talk of a teen hero. Ghoulardi, a Cleveland television semicomedian of the mid-1960s, invented the word *Knif* (fink spelled backward) and began offering Knif buttons. The teenage television audience immediately accepted the neologism, spread the vogue, and bought thousands of buttons. In one show, Ghoulardi coined the expression "All the world's a purple Knif." The idiom spread throughout the region and became a popular saying of the teenagers. Similarly, he named a pet crow Oxnard, and subsequently Cleveland's teenagers called each other Oxnard.[10]

A deliberate experiment to generate argot was attempted by students in a Phoenix high school communications class to study the process of word acceptance. The students invented a number of new words (*thacka, verk, greazums, shigbig,* and *bahamas*) and spread them around their school in personal conversations and in announcements on popular teenage radio stations. After two months, the experimenters visited more than fifty English classes to assess the results of the experiment. They discovered that *bahamas*

---

[8]Jacques Barzun, *Simple and Direct; A Rhetoric for Writers* (New York, Harper & Row, 1975), p. 38. See also two witty essays on this topic: Sam Hinton, "Moribund Metaphors Rise Again," *Verbatim*, 5 (February 1978): pp. 3–4; Lance Morrow, "If Slang is not Sin," *Time*, November 8, 1982, pp. 91–92.

[9]"It's Like Tubular!" *Newsweek*, August 2, 1982, p. 61.

[10]"What Catches the Teen-Age Mind?" *Time*, September 27, 1963, p. 55.

(meaning "underwear") was the most widely accepted. *Verk* ("punk"), *greazums* ("French fries") and *thacka* ("turn on") followed second, third, and fourth in acceptance. The reactions of the students to the invented terms were varied, but several remarked that the words were "dumb and weird." The linguistic innovations did not get a firm foothold in the community, and within two months the use of the words died out.[11]

There is notable lack of research in the genesis of argot vocabulary, and the question of etiology awaits more exploration.

CHANNELS OF MASS COMMUNICATION

Subcultures need channels of communication to maintain a sense of solidarity. Communication can proceed through various media, the simplest being direct person-to-person communication and general milling on America's high school and college campuses. Some of the communication in such situations does not need to be verbal; mere appearance is sufficient to convey a sense of belonging.

However, direct interaction within these ghettos is not sufficient to sustain the type of nationwide subculture that American teenagers form today. Various mass media come into play to accomplish that. It is no empty slogan to say that the media become the message: TV, radio, magazines, and the lyrics of music bombard the teen population with ideas and values that become singularly adolescent property. The media and their contents become the world of the teenage subculture.

The role of TV is most likely primary in encouraging conformist ideas and styles. It could hardly be otherwise, since its influence can be felt in virtually every living room.

Equally tangible is the medium of the record industry, which conveys lyrics, the ideas of teen heroes, subcultural values, and common joy and pain. Whether heard on the radio or on the stereo at home, records constitute a form of mass communication. The power of this medium is illustrated by over ninety record companies who release more than 9,000 pop records, including a total of 52,000 songs, each year.[12] Closely related are the music festivals and rock concerts where many heroes appear in person.

A medium of considerable importance to teens is magazines. Influential teen magazines are available at newsstands and drugstores. They try to attract attention by "teen"-connoting titles like *Teen World, Modern Teen, Teen Time, Teens Today, Teen Parade, Seventeen,* and, simply, *Teen.* Other magazines have taken their titles from slang vocabulary and have assumed

[11]"Students Buy, Soon Forget Slang Words," *Arizona Republic*, January 1, 1968, p. 35.
[12]R. Serge Denisoff, *Solid Gold* (New Brunswick, NJ: Transaction Books, 1975).

that such terms as *Dig* and *Flip* would appeal to teenagers. A survey revealed that most of these magazines have limited circulations. Typical examples are *Dig*, founded in 1955, with approximately 171,000 purchasers, *Teen*, with about 245,000, and *Modern Teen*, with about 221,000. One reason for limited circulation is the fact that these magazines are aimed at specific readership within the teenage population. Some of them are for young teenagers, some for girls only, some for middle teenagers, others for older teenagers including college students. Still others have a certain socioeconomic slant, as for example *Seventeen*, which caters to upper-middle-class girls. One of the variables that distinguishes one category from another is the degree of sophistication, usually reflected in the style of humor. While publications for younger teenagers appear intense and humorless, a more relaxed style emerges for older readers.

The diversity of youth publications can be illustrated by juxtaposing *Kids*, "The Magazine by Kids for Kids," and *Rolling Stone*, a newsmagazine with some political sophistication. The former addresses teenagers younger than fifteen, and in 1975 prided itself on being the "only national magazine written and illustrated totally by kids for kids." Its objective is to give children and teenagers a medium through which they can learn from each other and about each other, and at the same time enjoy working on a common communication project.

The biweekly *Rolling Stone*, however, which addresses the eighteen-to-twenty-five-year-old category, emphasizes modern music, offers views on a lifestyle that is a combination of counterculture and rock world, and publishes "personal ads" reminiscent of the style of the underground press. It is a heavily politicized publication that used to be part of the "youth revolution."

These publications are probably at opposite ends of the spectrum of youth magazines. In between lies a colorful array of printed matter, all vying for a segment of the youth population.

The factor that remains constant throughout all youth publications, and that is of foremost sociological importance, is the magazine's function of conveying a sense of collective identity. This unity function can be illustrated by the large volume of "Letters to the Editor," in which young people describe themselves, talk about their problems, and give and ask advice. In addition, the magazines organize fan club and pen pal departments. The close communication within the world of peers is strikingly illustrated by the exchange of personal views and problems.

Besides its subcultural role, the magazine market is of course also big business. A recent newcomer to the teen market, *Sports Illustrated for Kids*, began publication in January 1989; it illustrates the point. The magazine distributed 250,000 copies of each monthly issue free to 1,200 underfunded schools, presumably to encourage literacy. At the same time, it took advantage of the lucrative commercial opportunity and within the first four months sold nearly $8 million in advertising to tap the estimated $5 billion spent annually by American youngsters aged 9 to 12—who, in addition to their own spending, heavily influence their parents' annual spending, which is estimated to amount to $45 billion.[13]

FADS AND STYLES

Peer-group belonging can also be signified through clothing, grooming, music, dancing, and lingo. While these media are timeless, the specific content can be quite ephemeral. And this is where the definition of fad enters the picture. Ray Gold defines *fad* as "markedly novel, trivial, and ephemeral behavior which spreads rapidly through whatever portions of society choose to adopt it. Fad behavior involves crowd-like imitation directed toward momentary circumvention of folkways and mores; it also provides substitute ways of expressing normatively thwarted emotions, such as status yearning and sexual drives."[14]

The major elements of the definition include ephemerality, novelty, triviality, creation of status criteria, identification with the in-group, compensation (for powerlessness, alienation, and sexual frustrations), and the security of "sameness."

These elements can be recognized in the fads of American youth:

1. Almost all youth vogues are *shortlived,* one displacing the next in rapid sequence. It is difficult to determine the average duration of a youth fad; it may range from a few months to several years.
2. For a behavior style to qualify as a fad, it must introduce a relatively *new* way of doing, speaking, grooming, or dressing. It must draw attention and be clearly distinguishable from both the preceding habit in the given behavior area and the customary folkway in the adult world.
3. The significance of the fad is usually *trivial* compared with the mores of society. This implies that fads are "odd" forms of existing folkways, normally within the range of the permissible and not violating the mores. However, one can find instances where society has reacted with a severity toward teen fads that ordinarily is reserved for punishment of infractions of the mores. For example, the vogue of shoulder-length hair for boys during the late 1960s was judged so negatively by some school administrators that suspension from school was threatened or actually enforced.
4. Teenagers use fads as *status measurements.* Fads allow them to achieve prestige in the eyes of their peers by conforming and excelling in observance of the vogue.
5. Teen fads are considered in-group property. This exclusivity is both crescive and deliberate; that is, fads spring up more or less spontaneously and are imitated by teenagers without particular scrutiny of their purpose. However,

[13]Laurence Zuckerman, "Tapping the Kiddie Market," *Time,* April 24, 1989, p. 74.

[14]Ray L. Gold, "Fad," in A *Dictionary of the Social Sciences,* ed. Julius Gould and William L. Kolb (New York: Free Press, 1964), pp. 256–57.

once established, a fad is jealously guarded and deliberately kept from adults. In fact, it has been observed that as soon as adults accept and imitate a teen faddist style, teenagers reject it. The fad is part of the *identification function* of the subculture, using the uniform appearance or habit as a boundary-maintaining device.

6. Fads serve as *outlets for thwarted creativity* and as compensations for various frustrations. An example would be rechanneling of sexual aggressiveness into harmless, "safe," and culturally tolerated behavior forms (for example, teenage dancing). Also, compensatory fads may harness hostility into tolerable forms of rebelliousness.

7. There is psychological, and maybe even physical, *security* in uniformity of looks and behavior patterns. The young can feel safely ensconced in a peer group, are not only accepted but also protected by sameness, and do not suffer feelings of standing out and being vulnerable to outside forces. Apparently fad adherence serves the same universal function as the uniform: submergence of the individual into a protective body of collective sameness.

With these theoretical background remarks in mind, specific areas of youth fads and styles are now examined.

Clothing.   Clothing is a visual means of communication. Teenagers are able to identify in-group members by their appearance. Once clothing has given a teenager an idea of the social identity of a person, he or she is able to pattern his or her behavior and responses accordingly. If a teenager looks like a teenager, he or she is likely to be treated as a teenager, just as a schoolteacher who looks like a schoolteacher is likely to be treated as a schoolteacher. It can therefore be concluded that clothing influences the type of social interaction a person experiences.[15]

Clothing fads serve three additional functions beside the main functions of identification and protective "sameness." First, they serve as a medium of rebellion against the adult world; second, they often afford utilitarian comfort; and third, they allow for aesthetic expression.

Of these functions the one signaling rebellion is of primary interest here. Rebelliousness of youth has varied roots. Partly it is the age-old hedonistic resistance to being reined in by cultural dicta. Such rebelliousness becomes particularly accentuated, virtually provoked, if the culture is low in self-confidence and proceeds with diffident permissiveness in socializing its young. This condition seems to prevail, unlike in simpler societies, in most postindustrial countries. Additional roots of rebelliousness are found in the many adolescence-creating conditions that age-segregate, frighten, and confuse teenagers vis-à-vis a complex social system.

[15]Social-psychological functions of clothes have been examined by such writers as John Brooks, *Showing off in America: From Conspicuous Consumption to Parody Display* (New York: Little, Brown, 1981); Hilda M. Buckley and Mary E. Roach, "Clothing as a Nonverbal Communication of Social and Political Attitudes," *Home Economics Research Journal*, 3 (December 1974): 94–102.

It appears that the hippie movement, emerging in the mid 1960s, was originally based on just such a rebelliousness. What took form was not a mere faddist mood, but a social movement; it rejected not only conventional clothing but also middle-class art, philosophy, and values. The hippies conveyed a studiedly worn and bedraggled image, usually including regulation denim, regulation ornamentation (medallions and the popular Indian beads), and regulation hiking boots.

Occasionally, a leading member of some teenage subgroup asserts his or her ideas, or the ideas of the group, by adding special adornments to his or her clothing. Examples were (and still are) T-shirts that sported slogans and/or pictures on the front and/or the back. It was a medium through which the wearer could express serious or not-so-serious whims, concerns, complaints, political and philosophical views, and anything else he or she wanted to proclaim ("Don't Bother Me, I Can't Cope," "Fly Me, I'm Henry," "Cocaine, The Real Thing"). Major department stores, as well as thousands of small T-shirt shops across the country, are cashing in on the craze that has consumed millions of decorated T-shirts.

This again brings to mind the commercial exploitation of style-conscious youth. A fundamental rule of Madison Avenue strategy is that "the younger you reach them the more impressionable they are" and the more lucrative the return in the long run. For this purpose a large portion of American advertising aims at preschoolers, which at the beginning of the 1990s numbered approximately 23 million, the offspring of the baby-boom generation.

A typical example was observable during the early 1990s when, rather suddenly, somber black became the preferred hue of children's clothes—from toddlers to teenagers. The trendiness was quickly supported, if not instigated, by the industry which unloaded tons of black garments from black leather jackets, unitards, leggings, jogging outfits, to shirts and blouses.[16]

Vestiges of many if not all fads are still found. Perhaps no fad ever dies completely; it only slumbers to be reawakened, and often goes through fascinating metamorphoses to reappear in a slightly altered form.

Music.   Unlike clothing fads, music styles have proved of longer duration. Popular music, once primarily an adult-oriented entertainment, underwent radical changes in the mid-1950s and emerged at the end of that decade as the almost exclusive property of youth. The driving force behind this development was a combination of musical styles that fused the sounds of country and western music and rhythm and blues into rock 'n' roll. This original musical hybrid sired a number of offshoots, such as rock, soul, psychedelic, bubblegum, and even punk music. Compared with the music of

[16]Elisabeth Snead, "Babies in Black," *USA Today*, November 29, 1990, p. 1.

the Roaring Twenties, which lasted only about ten years, the rock 'n' roll tradition has endured much longer.

Adult reactions to youth-oriented popular music were severe and swift in coming. Frank Sinatra condemned it as a "rancid-smelling aphrodisiac"; Samuel Cardinal Stritch compared it to "tribal rhythms"; Pablo Casals publicly called rock "poison put to sound"; a group of psychologists, mindful of teenagers' frenzied response to Elvis Presley, called it a "medieval type of spontaneous lunacy"; and a United States Senate subcommittee started investigations of possible connection between rock and juvenile delinquency.[17]

Part of the reason for the virulent reaction had to do with the personality cult, the riots by fans, and the sexual innuendos associated with the new music. Elvis Presley is indelibly associated with the early history of rock 'n' roll, having helped introduce the new style to the teen world. The initiation was ecstatic and often unruly, causing numerous fan riots—not only in this country but around the world. The authorities took a dim view of this novel lack of inhibition and restraint. This was also the time when scientists started to voice concern about the physiological effects of the onslaught of the up-to-then unheard-of-decibels characteristic of the new style; they exceeded 100 decibels in front of a rock band—equal to the noise level of a moon rocket blastoff.

Chubby Checker introduced the twist in 1960. For the first time since the decline of the jitterbug, American teenagers had their own dance. But about two or three years later the twist became obsolete and taboo for connoisseurs, and such free-style versions as the "Watusi," "hitchhiker," "frug," "jerk," and the "monkey" appeared.

Versions of rock 'n' roll spread and became an international fad. Some English musicians were particularly influenced by American rock 'n' roll and began to refertilize the American mainland with their own versions. In 1964 the Beatles appeared on the Ed Sullivan Show before a television audience of almost 70 million, received one of television's biggest publicity coverages, and embarked on one of the most successful show business careers in history. With the Beatles began the actual rock revolution that subsequently defined an emerging segment of the American population, literally financed a counterculture, spawned a $2 billion industry, and gave young Americans a common means of expression—a common music, a common language, and even a common dramaturgy with roles of heroes and martyrs.[18]

Rock style has not remained uniform over the years. The folk rock of Bob Dylan was different from the more sentimental eloquence of the Beatles

[17]"The Sound of the Sixties," *Time*, May 21, 1965, p. 85.

[18]Bernice Martin, "The Sacralization of Disorder: Symbolism in Rock Music," *Sociological Analysis*, 40 (1979): 87–124.

at the height of their career; the acid rock of the Rolling Stones became more sophisticated over the years; the mid-1970s brought a gentler variety of rock sounds with soothing melodies and reconciliatory lyrics; and the early 1980s saw the spread of the cacophonous, nihilistic Punk, New Wave spinoff, and heavy metal.

It may be this flexibility that made rock the viable musical form it turned out to be and that allowed it the retention of certain basic characteristics since the 1950s.

Throughout the 1980s and into the early 1990s, American pop music hardly strayed from generic rock—be it in the form of the more sonorous and Establishment-approved Michael Jackson or in the form of the vituperously snarling Ozzy Osbourne. But what seemed to prevail in the end was an overreaction to the heavy-metal groups, such as Motley Crüe with its satanic symbolism, and the Beastie Boys and the 2 Live Crew with their studied vulgarisms. Despite the fact that the vast majority of teenagers listening to heavy metal are more enthralled by decibels and rhythms than by lyrics, the words of which they rarely hear or understand, the infuriated moral right wing of American society called for censorship of what they considered unwholesome music and lyrics.[19]

In the meantime, the opinions have polarized once more. On one side are rallying the liberal attitudes, insisting that art forms are entitled to attack and to shock and disagree with the prejudices of the powers-that-be; on the other side are the defenders of traditional values (including such voices as John Cardinal O'Connor of New York and Senator Jesse Helms) who feel that adult society has the responsibility to educate, preserve human dignity, and point the way to constructive values. No doubt this sort of confrontation and dispute will rage on as long as we have adolescents with the indomitable inclination to challenge tradition and experiment with styles purposely intended to produce shock and outrage.

It must be added that rock did not remain the sole domain of teenagers—it captured a large adult following, adults who fervently, and in a sense uninvitedly, imitated the youngsters, forming an adult fan club that was unwanted and embarrassing to the teenagers. More than 40 percent of the "teen beat" records sold in the United States at one time were bought by persons over twenty years old. Teenagers complained about adult intrusion and felt that their "sacred" domain was invaded by uninvited parents.[20]

Dancing. Obviously, this type of music was inseparable from dancing. The simple beat seemed monotonous to the musicologist and too loud for the sensitive, but it had a kinetic effect on dancers that proved compelling to

[19]Richard Corliss, "X-Rated," *Time*, May 7, 1990, pp. 92–99.
[20]"The Sound of the Sixties."

teenagers and adults alike. As a result, the discotheques, places of sustained rock 'n' roll rhythm and performing go-go girls, multiplied throughout the nation.

Dancing itself was a private choreography, enabling the dancer to be creative in steps, gestures, and motions. A partner was not really necessary since no bodily coordination between partners was needed. In essence, the partners danced by and for themselves, most of the time paying little attention to each other. Some observers called it a kind of "fertility rite," intended to alleviate the sterility of urban-industrial life.[21] However, it was "fertility rite" minus sexual contact—a paradox. On one hand, modern dance openly displays a degree of sexual suggestiveness that no other Western dance forms have dared before; on the other hand, it cooly refrains from any bodily contact with the partner—in fact, it studiously ignores the partner altogether. It sounds like a contradiction. Why do young Americans in an age of relative sexual permissiveness choose to dance in isolation?

Several explanations are possible and probably make a stronger point in combination. One is that our age of liberation is also reflected in dancing behavior. Each dancer is "doing his or her thing," expressing rhythms and improvisations without having either to lead or follow a partner. This development has been supported, on an unconscious level, of course, by the female's general surge toward emancipation. It may be part of her general revolt against having to follow the male lead. A second reason deals with American youth's increasing presumption that instantness in all things is possible, including dancing skill. Old-fashioned dance forms required learning and effort. Dancing apart from one another required none of the initially tedious synchronization of steps and movements. Modern dancing could be achieved instantly! A third reason assumes that, insofar as today's dancing has no rules, none of the participants are held responsible for "proper" steps and movements, in fact, none care about rules—it represents a miniature model of present-day society, characterized by anomie and alienation. Dancing, then, consists of an isolated, gyrating body unaccompanied by an identity.[22] Still another encouragement for this dance style comes from the awkwardness and inexperience that many adolescents bring to a situation where they have to intimately interact with the other sex. Rock dancing largely eliminates the embarrassment of sweaty hands, missing a beat, stepping on the partner's toes, and not knowing what to say. Dancing in isolation to music usually too loud for conversation lets the adolescent off the hook.

Given these "safety" factors, inhibitions all but disappear and raw, sensual expressions can be observed, the anatomical gyrations of the dancers

---

[21]Samuel Grafton, "The Twisted Age," *Look,* December 15, 1964, pp. 37–38.

[22]An interesting study, examining the parallelism between dance form and civilization form throughout Western history, has been completed by Gabriele Klein, *Über die Zivilisationsgeschichte des Tanzes,* Ph.D. Dissertation, Ruhr-Universität, Bochum, Germany, 1990.

sometimes frankly suggesting copulatory motions. Judgments concerning the sexual expression of rock 'n' roll dancing vary widely. Some parents condemn it completely; others think that some of the dances are acceptable. Analytical observers conclude that this type of dancing is "safe sex" for teenagers. Harvard psychiatrist Philip Solomon sees these dances as healthy outlets for youthful restlessness and as sublimated sexual desires.[23]

Studies have revealed that the predominant feelings experienced by young dancers are *release* and *abandon,* sensations that social scientists explain by the dancers' temporary retreat from the tensions and frustrations of being status-deprived adolescents. It was also found that teenagers considered adults at a discotheque to be trespassers and intruders.[24]

It seems, then, that rock 'n' roll music meets a number of teenagers' needs—their desire to express themselves bodily without limiting coordination to another moving body, without the need to converse, and without the fear of getting out of step. Moreover, erotic expressions pass with impunity and are rendered relatively inoffensive because of the dancers' abstention from physical contact.

Explained on the basis of these various functions, the longevity of rock 'n' roll is not surprising.

Hair style.   The youth style fomenting extremely hostile reactions on the part of adults and frequently jolting authorities into severe countermeasures was young males' infatuation with long hair. Of all the fads and styles of the past decades, long hair seemed to offend the mores and the aesthetic sensibilities of the Establishment most profoundly. The new hairstyle was not perceived as a fad but as a perversion.

It is not ascertainable how and why the fad of long hair for boys developed. Coincidentally or causatively, the style started around 1964, when the Beatles exhibited their trademark, long hairdos, in the United States.

The controversy over long hair applied exclusively to boys. Girls, it seems, enjoy almost unlimited license to fashion their hair in any way they wish, whether short or long, bleached or colored, ribboned or loose. To be sure, feminine hairdos go through fashions too, but since, by societal consensus, *all* of their styles pass as acceptable, deviant or "odd" fads are rarely ascribed to them. The difference between male and female hair styles is that the former are described as fads or deviations and the latter as fashions. Fashion, by definition, is a style approved or at least tolerated by the larger society and should therefore not be equated with fad.

In their own defense, boys point out that long hair has been a symbol of virility ever since biblical days and confess that they often grow luxuriant tops

[23]"The Sound of the Sixties," p. 88.

[24]Lucille H. Blum, "The Discotheque and the Phenomenon of Alone-Togetherness," *Adolescence,* 1 (Winter 1966): 351–66.

because their girlfriends admire them. They complain that a more liberal policy on hair styling is necessary to provide them with an opportunity to create more individualistic appearances to compete with girls, who traditionally are allowed more styling alternatives concerning not only hair but also dress, colors, shoes, hats, scarfs, make-up, and jewelry. Finally, some youngsters added that they wear long hair simply because they *want to* and because they want to look *different* from others, especially adults.

As the opposition grew, so did the hair—and with a fascinating display of obstinacy, the style spread, persisted, and even eventually influenced adult hairstyles to some degree.

The path of the new style abounded with innumerable clashes—many comical, others sordid, and some outright tragic. Examples from the earlier period include the action by the dean of Cardinal Hayes High School in the Bronx, who met students returning for the fall semester with a pair of scissors and shortened the locks of several boys; the refusal of the Kenosha, Wisconsin high school to admit nearly 200 boys because of their long hair; the order by Federal Judge Richard Duncan of Kansas City that a young delinquent get a haircut because "I refuse to sentence anyone I can't see"; and hundreds of teachers who apparently agreed with the judge and refused to teach students whose visibility was obstructed by a surplus of hirsute resources.[25]

Some extreme outcomes include the cases of a California father, who, after a longstanding feud over his son's long hair, shot the boy to death in anger;[26] two Texas brothers, thirteen and sixteen, who fatally shot their father, an Air Force officer, when he was asleep because he objected to their long hair and refused to buy motorbikes for them;[27] and a fifteen-year-old Rolling Stones fan who threw himself to his death under a train after he had been forced to have his long hair cut.[28]

The controversy raged between students and school administrators, employers and employees, and especially between parents and offspring. It continued long after the rebellious counterculture had ceased agitation. By the late 1970s two convergent trends seemed to resolve the controversy: the public turned more accepting, and teenagers' insistence on long hair dissipated, possibly because adults had gradually imitated it to some extent.

But peace was to be short-lived. The last decade of the twentieth century to some extent reintroduced the issue. Increasing number of children and teenagers again insisted on long hairdos, particularly the male ponytail. Again tempers flared across the nation. As mentioned earlier, in one case a Texas school barred a boy from regular class attendance because of his

[25]Reported by Hal Cooper in an AP report (New York, December 3, 1965), and by "The Unkindest Cut for Student Moptops," *Life*, August 24, 1965, p. 4.

[26]UPI Report (April 24, 1971).

[27]UPI Report (November 10, 1972).

[28]AP Report (January 19, 1966).

7-inch ponytail. The disciplinary action was appealed by the parents of the boy, but the court upheld the school's decision. The mysterious vehemence shown by the authorities, especially school authorities, against boys' "deviant" coiffures turns out to be a battle without end.

Besides fad formation in the areas discussed above, there have been many additional youth fads that were minor, regional, or very short-lived. They range from the 1960s wave of wearing Nazi medals to the 1970s "streaking" (a craze perhaps short-lived but hardly minor) to the mock violence of Punk style in the 1980s. The examples mentioned in the above discussions are just that—examples. They are not intended to catalog the innumerable fads that have delighted, dismayed, or left this nation indifferent over the past decades.

SENSE OF SOLIDARITY

The youthful sense of solidarity emanates from all the dimensions discussed so far. There is really no separate dimension by which this *esprit de corps* can be measured; it is conveyed through teenagers' attitudes, values, lingo, music, dancing, fads, styles, hero worship, status criteria, and subcultural institutionalization.

Their attempts to exclude adults from their activities and styles is one of the surest indications of youth's solidarity. This exclusion is frequently manifested by discontinuing a fad or style as soon as adults begin to accept and imitate it. The habitual reference to the impersonal third-person "they" (the adults, the Establishment) as distinct from the first-person "we" and "us" is a constant reminder of modern youth's practice of setting itself apart from the larger society.

Teen lingo in general is a good measure of how much an in-group awareness prevails and reinforces a separate identity. A sense of solidarity almost invariably results in a distinct lingo. Worshiping common heroes is another indication of solidarity. Such individuals serve as focal points for youth's need to consolidate feelings and values. Heroes are often defined as such because they represent alternative or even deviant values from the larger society and thus function as exponents of the youth collective's sense of solidarity.

Certain drugs—it used to be marijuana—served as a means of cultivating a sense of separateness. Engaging in a deviant or illicit practice is a powerful means of generating a feeling of being a distinct collectivity, a community of the "persecuted," "rejected," or "victimized." Some social scientists used to liken the typical setting of marijuana smoking and the stereotypical demeanor displayed at such times (the ritualistic passing of the "joint" around the circle of the initiated) to the passing of the Holy Eucharist among the believers to merge the participants into a common body. Such illicit, deviant, or at least unique, rituals play a powerful role in substantiating a feeling of belonging to the in-group and accentuating a feeling of alienation from the outgroup.

An unfailing sign of the youthful sense of solidarity is the fervent cultivation of the generation gap by word and deed. The frustrations growing out of the socialization process find their consolidating and consoling culmination in solidarity, using adults as scapegoats. The sense of solidarity is greatly enhanced if the in-group can identify a common adversary or "enemy," since it enables the followers to focus their dissatisfaction away from the in-group interaction and directs frustration and hostility to an out-group target. This habit also clarifies group boundaries, an important condition for maintaining cohesiveness.

A significant step toward measuring the concept of solidarity was made by James A. Cramer and Dean J. Champion, who believed that solidarity refers specifically to the *affective content* of group relations and is made up of the positive emotional elements prevailing among the members of a group, resulting in sentiments of "we-ness."[29] The researchers determined a number of items that are best suited for measurement of solidarity. These items included such statements as "Troubles and discouragements just draw us closer," "When we have a job to do, everybody pitches in," "Members are close knit, stick together through thick and thin," and "Spend lots of time together because we prefer each other's company."

STATUS CRITERIA

Just as in the case of the sense of solidarity, status criteria must be deduced from various dimensions of behavior. What is counted as status and prestige is directly correlated with success in such behavior as fads, drug use, dating, use of teen argot, and material acquisitions that reflect and enhance subcultural belonging.

Hence, a pair of faded jeans is not just clothing, it is a symbol of belonging and status; having a date with a member of the opposite sex is frequently not a human encounter based on personal attraction but on prestige derived from being seen with a popular girl or guy; flaunting possession of the latest popular hits does not necessarily mean enjoying them as personally meaningful, but means letting others know that you are up on the latest productions; participating in marijuana smoking frequently has nothing to do with the enjoyment of the elusive "high" (that is as often faked as it is actually experienced), but has something to do with the recognition by

---

[29]James A. Cramer and Dean J. Champion, "Toward the Clarification of Solidarity," *Pacific Sociological Review*, 18 (July 1975): 292–309.

peers that you are "cool"; fads are often enjoyed not because they gratify the youth's need for creativity, but because they achieve the necessary "look alike" and the acceptance as "one of the gang"; speaking the argot is not so much preference as coercion to live up to peer expectations; and joining in the worship of certain heroes is not always an expression of liking or respecting that individual, but an attempt to impress peers and to appear knowledgeable as to who is "great" and who is not, what is "in" and what is not, and in general to convey an air of appreciating the presumed spokespersons of their generation.

All of these behavior forms are part of the fine art of followership and correlated prestige. Beyond a certain point of following, the skill of leading emerges; that is, the teenager with the biggest achievement in these behavior patterns earns the highest prestige and qualifies for leadership status. However, to achieve true leadership requires additional personality features.

The desire for status among peers often seems to influence the choice of friends among teenagers. Boys and girls sometimes choose, or are chosen, "friends" on the basis of prestige. It appears that the prestige of a teenager carries over to his or her associates and, thus, a "friend" actually functions as a status criterion. In most cases, however, a modified process operates whereby teenagers look as much at personality features as the prestige potential of a friend-to-be.

Status criteria differ from peer group to peer group and depend heavily on the teenager's orientation. Hence, behavior that would be prestigious among delinquent youths would be rejected by nondelinquent youths. Significant items of prestige among middle-class youths might be different from those of working-class youngsters and, of course, the racial and minority groups imbue their young with still other status criteria.

However, certain items are used throughout most, if not all, groups to assess a teenager's standing. One of them is clothing and appearance. Research found that urban high school girls used these aspects in deciding whether new girls qualified as personal friends and as group members. However, when they discussed old friends, the question of appearance receded and personality, friendliness, and similar interests and involvements became more important. It followed, then, that once the appearance of a newcomer was assessed and a decision to pursue or not pursue a friendship was made, appearance was more or less taken for granted.[30]

The study also discovered that girls are able to infer socioeconomic background by the way a peer dresses. Girls in lower socioeconomic classes were found to be "improperly" dressed by more affluent girls and not accepted into certain groups. In most instances, the rejected girls were well

---

[30]Joanne B. Eicher et al., *A Longitudinal Study of High School Girls' Friendship Patterns, Social Class, and Clothing* (East Lansing, MI: Michigan State University Agricultural Experiment Station, 1974), p. 20.

aware of the ostracism but maintained their own ideas about clothing and appearance. They eventually formed their own groups, cultivated their own clothing styles, and thus avoided isolation.

The consequences that follow from this status behavior are of considerable significance to educators and social workers. The status criteria of clothing and appearance separated the high school girls to the disadvantage of students in lower socioeconomic classes. "The situation in the school was almost a case of 'never the twain shall meet,' so that girls were denied opportunities to learn ways different from those they had grown up with.[31] This implies that youthful status behavior reinforces and perpetuates the status quo. It is suspected that such labeling behavior contributes more to the isolation and eventual dropping out of lower-class youth than difficulties that are purely academic.

Being rejected by peers must be one of the most tragic experiences for a young person. That this occurs on the basis of "first impression" is particularly unfortunate because it means the decision of accepting or rejecting is not being made on grounds of more important factors. The moral of the story is that if teenagers from different social backgrounds want to be accepted by one another, they must learn to understand each other's views regarding dress.

There were some age differences, however, in the approach of choosing a friend. Ninth-graders considered personality as the most important basis on which a given girl would be judged. But twelfth-graders put personality in second place and considered "looks and appearance" as the first standard. These older teenagers relied more heavily on "first impression" and believed it gives them a realistic assessment of lasting reliability.

It is interesting that the opinions of teenagers concerning the criteria of popularity and what is sought in a friend have hardly changed over the past decade. The 1974 Eicher study (mentioned above) and the 1982 Sebald survey (see section on in-group values in Chapter 12) have come up with basically the same rank order of criteria.

Researchers have noted that determined status-seeking girls sometimes use sex as a means to enhance their prestige. They try to attract high-status boys for dates, and to do so they occasionally engage in rather intense petting without endangering their "reputation." The interaction consisted of a game of providing just so much sexual favor for so much prestige by association. On the other hand, boys' status behavior was found to primarily consist of drinking and dating practices through which "manhood" was tested and proved. In conjunction with the drinking behavior, a sort of daredevil approach to the problem of the purchase of beer or liquor developed, and accomplishing the illicit purchase was considered an act of cleverness and

[31]Ibid.

"having guts" that added to the status among peers. Such a purchase (with faked IDs or lying about one's age) was a battleground reserved for the courageous only, and the risk to the boys' self-esteem was great. If a boy revealed that he was afraid of showing a false ID or otherwise bluffing his way through demands to prove his age, he lost face within his peer group. This was the acid test of "keeping your cool." Any boy who failed to rise to the occasion had his claims to "coolness" ruthlessly deflated by his peers.[32]

Status expectations differ among groups. There is no *one* system with perfectly hierarchically arranged status positions for all. Studies seem to indicate that young people perceive of status as a set of ranked, slightly ambiguous prestige categories that are internally differentiated. This can be explained by pointing first to a horizontal dimension that is an array of different lifestyles heavily influenced by the teenagers' socioeconomic background. Each lifestyle differs somewhat in dress, speech, interpersonal demeanor, and prestige in the community (boys in a lower-class neighborhood, girls in a predominantly middle-class high school, college coeds, and rock 'n' roll groupies). Second, a vertical dimension can be visualized within each group according to which the members are assessed and status-ranked. While the horizontal dimension is qualitative, dividing teenagers into distinct categories that might be judged delinquent or nondelinquent, lower or upper class, the vertical dimension is a quantitative measure ascribing more or less popularity to a member of the group.

The process of status attribution is complex. Status does not simply derive from objective talents and characteristics, such as a boy's athletic ability or a girl's physical attractiveness. Teenagers acquire esteem in a variety of contexts and obtain subcultural validation by adherence to their group's standards. An element that seems to run through all modern peer groups is the presentation of oneself as "cool." To the extent that "coolness" becomes a part of a teenager's behavioral routine, peer acceptance and admiration will rise—and that, after all, is what status among teenagers is all about.

HERO WORSHIP

Most identifiable subcultures come equipped with leaders. Yet, when we look at the teen subculture in America on the national level, we find leadership conspicuously absent. Instead, heroes abound who are idols of the masses, passive figures of the world of entertainment, whose ability to lead is negligible and whose vision is myopic. With rare exceptions, they are profiteers cashing in on fads and styles that they have not created. Many of them

---

[32]Schwartz and Merten, "The Language of Adolescence," *American Journal of Sociology*, 72 (March 1967): 453–68.

become millionaires not because they are particularly talented or have something to say but because they were lucky enough to get into the limelight of the world of entertainment. This individual becomes the target of the teenagers' emotional accolades and their need for heroes. The result is hero worship—which is not to be confused with following a leader.

There are, however, certain segments of the youth population that have, or had, leaders. Among them are the spokespersons of the counterculture, the political activists and radicals (Joan Baez, David Harris, Jerry Rubin, Pete Seeger, Bob Dylan, Jane Fonda, and others) who stood up against the Establishment and in some cases became martyrs for their causes. There are also the leaders of the local teenage scene: the leaders of cliques, gangs, and crowds who rally their followers in the community, neighborhood, or school.

The present discussion focuses on the general, nationwide teen subculture and, because of the peculiar hero-orientation of the American teenagers, deals more with heroes from the entertainment world than leaders in the real sense of the word.

Hero worship is a timeless indulgence. It appears to be such a deep-seated need that if no real heroes are available, supernatural ones tend to be invented. This need is observable in both adults and teenagers. Depending on the cultural milieu, the hero may be a military figure, a political personality, an outstanding athlete, or a popular entertainer. Commensurate with the American ethos, which cherishes popularity more than Spartan values, teenagers in the United States exhibit special admiration for entertainers, singers, actors, and musicians. The worship of these popular heroes often proceeds in overt demonstrations. At concerts, cheering crowds manifest their loyalty; in teenagers' bedrooms, pictures on the wall silently testify admiration; in record stores, sales reveal listeners' adoration; and dress and hair styles often imitate popular idols.

The attractiveness that heroes have for the masses is composed of a number of complex elements. Some of them have been verified by research, and some have been assumed by theory. Major gratifications American teenagers derive from hero worship include:

Romanticism. Romanticism refers to emotions and attitudes that usually are insufficiently based on facts. The appeal of romantic emotions lies in the heroic, remote, mysterious, and idealized. This emotional disposition can be related to a number of areas in life, but it is most frequently observed in connection with attitudes toward love relationships. Teenagers are particularly prone to adhere to romantic perceptions of the male-female relationship because they lack the experience of the older generation and are reluctant to accept adult standards. As a result, teen heroes can easily capitalize on the romance hunger of their followers, reinforce unrealistic perceptions, and become tangible foci of romantic identifications.

Teenagers see in their heroes the incarnation of many of their fondest

dreams and desires. Since the unrealistic nature of the dreams makes implementation in the life of the individual teenager impossible, they are transferred to a person whose popularity seems to attest to their success in
materializing such dreams. Popularity is perceived by the teenage followers
as the *carte blanche* of all dreams and hopes.

Sex and fetishism. Expressions of hero worship have frequently been
interpreted as substitution and sublimation of sexual desire whereby some
material aspect of the popular hero, such as his or her clothing or hair,
becomes a fetish. In other words, a fetish is a tangible substitute for the
coveted person that provides a degree of erotic gratification. A mild, usually
socially acceptable, and widespread fetishistic practice is collecting and/or
pinning up pictures of heroes. Expressions of this romantic adulation can be
gleaned from almost all teen magazines, which provide fan departments,
print pin-ups, and advertise "real photos of rock stars."

American teenagers have established by now an impressive history of
fetishistic pursuits (often exploited by business). Frankie Avalon, an earlier
rock 'n' roll balladeer, was attacked by his fans numerous times. Once,
teenage girls pulled the shoes off his feet; another time, a crowd of excited
teenagers trampled him and sprained his back in an effort to touch him and
tear off pieces of his clothing.[33] On their 1966 return to the United States,
the Beatles were beleaguered at their hotels by hundreds of shrieking girls. A
teenager who let it be known that she had a lock from the head of one of the
Beatles was mobbed by the other girls who wanted to touch and kiss it. At
numerous performances, the Beatles' music and lyrics were completely
drowned out by the screaming teenage audiences, who were more interested
in seeing than hearing their idols. Several hotels at which the Beatles slept
turned the teenagers' fetishistic desires into lucrative business by cutting up
and selling square inches ($1.00 a piece) of the bed sheets used by the
heroes.[34] A similar fate awaited the sheets used by the Rolling Stones at a
1973 stopover in New Zealand, where businessmen purchased them to make
them into souvenir handkerchiefs and shirt panels.[35]

Some sexual expressions are less substitutional and more direct. Paul
Dean of the popular rock group Loverboy was asked how it felt to be a sex
idol for youngsters who aren't old enough to drive a car. "Well, I've got to
laugh when a 13-year-old is crying, 'I love you, I love you, I love you.' I say, 'No
you don't.' " According to Dean, then she screamed even louder, "Yes, I
dooooo!"[36]

---

[33]Thomas B. Morgan, "Teen-Age Heroes: Mirror of a Muddled Youth," *Esquire*, March
1960, pp. 65–73.

[34]UPI Report (Chicago, August 13, 1966).

[35]AP Report (Auckland, New Zealand, March 22, 1973).

[36]Lynn Pyne, "Rock Group," *Phoenix Gazette*, December 7, 1983, p. G1.

Dean added an observation of sociological acumen: "But I understand what's going on, because they don't have anything in their lives and they have this fantasy that they built up that we are superhuman and the perfect person, you know: 'This guy is unbelievable, how could I love anyone else?' "[37]

The scene is reminiscent of the so-called groupies, who constitute a special institution of teen subculture and are hero worshipers who, according to the simple definition of Frank Zappa (leader of the rock group called the Mothers of Invention) are "girls who go to bed with members of rock 'n' roll bands."[38] These girls are also known as "rock geishas" and engage in sexual activities with rock stars and their immediate entourages. Groupies cultivate numerous relationships, and it is not uncommon for them to extend sexual favors to several members of a group within one night. An internal status system has developed among the groupies that largely depends on which famous bands they can list as their "friends." Many of them travel with bands, staying with one for a week, then changing to another. These girls are a small minority. For the rest of the masses of teenagers, their heroes remain more distant, romantic figures with whom they stay in touch by various fetishistic practices.

Crowd ecstasy.   Heroes often serve as catalysts for the type of mass behavior that allows abandon and release. Youthful rambunctiousness and excitement find an outlet when heroes perform in front of large teen audiences. Concert settings give the young an opportunity to physically express exuberance by screaming, touching, and moving rhythmically. Being in a mass of peers is a visceral experience, not unlike dancing, and offers an outlet for tension. The behavior at teen concerts is governed by completely different rules (and maybe needs) than that at adult concerts. While the heroes perform, the audience is not expected to remain silent and motionless; band members are not usually disturbed by the noise their appreciative audience makes.

A good part of the behavior at such rallies is not intended as listening but as a testimony of *belonging.* A number of physical expressions of "worshiping," such as screaming, jumping, and even "fainting," have a mutually reinforcing effect in a crowd situation. The reinforcement is due to the rewards derived from the prestige assigned to such peer-approved and peer-encouraged actions. It is interesting that many vociferous teenagers are not looking at their heroes on such occasions, but at each other, apparently to make sure that they are seen screaming. Back rows usually do not scream,

[37]Ibid.
[38]"Manners and Morals," *Time*, February 28, 1969, p. 48.

but, merely applaud conventionally, since they are outside of the field of observation.

An interesting example of crowd-reinforced imitation comes from the early days of the rock 'n' roll era. Frankie Avalon's presence and singing would always induce some girls to faint—or to pretend to. It became the thing to do. During a Milwaukee presentation by Avalon, twenty-one girls ostentatiously fainted. At another performance on television, when Avalon sang "Boy Without a Girl," the camera showed a number of sobbing teenagers. *From then on,* this behavior became a routine and was imitated whenever Avalon appeared and sang that particular song.[39] Avalon's record was broken in 1975 when 250 young girls fainted ritualistically at a concert given by a Scottish group, the Bay City Rollers.

Michael Jackson exerted similar magnetism when he caused "fainting" on an international scope. When, in 1988, he performed in Vienna, Austria, approximately 130 girls (not one boy) fainted in homage to the U.S. superstar at a concert attended by 50,000 devotees.[40]

The fascination with the bizarre and the absurd.   Humans of any age category can be turned into a captive audience by the bizarre and the absurd. The heroes of modern American teenagers cultivate this fascination by a freak style that during previous epochs was confined to the semiunderground adult theatres à la Marquis de Sade. Today's teenage version is carried out by some (heavy metal) rock groups, wallowing in the macabre and the ghoulish. A particularly virulent form of combining the bizarre with the violent was the Punk style. Another version that never seems to lose its popularity, and one not totally deprived of humor, was/is the Rocky Horror Picture Show, a midnight movie of delight to young aficionados of the bizarre.

Such mid-1970s freak heroes as Alice Cooper, Mick Jagger, and Elton John devised freak gimmicks to win teen attention that included transvestic, surrealistic, sadomasochistic, and macabre appearance and performance. Among the most notable acts was Cooper's ritualistic suicide fake in front of shrieking teenage audiences with the tragic consequence of a number of imitations that proved fatal to teen fans.

Many teen aficionados are attracted to the freak shows because they find them "scary," "weird," and they make their skin "tingle" with excitement. Is the type of teenager attracted to the freak style an exceptional youth, characterized by deviant tendencies, or the quite normal youth who simply responds to the unusual, the bizarre, and the grotesque? The best one could do at this time is to reiterate that attraction to the bizarre is a phenomenon universal to all humans regardless of personality tendencies. However, one might hypothesize that persons with serious personality problems may go a

[39]Morgan, "Teen-Age Heroes," p. 65.
[40]"Jackson-Spannung war zuviel," *Eifeler Volkszeitung,* June 4, 1988, p. 5.

step further than merely enjoying the "weird and tingling" sensation that the vision of such fare induces and try to imitate the grotesque in their personal lives.

Identification. A hero is a ready model for imitation. He or she provides the "worshipers" with an image to which they can aspire. It must be noted that the first-class teen hero is a recording star and not a politician, businessman, or intellectual. Compared with the entertainer, even the top athlete is only moderately admired. It has been suggested that the reasons for this preference are the similarity in age and ability of many entertainers to the crowd-oriented teenagers. It seems easier for teenagers to identify with someone who is crowd-oriented like themselves, and is mediocre, "humble," and nonserious. Teenagers, due to the adolescent experience, need collective protection within which they feel safe from and invisible to adults. They are afraid of exposing themselves individually to evaluation and criticism, and they project this negative feeling onto personalities who are outstanding. Their aversion is aimed at the politician for his or her *principles,* the businessperson for his or her *enterprise and success,* and the intellectual for devotion to the *hard truths*—all representing values that tend to separate the individual from the crowd, expose him or her, possibly make him or her unpopular and therefore insecure. Teenagers try to escape exposure and seek the security of the crowd. They prefer virtues of conformity, mediocrity, and sincerity. Through their heroes, songs, and dances they can express themselves without leaving the secure environment of the group.

The Beatles, for example, were admired for their simplicity and sincerity. When asked whether they liked being idolized, they answered "we just like the money." Another important element that made the Beatles loved and admired heroes was the fact that they conveyed a nonserious image. By doing so, they enabled their fans to relax and meet them as equals. The Beatles admitted publicly that they did not think much of their own music but that they had "fun" entertaining and getting paid for it.

Another condition that induces identification with many of the teenage heroes is based on the subtle rivalry that girls introduce between the idols and their boyfriends. Directly or indirectly, boyfriends are frequently urged to look and act like teenage heroes, and they are rewarded, if they are successful in a certain degree of imitation, with some of the type of admiration that is ordinarily reserved for popular idols.

Heroes as "messengers." Heroes are significant others who have influence on teenagers' thinking and value-orientation. However, of all the functions American teen heroes perform, extending values is probably the least effective. The need to express and release emotional dispositions and the use of the hero as a catalyst for that purpose by far supersede the need for more rational formulations and value-orientations.

Nevertheless, one could classify some of the early "folk rock" heroes as advocates of certain values of adolescents—probably of the *older* and more intellectual adolescents. One of the best known was Bob Dylan, a young poet-songwriter who achieved popularity with such songs as "Tambourine Man," "Subterranean Homesick Blues," and "Like a Rolling Stone." His songs criticized social conditions and focused on civil rights, the threat of nuclear war, and the war in Vietnam. Although his singing made him a millionaire, he maintained an image that teenagers found acceptable and imitable. To his fans, the scruffy hair, wrinkled shirt, and faded jeans meant that he was one of them.

Others like Joan Baez, Judy Collins, Joni Mitchell, and Peter, Paul and Mary followed the lead of Dylan, expounded social commentary, and showed talent in distilling the moods of their time. The recurrent themes in their creations were justice for all, peace, brotherhood, love, sensitivity and the condemnation of urban-industrial conditions. Their collages pieced together images of tension between the generations, the loneliness of the young in an anomic society, the bittersweets of young love, the search for a stable and secure reality, and the fear of the fleeting and blurred meanings of our age.

While the charisma achieved by these heroes made their message credible to many, the majority of young teen fans approached the message more from the visceral, musical, and hero-worship angle, and the folk-rock following was never as broad as the rock 'n' roll enthusiasts in general. The political and philosophical messages of the protest heroes, however, made an impression on the older and more serious young population and contributed to countercultural development.

The early heroes of the American youth scene, especially as they were part of the counterculture, are ancient history to today's teenagers, who are much more interested in the immediacy and the sensateness of entertainment figures. If one would distill the late-twentieth-century American-teen-hero phenomenon to its core, the final essence would be that it must be "fun." And "fun" is antithetical to a serious value statement, because it would require thinking, self-examination, and it would set up demands of standards of behavior. Such demands are a threat to most teenagers. "Fun" is non-threatening because it leaves hedonism undisturbed. (The "fun syndrome" in American society is, of course, important to both teenagers and adults. Curiously enough, it has escaped serious analysis by behavioral scientists, though its exertion on American life is powerful.)

SUBCULTURAL INSTITUTIONALIZATION

All societies institutionalize the functions deemed necessary for taking care of basic needs. This means that behavior aimed at satisfying such important needs as sex, reproduction, training of the young, trading, protection, order, and leadership is not permitted to occur at random or by idiosyncratic preference, but is prescribed by the cultural blueprint, and is implemented, respectively, by marriage, family, education, business, police or the military, and government. Members of society must comply with specific structures, such as the monogamous relationship, the family group, the organization of public schools, and so forth.

If the main culture fails to provide an institutional framework for the gratification of a certain need, subcultural institutionalization may develop to facilitate fulfillment of the need. Subinstitutionalization is probably the most telling indicator of how far a collectivity has matured into a subculture. These new structures may or may not be in conflict with the larger society, may or may not totally replace the Establishment's procedure, and may be seen as deviant or as merely supplemental.

American adolescents have begun to develop several institutions of their own. By doing so, they manifest, more convincingly than by any other means, their attempt to be independent of the adult world. The manifestations can be recognized by regularities in behavior that indicate a surprising degree of organized social structure within the youth collectivity. It is the enmeshing of young people in their own segregated social structure that is of utmost sociological pertinence, because a structural proviso makes for regular patterns of social behavior.

Some subinstitutionalizations have already been mentioned. The whole area of youthful entertainment, including music, songs, dancing, and festivals, can be called institutions of the young. Of similar nature are teen magazines that promote hero worship and, most importantly, serve as channels of mass communication. A few more subinstitutions are:

Dating.   Dating is an example of a supplemental institution that is not necessarily in conflict with adult norms and institutions but rather defines the culturally accepted meeting ground between boys and girls and patterns their interaction. To a large extent, however, the specific norms and expectations are defined by the young people themselves, and certain aspects of the subinstitutional behavior border on the "forbidden," such as heavy petting and premarital sexual intercourse. Such behavior adjuncts exemplify the need fulfillment of young people who cannot find a legitimate outlet for sexual desires within the institutions of the Establishment, since such participation is reserved for adults and presumably limited to the institutions of marriage and the family.

Cohabitation.   We call it cohabitation when a boy and a girl or a man and a woman live together without being married. Generally, American society frowns on this type of arrangement, and, technically speaking, several states have laws against it. The nature of cohabitation differs on a wide spectrum; it can range from an ephemeral to a lasting relationship; from a noncommittal to a committal relationship. Since the U.S. Bureau of the

Census defines as cohabitation already such a short episode as living together for one weekend, a significant portion of American teenagers have had cohabitational experiences before they get married. In a sense, this amounts to subinstitutional behavior and falls far short of the approved main institution of marriage.

It has been speculated that one of the reasons increasing numbers of American youth experiment with cohabitation is their reluctance to make marital commitments in the face of perennially witnessing the breakups of adult marriages, possibly including those of their own parents.

Another reason, probably a more common one, is the young's fear of losing their independence and having to assume responsibilities. Such a loss would be out of line with the preponderant fun-morality that generally governs sexual activities. To many, whether they admit it or not, cohabitation is primarily a convenient sexual relationship that lasts as long as there is "fun" in it.

This is not to deny the benefits of a premarital moratorium that young people can use to get to know each other and to eventually base a more committal decision on such knowledge. The subinstitution of cohabitation can be used or abused as can any other institution; its most dismal abuse stands out when partners enter it with different motivations and objectives, so that sooner or later one or the other party gets hurt.

Social scientists who have foreseen the modern trend and the need for a marital-halfway institution have suggested the usefulness of an arrangement that provides the secure framework of a dyad without the presumedly absolute commitment of a marriage. Margaret Mead, for example, long ago proposed two different types of marriages, one for people who want to enjoy each other's company without children and the other for people who want children and plan the conventional marriage-family.[41] Under the "individual marriage," young people could enter and leave the unions relatively freely with a minimum of obligations to each other. In a sense, the modern cohabitational arrangement represents this idea (except that Mead had some contractual and legal agreements in mind) and provides sexual gratification, companionship, and, assuming the woman is employed, two contributors to the household expenses.

Commune.   A substitution for traditional family life was and, in a few instances still is, the commune. This subinstitutional structure experienced an upsurge during the counterculture years, but has noticeably receded since then. Similarly to cohabitation, there used to be a wide range of different types, but all had one thing in common: the legal and emotional commitments were at a minimum, with no legal pressure to enter or stay. The

[41]Margaret Mead, "Marriage in Two Steps," in *The Family in Search of a Future*, ed. Herbert A. Otto (New York: Prentice-Hall, 1970), pp. 75–84.

commune is a subinstitution ideally suited to accommodate young people who prefer a moratorium on marital and familial commitments and yet desire some of the benefits of the equivalent adult institution such as: (1) the experience of human intimacy, (2) a feeling of belonging, (3) a feeling of security, physical as well as psychological, (4) a chance to satisfy curiosity about other people, and, most prominently, (5) sexual gratification on a regular basis.

In summary, the subinstitutions of dating, cohabitating, and communal living meet the needs of modern youth who shy away from total self-surrender and hesitate to enter into the symbiotic fusion found in traditional marriage. Many apparently are no longer willing to give themselves completely to one person and no longer expect to get all of the emotional satisfaction they need from a single lifelong partner.

Business.   Ever since the counterculture, young Americans have been trying their hands at their own business ventures. They are establishments run by youth for youth; some are legal and others illegal. The former include stores dealing in clothes, jewelry, candles, records and tapes, posters, and antiques. In the vicinity of college campuses can be seen book exchanges, small boutiques, food co-ops, vegetarian restaurants, and often small workshops manufacturing furniture, leather goods, glassware, ceramics, and art work of all sorts.

Hovering between legality and illegality are shops that sell drug paraphernalia. The 1980s witnessed an onslaught of legislative bills which outlawed the sale of articles ostensibly meant to accompany or facilitate the use of illegal drugs.

Clearly illegal is the subinstitution that procures and often grows or manufactures illicit drugs, including marijuana, heroin, cocaine, and so forth. An intricate subterranean network, with well defined roles at various levels of procurement (including the roles of producing, smuggling, transporting, and retailing), caters to the desires of young and not so young Americans—desires not covered by the legitimate institutions of society.

The automobile.   The role of the automobile in the lives of American teenagers has been cited by some writers as another example of subinstitutionalization. While having or needing a car is, of course, not an exclusive youth syndrome—on the contrary, it is typically an adult pattern—the *purpose* for which teenagers use and desire "wheels" defines it as subinstitutionalized behavior. Teenagers use the car not so much as a utilitarian appliance but to promote status, as compensation for the feeling of powerlessness, and to make dating possible.

The role of the car can be best understood in terms of its functions for the teenager. Besides providing transportation to school and work, the car usually serves additional functions:

1. Owning or having regular access to a car is *prestigious* in the eyes of peers. The newer or more customized the car, the higher the prestige. A teenager may spend all savings on customizing and maintaining a car according to what his or her peers consider admirable.
2. The car is of great *instrumental* importance for dating and related activities. For the teenage boy, having a car is not only prestigious but usually imperative when asking a girl for a date. It allows for mobility and privacy, providing American teenagers with the most frequent setting for sexual experimentation.
3. For some boys a car is a *hobby*. In fact, researchers discovered that the most frequent hobby of high school boys was "working on their cars."[42]
4. Driving an automobile can provide a *sense of power*. Since the adolescent experience includes a feeling of restriction and powerlessness, some teenagers use the car as a symbol of freedom and escape from adult control. Psychiatrist J. M. Murray hypothesized that driving a powerful automobile allows teenagers to express frustration and hostility with a minimum of risk of punishment and often with complete anonymity.[43]
5. In some communities, *cruising* has evolved as a ritual on wheels, whereby hundreds of cars parade down a main street on certain nights, usually weekends. It is a noisy and odorous show of subcultural strength, whereby prestige can be measured on the basis of type and look of car, contacts/dates established, and a general sense of solidarity enjoyed. In some instances it has involved so many cars and generated so much noise and trash that local authorities tried to ban it, as, for example, in California's Alameda County. Phoenix tried a different solution by negotiating with the young cruisers, trying to persuade them to abandon the main avenue and change to a less congestable loop. In reaction to legal restrictions, the Bay Area's cruisers in 1984 declared a "National Cruise," which attracted 3000 cruising cars, additional thousands of onlookers, and 100 police in riot gear trying to disperse them.[44]

There are a number of additional behavior patterns among young Americans that can be defined as subinstitutionalized behavior, but they tend to prevail among older youths who have achieved some degree of political and philosophical sophistication and countercultural stature. Advanced youth or countercultural institutions include legal aid, "hot line" telephone centers, underground press, free schools, psychiatric "first aid," and many others.

SUMMARY

This chapter completes the discussion of eight dimensions of subculture. The first dimension, values and attitudes, was discussed in Chapter 12, and the remaining seven were presented in this chapter. The illustrations were

---

[42]James S. Coleman, *The Adolescent Society* (New York: Free Press, 1963), p. 12.

[43]J. M. Murray, "Emotional Problems in Relation to Driving," *Action Achievement Report*, 8th Annual Massachusetts Governor's Highway Safety Conference, Boston, May 25, 1954.

[44]Jonathan Alter and Richard Sandza, "Cruising Through California," *Newsweek*, September 10, 1984, p. 31.

usually interpreted in the perspective of structural-functional analysis in order to introduce the reader to the often-hidden meanings of behavior forms.

1. Teen argot is as puzzling to adults as it is functional to teenagers. Its functions include phonetic ease, relevance to the adolescent experience, maintenance of a sense of solidarity, provision of a status criterion, reflection of values, and a system of linguistic conditioning.

2. Subcultures depend on channels of communication for survival. The simplest and most direct communication center is the high school campus, where young people have ample opportunity to share ideas and attitudes. Other media include television, radio, teen magazines, the record industry, and rock festivals.

3. Teen fads and styles come and go. Their intentional as well as unintentional functions include status measurement, group identification, a relatively harmless expression of rebelliousness, security in uniformity of looks and behavior, and communication of belonging.

4. A sense of solidarity is reflected in almost all forms of teenage behavior. It becomes conspicuous in teenagers' effort to retain exclusivity of style and behavior forms, to preserve group authority and cohesiveness, and thereby maintain boundaries that clearly indicate the in- and the out-group. Solidarity is greatly enhanced by the identification of a common adversary and the common modes of defense and attack.

5. Status criteria must be deduced from various behavior forms within the peer group. Group members learn early what makes for prestige. Prestige depends on the type of friend, the type of clothes (especially for girls), the show of bravado (particularly for boys), the popularity of one's date, adherence to peer style and argot, and convincing demeanor of "coolness" in everyday life.

6. The American teenager is more oriented toward entertainment heroes than toward true leaders. The functions of hero worship include the fueling of romanticism, various sex-substitutions (including fetishism), cathartic crowd behavior, attraction to the bizarre, identification with youthful heroes, and the need for values.

7. Teenagers have devised structures for gratifying needs and desires not sanctioned by the Establishment. Subinstitutionalization centers on desires for sexual expression, drug use, the use of the automobile, and the world of entertainment. Subculturally institutionalized behavior is probably most indicative of the strength of a subculture. It is also a useful approach to understanding a counterculture or social movement.

We now move to a discussion of the more serious, goal- and action-oriented youth movements.

Author Index

Subject Index

394

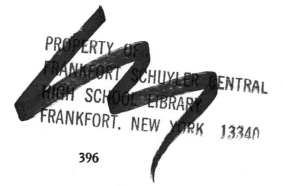